SEA

THE
OUTLAW LEGEND

THE
OUTLAW LEGEND

A Cultural Tradition in Britain, America and Australia

GRAHAM SEAL

Curtin University of Technology

CAMBRIDGE
UNIVERSITY PRESS

Published by the Press Syndicate of the University of Cambridge
The Pitt Building, Trumpington Street, Cambridge CB2 1RP, UK
40 West 20th Street, New York, NY 10011–4211, USA
10 Stamford Road, Oakleigh, Melbourne 3166, Australia

National Library of Australia cataloguing-in-publication data

Seal, Graham, 1950–   .
The outlaw legend : a cultural tradition in Britain,
America and Australia.
Bibliography.
Includes index.
1. Outlaws in popular culture. 2. Outlaws – United States.
3. Outlaws – Great Britain. 4. Outlaws – Australia.
5. Folk literature, American. 6. Folk literature, English.
7. Folk literature, Irish. 8. Folk literature, Australian.
I. Title.
306.08692

Library of Congress cataloguing-in-publication data

Seal, Graham, 1950–
The outlaw legend : a cultural tradition in Britain, America and
Australia / Graham Seal.
p.   cm.
Includes bibliographical references (p.   ) and index.
1. Brigands and robbers – Australia – Legends 2. Brigands and
robbers – Great Britain – Legends. 3. Brigands and robbers – United
States – Legends. 4. Folklore – Australia. 5. Folklore – Great
Britain. 6. Folklore – United States. I. Title.
GR365.S434 1996
398'.355–dc20   95–48971

A catalogue record for this book is available from the British Library.

ISBN 0 521 55317 2 Hardback
ISBN 0 521 55740 2 Paperback

Contents

CONTENTS

Illustrations

Ballads and Tales

*... it is certain that the populace of all countries look
with admiration upon great and successful thieves*

Charles Mackay, *Extraordinary Popular Delusions
and the Madness of Crowds* (1841)

*Ever since the good old days
Of Turpin and Duval,
The peoples' friends were outlaws too,
And so was bold Ben Hall*

'The Death of Ben Hall', Australian bushranging ballad

He stole from the rich and he gave to the poor ...

'Jesse James', American outlaw song

Preface

This book deals with the legends and the history of certain highwaymen, badmen and bushrangers who have become folk heroes. Beginning in medieval England and extending to the late twentieth century, this work covers three continents and ranges over seven centuries or so. This diachronic approach is balanced to some extent by an examination of the historical circumstances surrounding the activities of a number of outlaws, including Richard Turpin, Jesse James, William Bonney and, especially, Ned Kelly.

The strength and persistence of outlaw hero traditions in oral cultures of Britain, America and Australia is approached in relation to more mainstream treatments of the same heroes. While the folk image of the outlaw persists at the informal, unofficial levels of social discourse and interaction, particularly within those groups seeing themselves as the receivers of a heritage of discontent, such as the poorer agrarian classes, there is also a more official, popular representation of the outlaw hero. This representation is projected in various types of commercial and literary production, including the chapbook, the broadside ballad, the newspaper, pulp fiction, non-fiction and 'faction', film, television, art and literature. It is in the interactions between these two strands that the tradition of the outlaw hero is articulated and circulated over time and space.

The song and narrative texts discussed and analysed have been gleaned from a diversity of sources, as indicated in the references. Arranged in roughly chronological order, the book begins with an overview of the outlaw hero tradition. This is followed by a treatment of the balladry about the mythical outlaw of medieval legend, Robin Hood, together with the traditions of selected other non-historical outlaws. The British highwaymen are then considered as examples of the outlaw hero tradition in the seventeenth and eighteenth centuries. Australian bush-rangers and the American badmen of the nineteenth and early twentieth centuries are then discussed in terms of the outlaw hero tradition and the continuing fascination that these heroic criminals have in the modern world. Neither of these national sections claims to be comprehensive. A selection only has been made of those texts that seem most directly relevant to the arguments of the book. A focused study of any of the national outlaw traditions treated here would certainly turn up many further examples.

A more detailed chapter has been provided on the bushranger Ned Kelly. Although Jesse James survived a remarkably long criminal career of eighteen years, in many ways Kelly was the last of the outlaw heroes. More importantly, though, Kelly is the only outlaw hero to have transcended the status of folk hero, tourist attraction and mass media icon to become a national hero, an Australian culture hero. The details of this transcendence, while related in many ways to the specifics of Australian history, are also revealing of the broader, transnational implications of this study.

The study has a number of interlocking aims and aspirations. A fundamental aim is to examine the relationship between history and folklore. This is a complicated but central question for folklore studies and one that has ramifications in many other fields and in everyday life. While a full study of these latter aspects must await another time and opportunity, in this work the relationship of 'fact' to 'fiction', 'truth' and 'belief' is addressed in terms of the potent legendry of the outlaw hero.

The study also engages with some aspects of the opposing but interacting notions of 'law' and 'lore'. The argument is advanced that in those situations where the law of the state is found inadequate or oppressive certain individuals will, deliberately or through circumstances beyond their control, revolt against the power of the state. These individuals—'outlaws'—may be given the support of otherwise law-abiding citizens as long as they operate, or at least can be seen to be operating, in accordance with the moral code of the outlaw hero tradition. In short, outside the 'law' but inside the 'lore'. Outbreaks of 'social banditry' are the ideal circumstances for investigating this general proposition.

In the process of realising these aims, this book describes and analyses the major Anglophone manifestations of the outlaw hero tradition.

PREFACE

The texts selected here provide primary source evidence to support the various theoretical and other observations made throughout. They are presented with as much contextual information as seems necessary to understand them, both within the frameworks of the localised British, American and Australian milieux to which they belong, and within what has been identified as the broader cultural process of the outlaw hero tradition. The texts provide a basis for comparison of the stylistic and content consistencies and deviations of the English-language outlaw hero tradition. The book thus provides for the first time, as far as I am aware, a collection of related folklore texts from three Anglophone national cultures and some insight into the circulation of texts between traditions. This transnational approach is, presumably, of some intrinsic comparative interest and value, but more importantly allows the reader to ascertain for him or herself the accuracy of the observations made about and upon this material, and therefore the validity of the arguments derived from those observations. The notes to the texts attempt to indicate the diffusion of each text and, by implication, the extensive lodgements and resonances of the outlaw hero tradition within three distinct though related cultures. Consequently, some attention has been given to tracing and noting variants across time and space and indicating these in the notes. Such indications are not exhaustive, though within the limits of the sources, resources and facilities available, are reasonably comprehensive and salient to the general thesis argued here. The aim is to indicate the extent to which these closely similar fictions have been found convenient by many individuals and groups in many places and at many times.

Music has not been included, either as an object of study nor as the appropriate vehicles of the texts. While I am sensitive to the need for understanding such texts as part of the genre of song, rather than poetry, I have reluctantly, yet also with relief, excluded the musical dimension. The reasons for this exclusion are partly due to my own lack of expertise as a musicologist, partly due to the fact that tunes are only rarely indicated in many of the primary sources in which the texts are found, but more importantly to the absence of any convincing scholarly analytical mode that allows useful observations on the signification of song melodies in folk traditions. It is, or should be, well-known that while traditional texts generally retain a degree of coherence over time and space, the melodies that carry them are notoriously fickle, migrating from song to song. It is true that some songs retain a particular melody

as 'their' tune that will be recognised and rendered by most singers—
'The Wild Colonial Boy' is one relevant example. However, such songs
are also collected with other, unrelated and even apparently inappropriate
melodies, as is 'The Wild Colonial Boy'. (The noted Australian folklorist
and musicologist, John Manifold, delivered the opinion 'that "The Wild
Colonial Boy" has more tunes to it than any other song I have collected.')[1] What this means for cultural analysis is that nothing can—
yet—be generalised from the specific example with music. Singers clearly
use whatever tunes are to hand to carry their texts. It is the texts that
carry the message and the meaning of the broader tradition or cultural
process. It is the texts that persist over time and space. The tunes, which
often change with movements in popular music fashion, are significant
entirely and only within the context of the actual performance, the emotional moment of interaction between singer and listener. While such
moments, and their meanings, are important for folklorists to study, they
are of a different, micro-order to the broader and wider macro-cultural
processes discussed in this book.

Another regret is that this book has been unable to deal with the
outlaw hero in other countries with Anglophone traditions, such as
Canada, South Africa and New Zealand. There are indications that noble
robbers are not unknown in these cultures. Whether or not these individuals can be usefully viewed in terms of the tradition outlined here is
a matter for further study.

Acknowledgements

Work on this book has spanned many years. In that time I have become indebted to a large number of people. I wish to thank for their efforts on my behalf the staffs of the following libraries and other institutions: the British Library; the British Museum; Ralph Vaughan Williams Memorial Library, English Folk Dance and Song Society; the Folklore Society; the Mitchell Library, State Library of NSW; La Trobe Collection, State Library of Victoria; Deakin University Library; the National Library of Australia; Sheffield University Library; Leeds University Library; University of Kent at Canterbury Library; Goldsmiths College Library; Battye Library, Perth; Curtin University Library; National Film and Sound Archive, Canberra; Justice and Police Museum, NSW; National Archives (USA); University of New South Wales Press for permission to use 'The Death of Ben Hall'; Penguin Books Australia for permission to quote material from John Manifold's *Penguin Australian Songbook* and Russel Ward's *Penguin Book of Australian Ballads*.

I would also like to thank the following individuals, all of whom have contributed to this work: Patrick O'Farrell (History, University of New South Wales); John Widdowson (Centre for English Cultural Tradition and Language, University of Sheffield); Tony Green (then Institute of Dialectology and Folk Life Studies, University of Leeds); John McQuilton (currently University of Wollongong); Kenny Goldstein (then University of Philadelphia), Herbert Halpert and Martin Lovelace (Memorial University of Newfoundland); Don Grant and other colleagues in Communication and Cultural Studies at Curtin University; staff of Cambridge University Press, especially Phillipa McGuinness, Jane Farago and my editor Janet Mackenzie. I also thank—profoundly—

ACKNOWLEDGEMENTS

Maureen, Kylie and Jenna Seal: this is what the 'tap-tap-tapping' was all about. *The Outlaw Legend* is dedicated to the memories of Desmond and Arthur Seal, my father and my uncle.

NOTE ON CURRENCY AND MEASUREMENTS

In £.s.d. currency, as used in Britain and Australia during the period dealt with in this book, there were 12 pennies in one shilling, and 20 shillings in one pound (£). A guinea was equal to £1 1s.

Mass	Area
1 ounce = 28.3 g	1 acre = 0.4 ha
1 pound (lb) = 454 g	

CHAPTER ONE

The Outlaw Legend

Heroes come in all shapes, sizes, colours, creeds, nationalities and genders. They are, by definition, the focus of every kind of narrative, from cosmological myth to Mills and Boon romances. Heroes and heroines populate poems, paintings, plays, novels, histories, films, comics, cartoons and literary and popular productions of every kind, including the supposedly 'factual' reporting of the news media. Folklore too is peopled with heroes. Legends, myths, songs and narratives tell and retell the deeds of trickster heroes like the American Indian Coyote, occupational heroes like Crooked Mick of the Australian Speewah, military, pioneer, local and other heroes. There are few arenas of human activity in which heroic behaviour is unlikely. A world without heroes is unimaginable and would probably be unworkable, for heroes are at the very centre of cultural myth-making processes. Heroes reflect and reinforce the social, political and economic tensions within any community that celebrates such characters, real and imaginary.

Not only have heroes been with us for as long as history and myth have been recorded, they have also long been the object of serious study. Notable major works in this field include Lord Raglan's *The Hero*, the various volumes of Joseph Campbell's vast studies, libraries of studies and collections concerned with heroes and heroines of various mythologies, Norse, Greek, Roman, Celtic, Islamic, Hindu, to name only some. As well, the journals of comparative literature, mythology and folklore abound with shorter treatments of heroic figures.

Our fascination with heroism[1] is based on the dual status of the hero who is recognisably one of us, yet at the same time apart from us

1

by virtue of his (or far less frequently, her) actions or experiences. One heroic type to which this observation particularly applies is the outlaw hero. As well as carrying out deeds of daring and cunning usually associated with heroic figures, the ambivalent nature of the outlaw hero is extended by the fact that he is also a villain, a criminal living outside and against the law. He—and in the Anglophone traditions discussed here, it always is a male—is at once a representative of the dissatisfactions of the particular social groups who sympathise with him, and someone set apart from the other members of such groups by his outlawry.

The outlaw hero is a particular and very well-defined type of folk hero who inhabits the grey area between criminality and political or pre-political protest. His tradition can be traced as a cultural constant that persists over time and through space, and is available to be called into use whenever circumstances are appropriate. Outlaw heroes, real and fictional, exist in most of the world's folklores, celebrated particularly in song and narrative, as well as through other verbal folkloric genres. Islamic culture contains a Robin Hood-type hero named Kuroghli, the Son of the Blind Man, who is generous, manly, courageous, the friend of the poor and the enemy of the rich and powerful. Russian culture boasts the heroic bandit figures of Van'ka Kain and Sten'ka Razin. The Caucasus has, among others, Arsena of Marabda who operated during the first half of the nineteenth century; he was a friend of the poor, a great escaper and disguiser. Welsh tradition supports the figure of Thomas Jones, a sixteenth-century landowner, better-known as Twm Sion Cati, a highway robber adept at disguise and escapes. Scots tradition celebrates William Wallace, briefly Guardian of Scotland, in outlaw hero terms, and the English traditions of Hereward the Wake who fought against William the Conqueror are well-known. Mexican-American lore has, among others, the figures of Joaquin Murieta ('The Robin Hood of California') and Gregorio Cortez, whose life, times and legend were impressively documented and analysed by Amerigo Paredes.

The historian Eric Hobsbawm called such outlaw heroes 'social bandits', after investigating the careers and the legends of a variety of outlaws from a number of periods, cultures and nationalities.[2] Hobsbawm's thesis has been reinforced, refined and criticised in various ways[3] but his overall concept of a social bandit—one who has the sympathy and support of his own social group—has survived as a useful framework for understanding the activities and origins of historical figures as diverse as the Sicilian Salvatore Guiliano, the German Schinderhannes, the

French Vidocq, as well as more definite social movements and forces such as Indian Dacoits and Egyptian brigands. Hobsbawm's perceptive and erudite study shows a historian at work on a fascinating set of cross-cultural consistencies from which he is able to synthesise a compelling, if necessarily general, thesis. Indeed, the main criticisms of Hobsbawm's work in this area have been by anthropologists and others who insist that, while there may be a case for the identification of such cross-cultural continuities and parallels, the detailed field research on specific outbreaks of banditry shows that it is local circumstances and pressures that determine the degree of support for a bandit, rather than the operation of some abstract, meta-historical force tagged 'social banditry'.

While this criticism is no doubt valid in many cases, it remains true that the attributes of outlaw heroes are remarkably consistent, regardless of the economic basis of the society that supports such figures. Recurring cultural patterns of this type are not generally seen as the preserve of the historian, and it seems that the dynamics involved may be most usefully approached from the perspective of the folklorist. Indeed, although Hobsbawm made some reference to folklore in his work, he undertook no coherent and sustained investigation of such cultural expressions and practices. Ironically, perhaps, it is folklore rather than history that proves his case.

Others have also examined outlaw traditions, if usually in the more restricted geographical arenas of their own culture. American folklorists, sociologists and historians in particular have dealt with the figure of the outlaw or 'badman' in their culture. These investigators include Steckmesser (1966), Simeone (1958), Meyer (1980) and Roberts (1981). Each of these approaches the topic in a similar manner, even if their emphases differ somewhat. Simeone was concerned to compare and contrast the American outlaw hero with the legendary Robin Hood, and convincingly established the continuation of the Robin Hood image in American tradition. Steckmesser looked at a number of outlaws, noting both the similarities in their individual traditions and their historical contexts, an approach which he extended in his book-length study. Meyer identified twelve essential elements in the image of the American outlaw, most of which had been noted by previous commentators. Roberts applied these twelve elements to a discussion of the 'Railroad Bill' ballad(s) and their accompanying narrative complex, apparently without knowledge of the earlier work of Steckmesser and Simeone, or for that matter of Paredes' cognate work on Cortez.[4]

3

Most of these studies proceed by noting the similarities between the various traditions investigated and in drawing conclusions from these. While generally recognising the link between outlaw heroes and broadly similar, recurring socio-historical circumstances of perceived oppression, relatively little attention is paid to the historical, social, economic and political environments within which the various outlaws operated and in which outlaw hero traditions about them circulated. On the other hand, studies by historians and sociologists, such as White and, to a lesser extent, Hobsbawm, generally pay only limited attention to the processes of folkloric transmission and stereotyping involved in the creation and—most importantly—the perpetuation of an outlaw hero. This book seeks to combine both these approaches and, as far as possible, to situate the generation of outlaw heroes and the continuation of their traditions in specific political and economic circumstances. As well, not only are similarities between the various outlaw hero traditions noted, more or less in the manner of previous commentators, but also the differences between the originating British traditions and their recrudescences on the frontiers of America and Australia and, ultimately, on the new global frontier of the Internet.

DEEP CONTINUITIES

While Robin Hood is undoubtedly the archetypal figure of the outlaw hero,[5] this book concentrates mostly on the folklore associated with historical figures, particularly the British highwaymen William Nevison, Dick Turpin, William Brennan, Jeremiah Grant and others; the Australian bushrangers, including Ben Hall, Frank Gardiner, Ned Kelly, Thunderbolt and Daniel Morgan; and American badmen Sam Bass, William Bonney, Jesse James and a number of lesser-known but significant figures. Incidental reference is also made to other outlaw heroes, real or imaginary, though a primary purpose of this work is to make some observations on the intersection between the folkloric and the historic.

Comparison of folkloric expressions related to these real and legendary outlaw heroes in Britain, America and Australia reveals a number of common motifs or narrative elements. The single most important of these elements, indeed the defining motif, is that the outlaw hero 'robs the rich to help the poor'. This formulaic element may be expressed in a number of ways, depending on the circumstances. 'The rich' may be the forces of economic or social oppression, and injustice—the Sheriff of Nottingham's unjust taxes in the Robin Hood legend, the Union in the case of ex-Confederate raider Jesse James, the 'English' landlords in the case of Irish-Australian Ned Kelly. Similarly 'the poor' are generally those members of the social group that sympathises with and supports the outlaw hero, and from which he has usually arisen or for whom his activities are appealing. These groups perceive themselves as suffering under various forms of injustice and oppression, and see the activities of their outlaw hero as justified revenge against those forces and their representatives. In the case of Robin Hood, the poor are the archetypal peasants or serfs. One of the earliest Robin Hood ballads tells us that the outlaw 'dyde pore men moch god'.[6] According to his ballad, Jesse James 'stole from the rich and he gave to the poor',[7] in this case primarily the dirt farmers of the Kansas–Missouri border, many of whom believed themselves discriminated against in the aftermath of the Civil War.[8] In Australia 'the poor' are the rural workers, small landholders and, later, selectors, trying to maximise their economic positions on usually inferior land after the New South Wales and Victorian free selection acts of the 1860s.[9] Other Australian manifestations of this element of the outlaw hero tradition include bushrangers such as Ben Hall, who 'never robbed a needy chap',[10] and the bushranger of northern New South Wales known as 'Thunderbolt' or 'Captain Thunderbolt' (Frederick Ward), whose persona speaks in some of the few remaining lines of his ballad:

> My name is Frederick Ward,
>   I am a native of this isle;
> I rob the rich to feed the poor
>   And make the children smile.[11]

Numerous other examples are cited throughout,[12] and it is clear that the perception of deprivation or oppression is a fundamental aspect of the outlaw hero tradition. But while it may be expressed formulaically in the phrase 'he robbed the rich to help the poor' or some variation of that, the simple formula reflects a complex reality of intersecting political and economic factors and group perceptions. Its deployment, in combination with other elements of the tradition, is an indicator of deep and serious social tensions within a community rather than a mere narrative cliché.

The individuals, and the social groups to which they belonged, who told the tales and sang the ballads of outlaw heroes, were not simply celebrating criminal activity. In their hero's activities, the outlaw's supporters and sympathisers saw themselves and the articulation of their fears and frustrations in the form of an avenging force robbing the rich and powerful landowners, the despised police or military, and the banks or the railway companies that were often seen as economic oppressors. Outlaw heroes frequently appear among groups who, like those described above, are also deprived of adequate political representation, thus deepening and increasing their sense of oppression and frustration. Such people easily identified themselves as 'the poor' and said so in their songs. All outlaw heroes operate outside and against the official legal system of the state, but remain within the unofficial legal and moral code of those who see them as one of their own. Although the specific circumstances alter in each case, similar patterns of perceived injustice and suffering generate other historical outlaw heroes.

A second important element of the tradition is closely related to the first: it is generally found that the hero is driven to outlawry through no fault of his own. Robin Hood is usually said to have been a Saxon who fled to the forest to escape Norman tyranny; one of Ned Kelly's ballads points out: 'The Governor of Victoria was an enemy of this man.'[13] And even so unlikely a hero as William Bonney, 'Billy the Kid', was said to have killed his first man while in his early teens, knifing a man who insulted his mother, traditionally a justifiable form of homicide.[14] The folklore surrounding Jesse James is thick with explicit indications that Jesse, his companions and family and sympathisers were the victims of post-Civil War discrimination against those who, like the Jameses and the Youngers, had supported the Confederate cause.[15]

Almost invariably it is the oppression or injustice of others—usually those with authority and power—that compels the hero to take to the forest, bush or other marginal area where the control of the coercive oppressor is weak or non-existent. Not only is this peripheral or liminal space important from a logistic and tactical viewpoint, it is also a symbolic indication of the hero's change of social status. Before it, he is generally a reasonably law-abiding, occasionally model, citizen, acting within the bounds of his community's values and mores, if not always in accordance with the official legal system. After he becomes an outlaw, usually through some act of justifiable violence or vengeance against one or more representatives of the oppressors, the hero moves out of the everyday set of routine rights and obligations and passes to a different space outside the boundaries of the everyday. He is no longer controlled by the same laws and values but is outside them, literally an outlaw.

This is not to say that all constraints and obligations are removed. On the contrary, in order to maintain the respect, sympathy and the active support of his own social group, the outlaw must adhere to, or at least be seen to adhere to, a relatively rigid set of guidelines. Some actions are appropriate, even laudable, while others are reprehensible and may not be countenanced if the outlaw is to become a hero. The appropriate moral instructions are coded into the folkloric manifestations of the tradition and are therefore recurring elements within it. Outlaws who disregard these rules are not balladised and, more worryingly for them, are unlikely to have the sympathy and therefore the sustaining support of their own social group or groups. There are a number of British ballads about highway robbers who act in a manner that does not accord with tradition. They are shown to suffer the consequences of their failure to adhere to the appropriate moral guidelines. These include 'The Highwayman Outwitted' (also known as 'The Farmer of Chester'), in which a young woman outwits a highwayman with less-than-chivalrous intentions and benefits by attaining his treasure for herself and her family. Other songs that show the negative consequences of highwaymen not acting in accordance with the tradition are 'The Yorkshire Farmer', 'The Yorkshire Bite', and 'Two Jolly 'Butchers'.[16] It is worth noting that all these 'negative' highwayman hero songs concern non-historical villains.

One of the most important of the outlaw hero's moral guidelines is that he should never rob or in any way harm the poor, the weak or the otherwise unfortunate. This means, in Anglophone tradition at least, the safety of widows, orphans, cripples, fools and, generally, of women, who are not to be molested, even if rich. It is generally considered more than appropriate for the outlaw hero to treat women with the utmost courtesy. Robin Hood, of course, remains the exemplar in this area, while any highwayman worth his salt must act the gentleman, as does Turpin in his folklore and as do, according to tradition, most of the badmen and bushrangers. A number of outlaw heroes have traditions regarding their refusal to let members of their gangs rape or otherwise harm women.[17] True or fictional, the existence of such beliefs indicates the strength of this particular element of the tradition.

One persistent outlaw hero narrative encapsulates a number of the fundamental characteristics of the tradition. The story of the outlaw who comes across a poor woman—usually a widow—who is about to be evicted because she cannot pay the rent is a good example of the wish-fulfilment aspects of the outlaw hero tradition. Naturally, upon hearing of the widow's distress, the noble highwayman, badman or bushranger gives the widow the necessary amount so that she can pay the landlord's fee. As the landlord returns from the widow's hovel, the outlaw robs the rent back from him, usually returning it to the grateful widow. This story is attached to the folklores of outlaw heroes in England, Ireland and America; it reflects the essentials of respect for women, sympathy for the downtrodden, and robbing the rich, all presented in a narrative that shows the protagonist displaying the necessary panache of the outlaw hero.[18] The story does not seem to have become attached to any Australian bushranger heroes, perhaps a reflection of the effects of an especially entrenched patriarchy and a less rigid class structure.

The courteous 'gentleman robber' is a notion that has been pumped up in romantic fictional treatments of outlaw heroes to the point where it has the status of a defining generic feature. While courtesy is a fundamental element of outlaw hero folklore, it must be seen as only one of an interrelated set of characteristics that fuse to form the folklore of the outlaw. This folklore is not a closed system but also intersects with more formal effusions about outlaw heroes, such as those presented in literature and the mass media. In folklore, and in popular literary, filmic and artistic representations, courtesy is usually linked to manliness, an attribute of the outlaw hero expressed as 'bravery', 'boldness', or 'daring'. It is vital for the hero to act heroically, not only in relation to his constituency or support group, but also in relation to his enemies, the police, the sheriff's men, the troopers. However, despite his physical prowess, the outlaw hero must not be seen to offer unjustified violence, even to his enemies. The point is often made in outlaw balladry and narratives that the hero has 'never done murder nor killed'[19] (in this case William Nevison, also known as 'Swift Nicks'), or perpetrated any unjustified form of violence. Where the facts of a case make such statements difficult, murders committed by the hero or those around him are presented as acts of justified revenge or self-defence, given humorous treatment, or simply ignored. The traditions associated with Dick Turpin, Jesse James and Ned Kelly provide ample evidence of these techniques.

Turpin's career of crime included some unpleasantly violent and distinctly unchivalrous actions against women.[20] But Turpin's folkloric representation in song and story ignores these incidents. In the case of Ned Kelly, the murder of three policemen at Stringybark Creek in 1878 almost immediately became the subject of a song in which the bloody events are treated with a casual humour that is distinctly callous, even today. The song ends with Kelly saying of his shooting of Sergeant Kennedy: 'What a bloody pity that the bastard tried to run.'[21] Jesse James' acts of cold-blooded brutality are not mentioned in any of his songs or stories.

Related to the masculine notions of manliness and boldness is the requirement that the outlaw hero should 'die game'. That is, he must die bravely, preferably with his boots on and firing doggedly at the overwhelming police numbers arrayed against him, as does Australia's fictional 'Wild Colonial Boy' whose song, in its final verse, insists that he would rather die than 'live in slavery bound down by iron chains'.[22] One of the numerous Kelly ballads invokes an earlier outlaw hero in its penultimate verse:

> I'd rather die like Donohoe, that bushranger so brave,
> Than be taken by the Government and treated like a slave.[23]

If the outlaw is unable to manage such a glorious finale, his minimal responsibility is to go out at the end of a rope, bravely defiant and preferably uttering some resonant last words, as Ned Kelly is widely but inaccurately believed to have said before the trap was sprung: 'Such is life.' Outlaw heroes were well aware that they were expected to behave in an 'undaunted manner' at their executions. The annals of Tyburn and other hanging trees are full of the elaborate and often witty last speeches and gallows-jests that highwaymen, both famous and obscure, were said to have delivered at the drop, usually dressed in great and new finery. The utterances of highwaymen who were not celebrated as folk heroes also show the power of the traditional moral guidelines. The highwayman James Wright, executed in 1721, '... valued himself not a little that he had never injured any poor man'. A Thomas Easter, responding to the protests of his victim on Putney Heath, declared that he was an honest highwayman 'because I rob the Rich to give to the Poor'.[24]

The outlaw hero of tradition, and often of fact, is particularly adept at outwitting his captors, pursuers and oppressors, and is often a great escaper and disguiser. The Irish William Brennan, and Jeremiah Grant,[25] among others, were celebrated for their feats of escapology. As in so many other areas, the outlaw in Lincoln green is the archetype here, and there is clearly some affinity with another important form of folk hero, the trickster.[26] The ride from London to York in just one day, allegedly carried out by Dick Turpin, is another example of this, as is the use of disguise by Jesse James in the American tradition.[27] In Australia, the Kelly gang was believed to possess unusually good bush skills that allowed them to elude the considerable police numbers that tracked them for eighteen months between 1878 and 1880.[28] In general, the ability to escape, especially from difficult situations and preferably more than once, using skill, daring and various forms of trickery, including disguise, is usually a fundamental criterion of outlaw heroism.

Finally, though, the outlaw hero cannot escape and must face his fate. Intimately connected with the mode of the outlaw's death is the manner in which he is finally killed or captured. Where history does not allow a gallant and defiant exit by bullet or rope, the outlaw hero is generally betrayed by a trusted friend or accomplice. Outlaw heroes do not give themselves up: they are betrayed while sick, as Robin Hood was poisoned by the Abbess of Kirklees, or, like Jesse James, shot in the back by a member of his own gang:

> That dirty little coward that shot Mr Howard
> Has laid poor Jesse in his grave.[29]

A further instance—of many—is provided in the legendry of the bushranger Ben Hall, shot by police while sleeping, they having been led to the scene by a once-trusted friend:

> Savagely they murdered him,
> Those cowardly blue-coat imps,
> Who were laid on to where he slept
> By informing peelers' pimps.[30]

The Irish outlaws William Brennan and Jeremiah ('Captain') Grant are both betrayed in their ballads by women, as was the case, both in history and in legend, with the Australian bushranger Frank Gardiner.[31]

After death, and in common with some other types of folk hero, the outlaw hero is sometimes rumoured to live on, having escaped the noose or bullet by trick, perhaps by chance. Billy the Kid was widely believed to have survived his shooting by Pat Garrett.[32] Although Ned Kelly was definitely executed on 11 November 1880, legends about the survival of his younger brother and gang member, Dan, persisted in Australia until at least the 1920s.[33] Where survival legends do not occur, there may well be after-traces of the hero. Legend has it that in the case of bushranger Ben Hall, his sister-in-law gave birth to a child bearing the marks of the thirty-two bullets that the police had pumped into the sleeping bushranger.[34] There may be tales of the hero's still undiscovered treasure, as with 'Black Francis' in Ireland,[35] Sam Bass in Texas[36] and many of the New South Wales bushrangers of the 1860s.[37] These after-traces can be thought of as metaphorical transpositions of the persistent and widespread folkloric reluctance to accept the death of great heroes—or villains. Relatively recent examples of this tendency might be Adolf Hitler and Elvis Presley, though the claims of both these men to fame or infamy were not related to outlawry.

To summarise, the outlaw hero tradition consists of ten motifs or discrete but interacting narrative elements that can be referred to in shorthand as: friend of the poor, oppressed, forced into outlawry, brave, generous, courteous, does not indulge in unjustified violence, trickster, betrayed, lives on after death. These attributes may be expressed directly as in synonyms for manliness, boldness, bravery, defiance, or implied in the content of the song or narrative concerning an outlaw hero. For instance, while a particular outlaw hero may not be explicitly referred to as a friend of the poor, the victims of his robberies will invariably be the rich or powerful, often both.

These essential elements of the tradition constitute a dynamic and interacting group of well-defined motifs that can be used in varying combinations to construct narratives appropriate to a variety of historical events and characters. Not all the elements are present in every expression of a particular outlaw; but enough will be there to indicate to those who listen that an intricately balanced combination of traditional motifs, and the values and attitudes embedded within those motifs, is being invoked. The articulation of these elements in a variety of folkloric forms or genres reflects—and so reinforces—communal attitudes and expectations of those social groupings that support and/or sympathise with particular outlaw heroes. In short, we are not only dealing with a folk cultural tradition that generates songs, legends and so on from time to time, but also with a set of social, economic and political attitudes and activities that motivate the actions of individuals and groups enmeshed in specific historical circumstances. In the case of almost every individual outlaw hero tradition identified here, there is clear evidence of serious social, economic and political tensions within and between the various communities and groups involved.

DISCONTINUITIES

Having pointed to and discussed the parallels and similarities of the outlaw hero traditions of Britain, America and Australia, some attention must also be given to the differences between them. While the similarities are more pronounced and more important than the differences between these three national manifestations of the outlaw hero, some of the main differences between the traditions in the three cultures are significant.

One important difference is that while the British outlaw hero, whether in England or Ireland, is portrayed in folklore as a heroic individual, his American and Australian counterparts generally have strong family ties and influences. This is apparent both in the history of many bushrangers and badmen and in the ballads of their exploits. Historically it was the James–Younger gang, a confederation of related males, who formed the outlaw band of which Jesse James came to be the most prominent member. Jesse's mother and half-brother feature significantly in the James mythology as the relatively innocent victims of a Pinkerton bomb attack that maimed Mrs Samuels (née James) and killed Jesse's young half-brother. Likewise, Jesse's own domestic arrangements are commented on in his ballads:

> Jesse had a wife, the darling of his life
> Two children they were brave

as are his brothers:

> It was with his brother, Frank, he robbed the Glendale bank.

Billy the Kid was said to have committed his first murder on a man who insulted his mother, while the Australian bushranger Ned Kelly's mother and family play a central part in the events of 1878–80 and in the folklore that stemmed from them. Kelly folklore is riddled with signifiers of 'family', including the gang membership of Ned's younger brother, Dan, the judicial and police persecution of his mother and other family members, and the melodramatic, if historically inaccurate, heroinisation of Ned's younger sister, Kate Kelly, as an active provider and shield of the bushranger gang.[38] Family and romantic interrelationships also played a big role in the activities and folklore of the Gardiner–Hall gang in New South Wales during the 1860s.[39]

12

Threats—perceived and actual—to certain aspects of family structure and stability are therefore a common feature of the American and Australian experiences of the outlaw hero, yet are absent from that of the highwayman. In this, the New World outlaws bear a rather close resemblance to the structures and activities of the medieval outlaw gangs, which were also based largely on kinship ties.[40] It is tempting to speculate that the role of the family is particularly important in situations where the rule of law and order is weak or has been significantly eroded, as was the case in late medieval England and on the American and Australian frontiers.[41] In the early modern period in England, the administration and effect of law were extended and strengthened; in such circumstances the family may well have had less importance as an extra-legal structure, and so features little in the facts and the folklore of British outlawry.

A related possibility is that the legal and policing systems may have been operating to the satisfaction of the authorities and those economic groups within society closest to those authorities. But for those social groups that generated outlaw heroes, the same law and its systems of application had come to be seen as largely or seriously antagonistic to their own interests. The result was a loss of confidence in these systems, rapidly followed by cynicism and mounting discontent. In the case of convict outlaws of the early period, like Donohoe and others, it is not difficult to see such attitudes conditioning action. But even in the later eras of the 1860s and 1870s, outlaw heroes typically arose in circumstances where duly constituted authority, particularly as it was expressed in policing and judicial administration at the local and regional level, was a source of serious disaffection amongst certain groups. The historical studies of bushranging that have appeared in the last decade have convincingly demonstrated this to be the case in Australia.[42]

It could also be argued that the concentration on family in the American and Australian traditions merely reflects the era of their composition. The family, as currently constructed, is largely an invention of industrial capitalism, a replication of the hierarchical relationships of power and authority demanded for the continuation of modern modes of production and working life. The family therefore appears with increasing frequency in many forms of cultural production from the late eighteenth century onwards. While this may be true, it does not alter the fact that those involved in the American and Australian outbreaks perceived themselves and their actions in terms of their family relationships. Whether that perception was or was not the result of dominant ideology is not at issue here. Family relationships, ties and obligations were provably significant in the motivations and articulations of many of the outlaw heroes of this era; we are therefore entitled to see the reflection of these in the folkloric expressions as 'authentic', despite the wider ideological imperatives of the times.[43]

Consideration also must be given to the traditions that present outlaw heroes in rather less favourable light. In his discussion of the traditions surrounding Bass, Bonney, James and Floyd, Robert Meyer presents and refers to materials that are distinctly antagonistic to these characters. While the folkloric provenance of these materials is not established, there are enough of such expressions, not only in American tradition, but also in British and Australian tradition, to indicate the existence of a dissenting sub-genre. Such ballads and similar narrative expressions generally moralise about the outlaw's actions, lamenting the waste of a life and whatever talents the individual is thought to have possessed. Meyer quotes the following stanza of one such James ballad:

> So, good folks, what's the use of us pretending,
>> It doesn't pay to play these crooked games.
> Beware of any such unhappy ending,
>> Just profit by the death of Jesse James.[44]

There are similar articulations concerning Billy the Kid and Pretty Boy Floyd. In Australia a number of bushranger ballads strike much the same moralising notes. Such compositions seem always to evolve either away from the geographic location of the outlaw hero's activities or some time after his death, or both. They are clearly not motivated by the communal outrage and anger upon which the outlaw is buoyed at the time and place of his actions. Further, such articulations usually bear the marks of mass media popularisation of the outlaw hero. These 'media traditions' tend towards a double standard: glamorising the sensationally violent aspects of the outlaw's career, while being careful to present the proper moralising sentiments about him receiving his just deserts for defying the law. The interaction between the folkloric and the media traditions of the outlaw hero is a continuing theme in what follows.

One element important only in the Australian manifestation of the outlaw hero is an articulation of discontent regarding the British monarchy. Bushranger balladry either directly or indirectly expresses defiance of the duly constituted forces of authority, generally referred to comprehensively as 'the Crown'. Australia was until 1901 a collection of British colonies and is still effectively tied to Britain and the monarchy—Queen Elizabeth II, for instance, includes among her titles 'Queen of Australia'. While republican sentiments of one kind or another have continually waxed and waned in Australia, the influence of Irish attitudes in such matters has always been marked.[45] The strong presence of the Irish in all areas of Australian society from the beginning of European settlement has ensured that the unhappy legacy of English–Irish relationships has left traces, often deep, of discontent within Anglophone Australian folklore. The Irish and Irish-Australian backgrounds of many of the leading bushrangers—Donohoe, Kelly, and the fictional 'Wild Colonial Boy', to mention some—has often been noted, and has undoubtedly been the cause of this particularly Australian expression of the outlaw hero tradition. It is important to note that antagonism to the English Crown is not usually explicit in Irish articulations of the outlaw hero tradition.

FOLKLORE AND FACT

These considerations lead to the question of the relationship between the folkloric tradition of the outlaw hero and the historical events through which the tradition has continually been invoked. In the case of English highwaymen like Turpin and Nevison, it seems that their popular images—no matter how historically inaccurate—came to represent an eighteenth-century resonance of the Robin Hood tradition. While these figures are not known to have been involved in any direct form of social protest or political action, their escapades were a focus for popular discontent with the administration of justice and with general social and political issues. They were thus celebrated in terms of the outlaw hero tradition and, particularly in Turpin's case, continued to represent such traditions in both their popular and folkloric manifestations up to the present day.

The connection between political or pre-political protest and struggle is clear in the case of the Irish outlaw heroes Jeremiah Grant and William Brennan. Both were involved in the long conflict with the English for control of Ireland, as their folklore makes perfectly clear. These political forms of resistance easily shaded into the criminal, producing figures whose personae are an amalgam of the folkloric and the factual as well as an appropriately ambivalent amalgam of the hero and the villain typical of outlaw heroes in Britain, Australia and the United States.

In the case of Jesse James, the post-Civil War dislocation of the border states generated considerable conflict between supporters of the warring sides. Although, as Richard White and others[46] have shown, the James family and their supporters could by no stretch of the imagination be considered 'the poor', their post-war position of relative deprivation made them a convenient focus for the expression of deep discontents within their community. The view of the James family as victims was given considerable impetus by the Pinkerton bombing of the family home.

William Bonney's brief and brutal career as Billy the Kid saw him made the focus of another series of social tensions and conflicts in the Lincoln county area of New Mexico. Here there was a 'range war' between conflicting politico-criminal cliques vying for control of the local and lucrative cattle industry. Bonney worked as a hit-man for the Tunstall faction, gunning down opposing gang-members. This unpromising material for folk heroisation appears to have received a positive impetus from the plight of another local group that could, with considerable justification, call itself 'the poor'. The Mexican-Americans had been discriminated against and extorted to such an extent that even a 'gringo' gun-slinger who apparently performed some erratic act of kindness to one or more members of this despised group was acceptable as a hero. To these people, Billy the Kid became a kind of avenging angel, an outlet and a symbol of their own frustrations and hatreds.[47]

The Australian bushranger heroes—from the convict escapees or 'bolters', like Mathew Brady, Martin Cash, Mike Howe and Jack Donohoe of the early nineteenth century through the 1860s figures of Ben Hall, Frank Gardiner and Daniel Morgan, to the final notorious figure of Ned Kelly—were also intimately associated with episodes of social, political and economic tension. In the case of the early bushrangers, the realities of power were stark and simple. The bushrangers represented the hatreds and perpetrated the vengeance of the convicts upon their military and notoriously brutal gaolers. In the case of the 1860s bushrangers, conflict over control of the land and its livestock resources underlay the activities of Hall, Gardiner and the like, exacerbated by the rush for gold and the consequent demographic and economic dislocations. Similar conflicts over access to land, water, transportation (and hence markets) and the administration of law and order conditioned the north-east Victorian Kelly outbreak of 1878–80 and ensured that the Kellys, like their New South Wales predecessors of the 1860s, would become the focus for the expression of a range of local discontents and the centre of yet another permutation of the outlaw hero tradition. Ned Kelly injected an explicitly political Irish perspective of discontent and dispossession into his struggle, a factor that has no doubt contributed to his longevity as a folk and popular hero in Australia.

The continuations and extensions of the various outlaw hero traditions in folklore and in other forms of cultural representation, particularly the mass media and even emerging forms of electronic communication, also reinforce the link between outlaw heroes and political or social dissent. Billy the Kid, Jesse James, and Dick Turpin continue as characters in film, TV, books, board games and other products.[48] The best example of this is undoubtedly Ned Kelly, whose image, agglomerating many of the essential elements of Australian cultural identity, has transcended the status of local hero and even that of folk hero to become a truly national hero. At least, to many. To others, Kelly will always remain a villain—hardly surprising, given the ambivalent status essential to the generation and perpetuation of outlaw heroes. In the case of Kelly, the image of the outlaw as friend of the poor and downtrodden has persisted well into the twentieth century in folk speech, in folk poetry and in song.[49]

This consideration of the relationship between history and folklore strongly suggests that in pursuing the outlaw hero we are not dealing only with the folkloric recycling of traditional motifs whenever circumstances are appropriate. The interaction between fact and folklore is much more complex, involving also the conscious manipulation of elements of the tradition by individual outlaws and their sympathisers. The actors in significant—and insignificant—outlawry episodes determine many of their actions by their knowledge of the outlaw hero tradition, of its embedded moral code and the expectations of their sympathisers, also conditioned by their knowledge of the tradition. The outlaw hero tradition therefore provides a kind of 'cultural script' by which all the actors involved can plan and judge their attitudes and actions. Because those actions involve defiance of dominant power structures of one kind or another, it is necessary for outlaws and their supporters to follow an alternative, traditionally defined, moral code that acts to legitimise their defiance and violence in certain circumstances. The lore becomes the law, substituting an appropriate moral code for the legal system being directly challenged by particular outlaw heroes. In this way, the folkloric underpins, motivates and sanctions activities that rupture the social fabric as violently as outlawry and, ultimately, acts to control the potential excesses likely to stem from such activities, even as it sanctions and supports them.[50]

Confirmation of this way of looking at the folklore and history of outlaw heroes is provided by the fact that only a very few individuals become heroes. Of the vast numbers who embark on criminal activities like those described here, only those whose activities relate to—or can be interpreted as relating to—circumstances of perceived oppression are celebrated in song and story. Turpin, Nevison, Grant and Brennan— among very few others—became the foci of deep tensions and serious conflicts within their societies, both during and after their lives. The same observations apply to William Bonney, Jesse James, Sam Bass and a few other American badmen. In Australia it was Jack Donohoe, Ben Hall and Ned Kelly who were the main candidates selected from a very large pool for celebration as outlaw heroes. The traditions and the historical circumstances associated with these and other outlaw heroes in Britain, Australia and America are investigated in the following pages.

CHAPTER TWO

Outlaws of Myth

One of the main themes of this book is the interaction of the folkloric and the historical. The extent to which the values and attitudes embedded in folk traditions determine attitudes and actions in specific times and places—and the subsequent impact of these events on the continuation of the tradition—is a concern taken up at various points. Many of the folkloric expressions that constitute the outlaw hero tradition relate to historical figures and their real, imputed or imagined activities. These are discussed in some detail in subsequent chapters. At this preliminary stage, though, it is appropriate to look briefly at the non-historical or mythic characters and narratives that occur in the tradition and which provide an ongoing reservoir of outlaw hero elements, generally detached from the specifics of time, place and a particular human agency. Because these expressions do not generally deal with the activities of historical outlaws, they are applicable to many situations and easily adaptable across wide distances and long periods. They are universal enough in their outlaw essentials, yet vague enough in their historicity, to be appealing to a great diversity of potential singers/speakers and hearers. Most of these items are therefore extremely widespread in oral tradition. Their wide diffusion suggests strongly that they, in conjunction with the song, verse and narrative expressions relevant to each national tradition, have been an important means of preserving and transmitting the ethos of the noble robber in Anglophone tradition. As will be seen, this preservation and transmission has both 'positive' and 'negative' facets, which implies that the alternative moral code of outlawry—the lore—is not simply a chance grouping of beliefs but a coherent philosophy and a guide to appropriate action. This philosophy is generally articulated only in fragmentary form in any one expression, yet is clearly present when the corpus that makes up the outlaw hero tradition is examined as a whole. An appreciation of this mythical and widely transmissible 'core' of outlaw hero expressions is a necessary preliminary to the subsequent examination of the historical outlaw heroes of Britain, America and Australia.

MEDIEVAL OUTLAWRY

While the outlaw hero tradition motivates attitudes and actions of historical characters in the drama of history, the Anglophone archetype of the tradition remains a myth. 'Robin Hood', long looked for as a real person, has not yet been convincingly located in the shadows of medieval England where outlawry was made a legal state or, more accurately, a non-state. If an individual were declared an outlaw, his lands and goods were forfeit to the authorities, variously the king and the individual's lord. The outlaw, who was presumed to bear the wolf's head, and thus was no longer a human being, could also be arrested by any man. If the outlaw resisted arrest, it was lawful for him to be killed by the arrester. This situation persisted legally until 1329 when the king's judges decided that only a properly appointed justice could put an outlaw to death. However, outlaws were being killed in the belief that it was lawful until at least the end of the fourteenth century.

The outlaw, then, was literally cast out of human society and explicitly identified with the natural world, the domain of the animal. He was no longer human and could be slain by any (male) human with complete immunity from prosecution by the law. Although the severity of outlawry declined from the fifteenth century, outlawry legislation remained within the British legal code and was invoked against Ned Kelly in the colony of Victoria in 1879. During the American Civil War the members of Quantrill's Raiders were outlawed by the Federal authorities (see Chapter 4). The concept of the outlaw, and legal definitions and manipulations of the concept, are therefore continually involved in the lives and legends of many outlaw heroes.

While not designed specifically to deal with highway robbery, outlawry was typically the legal means used to deal with such lawbreaking. In medieval England, highway robbery was endemic; it was usually carried out by large gangs of criminals, the members of which were frequently of noble families. Some of the activities of gangs like the

Folville family were related to power and wealth—struggles within and between the aristocracy—and therefore had a political dimension. This dimension was generally restricted to the nobles themselves, who were often able to purchase, or otherwise obtain from the king, pardons from their outlawry. The fact that highway robbery was the focus of several attempts in the fourteenth and early fifteenth centuries—the latter being briefly successful—to declare it treasonous is an early indication of the continuing linkage between the actions of highway-robbing outlaws and political or pre-political dissent. The troubled state of the realm in the later medieval period was reflected in the 1283 Statute of Westminster, an attempt to reorganise and reinforce the legal system and reverse the corruption, depredation and civic strife that had become the norm. Wat Tyler's rebellion of 1381 was a reaction to a long period of legal and economic oppression which forms the social context in which we first hear of Robin Hood, around 1360.

It has sometimes been argued that Robin Hood was simply a convenient name upon which to hang accounts and legends of the doings of real and imaginary medieval outlaws. The period certainly had no lack of such gangs and legends, but there seems little in the activities of these politico-criminal federations likely to sustain a legend as pervasive and powerful as that of Robin Hood. Indeed, the activities of the medieval outlaws seem mostly to have outraged the conventions of the outlaw hero code. Perhaps the reality of the situation conditioned the ballads that were generated at this time about fictional outlaws, including Robin Hood, but also relating to, among others, Adam Bell and even one Mar Stig, a European outlaw. Regardless of the exact relationship between reality and romance in these cases, a cultural stereotype of some potency came into existence during this period and was available for refinement and adaptation in relation to the later figure of the highwayman.[1]

ROBIN HOOD

The predominantly aristocratic nature of medieval outlawry is reflected faithfully in the early ballads and 'A Mery Geste of Robyn Hoode' (going by various titles and usually referred to as the 'Geste').[2] Although Robin is a commoner in these works (he is not elevated to the aristocracy until the seventeenth century), the world of the Geste is clearly that of the rich and powerful. The Sheriff of Nottingham appears in his role of arch-villain. There are knights, abbots, sundry other nobles and notables

Title page of A Mery Geste of Robyn Hoode, *an early sixteenth-century treatment of the Robin Hood legend. (By permission of the British Library, C21c63.)*

and, of course, the king himself. In the end, Robin helps the king and is received into his service. But after a while the expense and his nostalgia for the greenwood compel him to ask the king for permission to visit his old haunts again. The king grants him a week. Robin returns to the forest, rejoins his band and his week's holiday extends for twenty-two years, a continuing refusal to accept the monarch's authority. In the end, he is betrayed to death by the Prioress and Sir Roger. The various versions of 'The Geste of Robyn Hoode' present Robin as a heroic figure and conclude unequivocally with the verse:

> Cryst haue mercy on his soule,
>   That dyed on the rode!
> For he was a good outlaw,
>   And dyde pore men moch god.

The Geste is a literary work of some sophistication, either compiled from existing ballads or using the same materials. The early ballads of the fifteenth century are certainly less literary (many perhaps being in oral circulation before their capture in print) and also tend to be more proletarian in their characterisation and plotting. While Robin has the scoundrelly but still relatively high-born Sheriff of Nottingham to outwit, and corrupt members of the clergy to deal with, he has encounters with commoners, such as a potter in 'Robin Hood and the Potter'. The potter bests Robin, after which Robin symbolically exchanges clothes with him and, in this trickster disguise, goes off to Nottingham for further adventures with the Sheriff and, as it happens, his wife. This is similar in some ways to the later 'Robin Hood and the Pedlar' in which a pedlar defeats Robin in a fight and is symbolically incorporated into the 'band of merry men'. In this ballad, Robin is still a leader of ordinary men, his heroic status dependent on his bravery, courteousness, fairness and skill. The greenwood hero of the ballads and the Geste, then, despite his increasing aristocratic connections, is still quite a way removed from the 'earl of Huntingdon', the awfully-named Robert Fitz Ooth, supposedly and conveniently descended from both Norman and Saxon forebears. This eighteenth-century fabrication influenced much subsequent thinking about Robin as a wronged noble.

Outside the fictions of balladry, Robin Hood was still making his way in the real world. While the earliest mention of Robin Hood in Langland's *Piers Plowman* of c. 1377 is not explicit on Robin's status as a robber of the rich and a potential threat to established order, by the first half of the following century, his political nature is apparently commonplace, as a 1439 petition to Parliament makes clear. The petition concerned one Piers Venables of Derbyshire, a fugitive who had gathered a band around him who 'beyng of his clothinge, and in manere of insurrection went into the wodes in that county like it hadde be Robyn Hode and his meynee'.[3] In Southacre, Norfolk, during 1441, labourers and yeomen threaten to kill a Sir John Harsyk. They block the road and chant 'We are Robynhodesmen. War, war, war.'[4] And there are numerous other small but significant instances where Robin Hood is connected with political discontent and action, including the Poll Tax rioters of 1993, who invaded Nottingham Council Chambers disguising themselves in hoods of Lincoln green.[5]

Regardless of the historicity of Robin Hood, his image, both popular and folkloric, is that of the outlaw hero, and he is clearly viewed in such terms from a very early period. The courteous archer in Lincoln green is therefore justifiably seen as the archetype against which all subsequent Anglophone outlaw heroes are measured. That this is so is made elegantly clear in F. J. Child's account and editing of the Robin Hood ballads, where he presents evidence that these songs celebrating the real or mythical outlaw's exploits were widely sung in England, and beyond, around 1400 and, given the Piers Plowman reference, almost certainly much earlier.[6] While, according to Child's view, the later balladic treatments of this figure 'debase' it in various ways, it is clear when viewed from the perspective of the outlaw hero tradition that this 'debasement' is in fact a sharpening and refining of the image of Robin Hood. Whereas he is certainly a friend of the poor in the Geste and, presumably, in the earlier traditions, by the time of a seventeenth-century treatment titled 'The True Tale of Robin Hood' (1632)[7] he is a fully-fledged outlaw hero, with all the characteristics likely to be attributed to such a persona. Here the outlaw is definitely a morally upright friend of the poor—'all poore men pray for him, / And wish he well might spede.' He helps distressed travellers on the road, assists widows and orphans, protects women, generally operates against the established power and corruption of the church, and robs the rich, particularly those who 'did the poore oppresse'. He does not harm the humble workers nor harm any man 'That him invaded not'. He is finally betrayed to death by 'A faithlesse fryer'. Here Robin Hood has reached his status as the defining type of the outlaw hero. The image is reinforced in another seventeenth-century ballad, 'The Noble Fisherman' or 'Robin Hood's preferment' (Child, No. 148), which has Robin saying:

It shall be so, as I have said;
    And, with this gold, for the oprest
An habitation I will build,
    Where they shall live in peace and rest.[8]

In his influential discussions of the Robin Hood ballads, Child usefully summarised the salient characteristics of the Robin Hood portrayed in those works, in many respects anticipating Hobsbawm by some sixty years:

> Robin Hood is a yeoman, outlawed for reasons not given but
> easily surmised. 'Courteous and free', religious in sentiment, and
> above all reverent of the Virgin, for the love of whom he is
> respectful to all women. He lives by the King's deer (though he
> loves no man in the world so much as his King) and by levies on
> the superfluity of the higher orders, secular and spiritual, bishops
> and archbishops, abbots, bold barons and knights, but harms no
> husbandman or yeoman, and is friendly to poor men generally,
> imparting to them of what he takes from the rich. Courtesy,
> good temper, liberality and manliness are his chief marks; for
> courtesy and good temper he is a popular Gawain. Yeoman as he
> is, he has a kind of royal dignity, a princely grace, and a
> gentleman-like refinement of humour.[9]

Here, with the exception of the outlaw's reputed religious and monarchist sentiments, are the ideal features of the outlaw hero or 'social bandit' as delineated so compellingly by Hobsbawm. The ballad Robin Hood is bold, manly, free, courteous to women, a robber of the rich and a friend to the poor. The forest outlaw of the ballads and of other oral traditions is an archetype of the 'noble robber', a characterisation that parallels the presentations of Robin Hood in literature, film and other popular forms of Anglophone cultural tradition. Much time and learned effort has been devoted to the study of this character—sometimes with the aim of discovering his true identity, sometimes with an interest in the more general mythic significance of the green archer.[10] The most recent research and its conclusions are that Robin remains a figure of uncertain historicity but is a cultural symbol of considerable potency in the English-speaking world. Dobson and Taylor's revised and reissued

Rymes of Robin Hood discusses Robin Hood place-names, linguistic terms, films and other evidence of the enduring popularity of the outlaw, as well as a representative selection of mostly literary Robin Hood ballads.[11] Although Dobson and Taylor's work deals only briefly with the folkloric aspects of Robin Hood, it provides proof, if more were needed, of the persistence of particular cultural motifs over long periods of time and across great distances.

As well as proving his virility in past as well as present popular and high culture, Robin Hood has persisted to some extent in folksong. A few oral versions of Robin Hood ballads were retrieved by English folk-song collector Alfred Williams early this century, and they provide evidence, if in somewhat fragmentary form, of the persistence of Robin Hood's image in British tradition.

BOLD ROBIN HOOD[12]

Of great popularity with the more aged men. Words of Elijah Idles, Inglesham.

> Bold Robin Hood was a forester good,
> As ever drew bow in the merry green-wood,
> And the wild deer did follow, did follow,
> And the wild deer did follow:
> There's none so bonny, blithe, and gay
> As Mary, the pride of the morning.
>
> Then up came Little John with his courage so strong,
> He conquered them all with his hey-ding-dong,
> While the bugle horn he echoed, he echoed,
> While the bugle horn he echoed:
> There's none so bonny, blithe, and gay
> As Mary, the pride of the morning.

While it is difficult to attribute too much to these obviously attenuated versions, it is clear that both celebrate the archer in traditional manner. 'Bold Robin Hood' seems to have picked up elements of nineteenth-century music hall, but 'Robin Hood and Little John' can be identified as the remnants of a ballad already in existence by the end of the sixteenth century and included in Child's great collection under the same title (No. 125). The scene is a favourite of filmmakers and also, it seems, of singers, with Little John and Robin meeting on the famous bridge that can only carry one of them at a time. They fight and, depending on the version of the story or ballad, Little John wins or Little John wins at first but is subsequently tricked by Robin into losing. In any case, it all ends in a display of bonhomie in which Little John is taken into Robin's band, at once an incorporation of valuable skills and a symbolic gesture towards the community represented by 'the merry men'—a 'resistant community', in Knight's useful phrase.[13]

ROBIN HOOD AND LITTLE JOHN[14]

Fragment. This ancient song was sung at Quenington; the following is all I could obtain. Words of Mrs Timbrel, Quenington.

> When bold Robin Hood was about twenty years old,
>   He happened to meet Little John,
> For he was a blade right fit for the trade,
>   And he was a lusty young man.
>
> They happened to meet on a long, narrow bridge,
>   Where never a one gave way;
> Says bold Robin Hood, as he right gallantly stood,
>   'Now we'll have a fight and away.'
>
> They fought, they fought, up hill and down.

It seems from these fragmentary texts and Williams' observations on them and the age of their singers that Robin Hood may have been in decline as a central figure of rural English folksong by the early part of the century. As A. L. Lloyd has pointed out, only seven or so of the nearly forty Robin Hood ballads in Child have been collected in British oral tradition, and a further three in America.[15] These turn up in various states of completeness in the collections of the late and early nineteenth centuries,[16] usually derived from nineteenth-century broadside versions, especially those printed by Such and Catnach. It seems fair to say from the available evidence that, while Robin Hood retained a definite niche in oral tradition, he can hardly be said to be a major figure of British folksong. Nor of American or Australian traditions. In all these places Robin Hood the outlaw hero was supplanted in oral tradition by highwaymen, badmen and bushrangers.

But a glance at the catalogues of the broadside printers of the 1830s shows that Robin Hood lived on in popular fictions—the publisher Catnach featured two Robin Hood ballads in his 1832 catalogue, and only one on Turpin.[17] And while the outlaw of Sherwood may have relinquished whatever place he had in the sung traditions of England, he was being put to a variety of uses by both popular and elite artists from the early fifteenth century onwards.

In a comprehensive and careful study, *Robin Hood: A Complete Study of the English Outlaw,*[18] Stephen Knight has diligently traced the outlaw's career in literature, film and popular culture up to the present time. Knight shows how the Robin Hood mythology underwent changes related to social, economic and ideological pressures. Robin's original folkloric presence is in legends, place-names, proverbs, drama and, presumably, ballads[19] as a symbolic figure of resistance to authority and of communal solidarity. While these notions have persisted, they have been overlaid and extended by narrative treatments that variously gentrify, politicise, nationalise and romanticise the story and its hero. Knight provides convincing evidence of these processes and the historical contexts in which they occurred. What is especially noteworthy about Knight's approach, though, is that, unlike most previous commentators, he is aware that such changes do not necessarily supersede any previous interpretations. There is no necessary chronology, no neat or even messy succession from one treatment of Robin Hood to another. Rather, many such treatments may co-exist, providing different meanings for different social groups. While Alfred Williams' rustic ancients were trying to recall the lusty Robin Hood songs of their youth, the Newbolt reforms of English education were generating then-politically correct texts for the edification of 'young England'. Still in circulation was the Aldine series, 'The Robin Hood Library'(1901–06), a series of twopenny pamphlets aimed at the *Boys' Own* readership, but with a veneer of classicism. It is this ability of a character or narrative to lodge in diverse cultural niches and mean various, often conflicting, things to various groups, even at the same historical moment, that is a marker of myth. Knight pins down the Robin Hood myth in its various incarnations through the centuries, clarifying its sometimes strong, sometimes weak interactions with notions and needs of rebellion and resistance.

At first Robin Hood is a forest fugitive, which as noted above was a common figure in the twelfth and thirteenth centuries. In this guise Robin is a shadowy opponent of authority and law, as well as a symbol of communal solidarity. There is a decided aura of raffishness and the demotic in the fourteenth-century references, involving both robbery and ribaldry. The resistant elements, consistent with the image of the outlaw hero, are developed and refined in the ballads of the fourteenth century and after, and also in the widespread Robin Hood plays and games that are first recorded in the early fifteenth century (at Exeter, 1426–27). These performances were closely associated with the ritual calendar and with traditional activities, including raising funds, sports, competitions and other festive activities. The records of Robin Hood plays increase throughout the 1500s, as does official concern about them. By around 1600 most of these plays have quietly faded away or been actively suppressed through a combination of growing Puritanism and civic alarm.

It is the civic alarm that is of most interest here. The suppression of the plays was part of a long process of official elimination or sanitisation of popular revels. The authorities were concerned about what they considered undesirable social aspects of these events, such as drunkenness, gluttony, violence, 'levying' (essentially, demanding money with menaces, a traditional form of obtaining funds in economies lacking social security), petty crime, damage to property and so on. These were usually the reasons given for the banning of popular fairs and festivities. A rarely expressed reason was the propensity of such events to focus social and economic disaffection, and to provide vehicles for the active demonstration of discontent. Riots were a frequent accompaniment of folk customs, and while these were generally poorly organised and ill-articulated, they were nevertheless seen as a threat to social order. Robin Hood's definite, if fuzzily defined, resistance to authority was in this context an unwelcome development. While subsequent redefinitions of Robin Hood by professional dramatists, poets, historians and other writers generally tended away from these folkloric discontents, the association of Robin Hood with opposition to injustice and with the communality of 'the merry men in the greenwood' remained as one of those continuing, if gradually submerging, elements of the myth.

The medieval archer has certainly lived on in a multitude of cultural representations, and in popular memory, from the thirteenth century to the present. In 1991 *The Adventures of Robin Hood*, a British production, screened at cinemas around the English-speaking world. At about the same time Hollywood produced yet another treatment of the outlaw, starring Kevin Costner. Having burned out their cost-effective time on the silver screen, both these productions are now being narrowcast on

The Sword of Sherwood Forest. *(Copyright © 1960 Columbia Pictures Industries, Inc. All Rights Reserved. Courtesy of Columbia Pictures.)*

thousands of living-room VCRs in Britain, Australia and the United States, and elsewhere in the world. In 1993 Mel Brookes produced a filmic parody of the Robin Hood mythology: *Robin Hood—Men in Tights.* These film versions of Robin Hood continue a Hollywood tradition of regularly celebrating the English outlaw every few years, a tradition beginning in 1909 with 'Robin Hood and His Merry Men' and involving well over thirty productions to date. The outlaw has also had an enduring career in the theatre, in dramatic, comic and musical forms and, as with some other noble robbers, is celebrated, commemorated and commodified in the places of his passing. There are three tourist theme parks and recreations of the Robin Hood myth in and around Nottingham.

But it is a tamed and domesticated image that emerges from these representations; one so familiar and even warm that the outlaw is able to lead a healthy existence in mainstream children's literature, theatre and animation. For adults, Robin Hood is simply a familiar figure of adventure, romance and vicarious freedom from obvious forms of tyranny and oppression. This is some distance from armed defiance of the forces of law and order that spearhead the entire apparatus of civil society. The fiercer and more unequivocally resistant strands of the outlaw hero tradition in Britain have for some centuries involved the highwayman rather than the forest outlaw. The highwayman, armed with the technology of impersonal death and mounted on steeds able to quickly traverse the rapidly growing networks of roads required for economic expansion, was the unlikely heir of Robin Hood's noble robber image. Like the medieval outlaws, the early modern highwaymen were both mythic and real. Like Robin, many of these celebrated highwaymen heroes lived only in ballads.

NON-HISTORICAL OUTLAWS

Historical figures who became celebrated in terms of the outlaw hero tradition are discussed in a later chapter. The material presented here indicates the continuity of the essential elements of the outlaw hero in British folk tradition through a number of examples selected from a substantial repertoire of fictional outlaw ballads. Many of these songs are very widely distributed throughout Britain, and some are well-known in America and Australia. Not all can be considered part of the outlaw song genre, belonging to other, though related, groups, such as 'the dying rake' or the 'country bumpkin outwitting the urban thief'. These various texts—either positive or negative—nevertheless reveal essential aspects of outlaw hero folklore.

Positive Highwayman Ballads

The positive texts are those in which unnamed highwaymen figures perform robberies and other acts in accordance with the code of the outlaw hero tradition. The examples selected here are 'The Highwayman', 'The Jolly Highwayman', 'The Maltman and the Highwayman', 'The Flying Highwayman', and 'The Wild Colonial Boy'. The protagonists of these sung narratives are best seen as idealised representations of the outlaw hero,[20] robbing only the rich, sometimes giving to the poor, acting courteously to women, and generally being portrayed as heroes rather than as villains.

The most common motif in these ballads is the avowal that the outlaw robs the rich and not the poor, as in 'The Highwayman'. More widely-known as 'Newry Town', this song relates to that body of songs dealing with the sad fate of the rakish blade, usually brought undone by the pox or some other dire fate. The hero of this ballad justifies his criminal activities by the need he feels to maintain his wife in proper style. The hero is also at pains to point out that:

> I never robbed a poor man yet,
> Or caused a tradesman for to fret,
> I robbed the rich, but I served the poor . . .

And, although he robs the rich, like Robin Hood, he avowedly helps the poor.[21]

THE HIGHWAYMAN[22]

> In Newry town I was bred and born,
> In London town I die in scorn,
> I was brought up to the saddle trade,
> I was always thought a roving blade.
>
> At seventeen I took a wife,
> I loved her dearly as my life,
> And to maintain her both fine and gay,
> I robbed upon the King's highway.
>
> I robbed Lord Mansfield I do declare,
> His Lady fair in Grosvenor Square,
> I gave three cheers; bidding them goodnight,
> And went to the play in great delight.
>
> Through Covent Garden was my way,
> I and my girl to see the play,
> But Fielding's gang did me swift pursue,
> They took me then, the cursed crew.
>
> I never robbed a poor man yet,
> Or caused a tradesman for to fret,
> I robbed the rich, but I served the poor,
> Which brings me to this dismal door.

When I am dead and for the grave
Let me a splendid funeral have,
Let none but robbers go with me,
Give them I pray their liberty.

While the protagonist of the brief ballad 'The Jolly Highwayman'
does not have much interest in the poor, he robs only the rich, it seems,
and does enunciate the traditional outlaw hero justification of supporting
his aged mother. As in many outlaw hero expressions—'The Wild Colonial Boy', for instance—the robbing and humiliation of the powerful
and wealthy is a central plot element.

THE JOLLY HIGHWAYMAN[23]

It's a jolly highwayman, likewise a noted rover,
I drove my parents almost wild when I first went a roving
I robbed lords, I robbed dukes in a very rakish manner,
Not only to maintain myself, likewise my aged mother.

The very first man that I did rob, it being a lord of honour,
I did abuse that mighty lord in a very rakish manner,
'Deliver your money, my lord, without any more desire,
For, if you don't it's my desire with powder and shot to fire.'

I put a pistol to his breast, which made him for to shiver,
Ten thousand guineas all in bright gold to me he did deliver,
Besides a gold repeater watch to me he did surrender,
I thought I had a noble prize to me he did deliver.

The very next man that I did rob was down in Kelpin's garden,
And not long after he was robbed, in Newgate I was fastened,
To hear the turnkeys and the locks and bolts at six o'clock in the
    morning,
Glad was I, resolved to die, so fare you well, companions.

The redoubtable Alfred Williams also collected a version of 'The
Maltman and the Highwayman', a song in which the maltman is robbed
and stabbed by a 'gentleman thief' in clear contravention of the code of
the noble robber. A helpful miller sends the thief to a just end and is
exonerated from the crime of murder by the testimony of the recovered

maltman. It is something of a fantasy, but a revealing one in terms of the arguments advanced here.

THE MALTMAN AND THE HIGHWAYMAN[24]

I will tell you a story at large,
   When a maltman was riding along,
He had in his pocket great charge,
   Not thinking any man would him wrong.

He was met by a gentleman thief,
   Who bid him a civil salute,
Who bid him deliver in brief,
   For there was no time for dispute.

Then in silver he gave him three pounds,
   But that little sum would not do,
Till he did oblige him with wounds,
   And his broadsword he presently drew.

He cut him without more delay,
   Till twenty bright guineas he'd got,
Then the rogue he went laughing away,
   And he left him to bleed on the spot.

A Salisbury miller came by,
   A man of wonderful size,
Seeing his neighbour lying there,
   Dismounted and bleeding likewise—

'Oh, what is the matter?' calls he.
   'Kind sir! I am robbed of my store,
My silver and guineas to boot,
   And the rogue is gone jogging before.'

'Oh, lend me but thy nimble nag,
   More swifter than my heavy Ball,
And if I don't recover thy loss,
   Odzooks! it shall cause me a fall.'

Then me [*sic*] mounted on his nimble nag,
   And he rode through the night and the day,

And the highwayman at him let fly,
    But a miss was as good as a mile.

Then he stepped up with all speed,
    And lent him a knock on his crown,
His club was so heavy and great,
    Which it made him come tumbling down.

'Now we'll hang him on yonder high tree,
    For fear of some sudden uproar:
But now he's stone dead you may see,
    He will never rob gentlemen more.'

Then at Salisbury the miller was tried,
    For hanging the highwayman there;
But the maltman went in at his side,
    So poor Joseph the miller got clear.

'The Flying Highwayman' is an undated broadside, possibly referring to any of a number of 'flying' highwaymen from the seventeenth
and eighteenth centuries, or to a complete fiction. Nevertheless, the
appropriate outlaw hero sentiments have become attached to this song.
The protagonist is youthful and bold; he robs only the rich, believing it
is his 'duty' not to rob the poor; and he meets his execution with the
required bravado. Improbably, 'Young Morgan' is pardoned by the king
in the nick of time.

THE FLYING HIGHWAYMAN[25]

Come all ye bold and swaggering Blades,
    That go in search of plunder,
With Pistols cock'd and courage bold,
    Have Voices loud as thunder.

Young MORGAN was a flashy blade
    No youth had better courage,
Much gold he got on the highway,
    That made him daily flourish.

Grand Bagnios was his lodging then,
    Among the flashy Lasses;

35

Soon he became a Gentleman,
   And left off driving Asses.

I scorn poor people for to rob,
   I thought it so my duty;
But when I met the rich and gay,
   On them I made my Booty.

Stand and deliver was the word,
   We must have no denial;
But alas, poor Morgan chang'd his note,
   And soon was brought to trial.

I robb'd for gold and silver bright,
   For to maintain my Misses,
And we saluted when we met,
   With most melodious kisses.

After sweet meat comes sour sauce,
   Which brought me to repentance,
For now at last I'm try'd and cast,
   And going to receive my sentence.

Up Hounslow Heath and Putney too,
   I oft made my approaches;
Like lightning I and my horse did fly,
   When I heard the sound of Coaches:

When first of all I was call'd up,
   In order for my trial,
With my beaver hat and surtout coat,
   I stood a bold denial.

I stood as bold as John of Gaunt,
   All in my rich attire;
I ne'er seem'd daunted in the least,
   Which made the court admire.

From Newgate to St. Giles's pound,
   Me and my Moll was carted;
But when we came to the gallows tree,
   Me and my Moll were parted:

So I took leave of all my friends,
  Likewise my flashy Blowen;
But now at last I'm try'd and cast,
  Out of the world I'm going.

I thought I heard the people say
  As I rode through the city,
That such a clever Youth as I,
  To die it was a pity:

I thought I heard such cries as those,
  Which set my tears a flowing;
But now alas, I'm try'd and cast,
  And out of the world I'm going.

I'm the Captain of the gang,
  All in a low condition;
But now I'm going to be hang'd,
  I'll throw up my commission.

So why should I refuse to die,
  Now here or ever after;
The Captain he must lead the way,
  His men must follow after:

The King was pleased to pardon me,
  And on me took compassion,
And freed me from the gallows tree,
  All in my low condition.

Perhaps the single most important example of the positive non-historical highwayman ballad is the 'The Wild Colonial Boy'.[26] Although closely related to the British highwayman ballad in style, it is not British in origin. Appearing in Australia during the gold rush period of the 1850s and 1860s, this ballad is widely sung throughout the British Isles, as it is in America, and elsewhere. The Wild Colonial Boy is a mythical bushranger who, like certain historical bushrangers discussed later, belongs firmly to the outlaw hero tradition, robbing the rich to help the poor and bravely defying the forces of authority to the bitter end.

This song is probably the most widespread of all outlaw hero ballads and so is particularly important. It is discussed in more detail at a number of points throughout this book, but here it is worth noting that the song is rich in the elements of the outlaw hero tradition already outlined. The Wild Colonial Boy is a member of a nationality that is widely represented as oppressed;[27] he is brave and defiant; he robs the wealthy squatters or, in some versions, a judge. In an American-Irish version he is said to have 'helped the poor';[28] he is adept at disguise, eluding pursuers and escaping from tricky situations.[29] In the end, he dies game. While he is not betrayed in a direct sense, many versions of the song have him being deserted by his cowardly companions in the ultimate moment of need.

But as well as these considerations, it is arguably the very clearly articulated revolt of the Wild Colonial Boy against the powers of authority and law that makes the song, in all its variants, so transnationally appealing. Given the close connection already observed between dissent, protest and the heroisation of certain outlawed individuals, it would seem that the particular permutation of the outlaw hero tradition evinced in the ballad of 'The Wild Colonial Boy' is ideally suited to just about any situation of perceived injustice and oppression.

THE WILD COLONIAL BOY[30]

'Tis of a Wild Colonial Boy, Jack Doolan was his name,
Of poor but honest parents he was born in Castlemaine.
He was his father's only hope, his mother's only joy,
And dearly did his parents love the Wild Colonial Boy.

CHORUS
Come, all my hearties, we'll roam the mountains high,
Together we will plunder, together we will die.
We'll wander over valleys, and gallop over plains,
And we'll scorn to live in slavery, bound down with iron chains.

He was scarcely sixteen years of age when he left his father's home,
And through Australia's sunny clime a bushranger did roam.
He robbed those wealthy squatters, their stock he did destroy,
And a terror to Australia was the Wild Colonial Boy.

In sixty-one this daring youth commenced his wild career,
With a heart that knew no danger, no foemen did he fear.
He stuck up the Beechworth mail-coach, and robbed Judge
    MacEvoy,
Who trembled, and gave up his gold to the Wild Colonial Boy.

38

He bade the judge 'Good morning', and told him to beware,
That he'd never rob a hearty chap that acted on the square,
And never to rob a mother of her son and only joy,
Or else you may turn outlaw, like the Wild Colonial Boy.

One day as he was riding the mountain-side along,
A-listening to the little birds, their pleasant laughing song,
Three mounted troopers rode along—Kelly, Davis and Fitzroy—
They thought that they would capture him, the Wild Colonial
    Boy.

'Surrender now, Jack Doolan, you see we're three to one.
Surrender now, Jack Doolan, you daring highwayman.'
He drew a pistol from his belt, and shook the little toy,
'I'll fight, but not surrender', said the Wild Colonial Boy.

He fired at Trooper Kelly and brought him to the ground,
And in return from Davis received a mortal wound.
All shattered through the jaws he lay still firing at Fitzroy,
And that's the way they captured him—the Wild Colonial Boy.

Negative Highwayman Ballads

The second category of ballads consists of 'negative' texts in which highwaymen are portrayed acting against or outside the code of the outlaw
hero tradition and suffer appropriate consequences. There are a number
of such songs, including 'The Yorkshire Farmer', 'The Yorkshire Bite',
'The Highwayman Outwitted', and 'The Two Jolly Butchers', reproduced here. In 'The Three Butchers', up to nine unheroic highwaymen
are defeated by a 'Young Johnston', and in 'The Bold Robber', a highwayman attempts to rob a 'poor sailor', who kills the highwayman. Most
of these songs belong to genres other than those of the outlaw hero. But
their portrayal and disapproval of 'un-highwayman-like' actions reveals
the obverse of the outlaw hero tradition, and therefore its potency as an
approved or sanctioned code of behaviour for those outside the law.

In 'The Yorkshire Farmer', for example, yet another 'gentleman
thief' preys upon the apparent gullibility of a 'silly old man'. However,
the farmer is not so silly and, realising the intent of the thief, leads him
to believe that his money is hidden in his saddle. When the thief
demands it, the farmer throws the saddle away, obliging the thief to get
off his horse to retrieve it and the loot. The farmer takes the opportunity

to send the thief's horse on its way and to escape himself—presumably still in possession of his goods—leaving the outwitted robber to fruit-lessly search the saddle.

THE YORKSHIRE FARMER[31]

A song I will sing unto you,
  A song of a merry intent,
It is of a silly old man
  Who went for to pay his rent.

As he was a-riding along,
  A-riding along the highway,
A gentleman thief overtook him
  And this unto him did say:

'How far are you going on this way?'
  It made the old man for to smile,
'To tell you the truth, kind Sir,
  I just am a-going two mile.

'I'm but a poor silly old man
  Who farms a good piece of ground.
My half year's rent, kind Sir,
  It just comes to forty odd pound.'

'But oh never mind,' said the farmer,
  'I do not fear thieves on my side,
My money is put in two bags,
  And hid in the saddle I ride.'

As they were riding along,
  A-riding all down a steep gyll,
The thief pulled out a pistol,
  And bade the old man stand still.

The old man was crafty and false,
  As in this wide world there are many,
His saddle he threw over t' hedge,
  Said, 'Fetch it if thou wilt have any.'

The thief he got off his brown horse,
  His courage was stout and was bold,

To search for the farmer's two bags,
 He gave him his horse to hold.

The farmer put foot in the stirrup,
 When once he had got him astride
He set the thief's horse in a gallop,
 You need not have bid him to ride.

The thief he was not content,
 He thought he must have the two bags,
So he took out his rusty old sword
 And chopped the old saddle to rags.

In an eighteenth-century broadside usually known as 'The Yorkshire
Bite', the deceitful highwayman is outwitted by a young boy, who gains the
robber's booty for his justified reward. The highwayman appears as a straightforward and not very clever thief attempting to take advantage of the boy's
youth and apparent naivety. The highwayman tries to rob 'the poor' and
displays no heroism at all, while his intended victim exhibits cunning and
boldness, winning the approbation of his master and a generous portion of
the undeserving highwayman's booty. The version given here is an oral one,
collected early this century. The song is also known in America.

THE YORKSHIRE BITE[32]

It's of an old farmer who kept for his man
A bright Yorkshire lad, as you well understand;
Said he, 'Go and take this old cow to the fair,
She is in good order, and that I swear.'

Away went the cow with her head in a band,
And away went the lad, as you well understand;
When he got to the fair he met with three men,
And sold the old cow for six pound ten.

Then he went to an alehouse, where he asked to drink,
And counting his change, how the money did clink!
'Oh, what am I to do with this money?' said he,
'For fear on the road some robbers might be.'

'Sew it in your coat-lining,' the landlord did say,
'Or you might be robbed upon the highway.'

There sat a highwayman a-drinking his wine,
Said he to himself, 'That money is mine.'

The lad he jumped up, and away he did go,
The highwayman quick followed after also;
'You're well overtaken, young man,' he did say,
'You're well overtaken all on the highway.'

'How far are you going?' the highwayman cried.
'Oh, it's four or five miles,' the lad he replied,
'Oh, it's four or five miles, for what I do know.'
'Then jump up behind, and away we will go.'

They rode till they came to a very dark lane
Where there was no one to be heard or be seen;
'Now deliver up thy money, without fear or strife,
Or else this very moment I'll take thy sweet life.'

His hand in his pocket the money pulled out,
And among the long grasses he threw it about;
And while the highwayman held it in his purse,
The lad made no mention but rode off with his horse.

The highwayman holloaed and begged him to stay,
But the lad would not listen, but kept on his way
All home to his master, and to him did bring
Horse bridle, and saddle—a very fine thing!

'Odzooks!' cried the farmer. 'What's this to my loss?
Odpox! What! my cow turned into a hoss?'
'Oh no, my good master! Your cow I have sold,
But I have been robbed by some highwayman bold.'

They searched in the bags, and within them they found
Three handsome gold watches, and four hundred pound
And a brace of new pistols, I swear and I vow—
'So I think, my good master, I've well sold your cow.'

'And now, my good lad, for thou'st been bold and rare,
Three parts of this money shall run to thy share;
And, since the highwayman has lost all his store,
So let him go robbing until he gets more.'

Also known in other versions as 'The Farmer of Chester', 'The Highwayman Outwitted' deals with a highwayman who does not adhere to the code of the outlaw hero. Although the robber begins well by waylaying a rich farmer's daughter, he then strips her of clothes in a decidedly unheroic manner. She easily outwits this not very intelligent robber, and so gains his booty for herself in much the same way as the hero of 'The Yorkshire Bite'. Versions of this song have been extremely frequent in broadside form and in oral tradition in Britain. It is also sung in the United States.

THE HIGHWAYMAN OUTWITTED[33]

It's of a rich farmer in Cheshire,
    To the market his daughter would go
Not thinking that any would harm her
    She often been that way before.

She was met by a rusty [or ruffian] highwayman
    Who caused the young damsel to stand [or stay]
'Your money and clothes now deliver
    Or else your sweet life is at hand [or you must pay].'

He stripped this fair maid stark naked
    And gave her his bridle to hold
And there she stood shivering and shaking,
    Near starved unto death with the cold.

She put her left foot in the stirrup
    And mounted like a man
Over hedges and ditches she galloped
    Crying, 'Catch me, bold rogue, if you can.'

The bold rogue he soon followed after
    Which caused him to puff and to blow
Thank God that he never did catch her
    Till she came to her father's door.

'Oh daughter! dear daughter! what's happened?'
    'Oh father! to you I will tell;
I was met by a rusty highwayman
    Thank God! he has done me no harm.'

43

'Put the grey mare in the stable,
   And spread the white sheet on the floor.'
She stood there and counted the money,
   She counted five thousand and more.

'The Two Jolly Butchers' is a version of an often-collected and published ballad, 'The Three Butchers'. The song derives from a broadside ballad of c. 1685, probably based on fact, and titled, in part,

> A New Ballad Of the Three Merry Butchers, and ten Highway
> Men, how three butchers went to pay five Hundred pounds
> away, and hearing a Woman crying in the Wood went to Relieve
> her, and was there set upon by these Ten High-Way Men; and
> how only stout Johnson fought with them all, who killed Eight
> of the Ten, and at last was killed by the woman he went to save
> in the wood—To an Excellent New Tune . . .

It was published by J. Bissell, London. Versions of the ballad are common in broadside collections.

THE TWO JOLLY BUTCHERS[34]

It's of two jolly butchers, as I have heard them say,
Who started out from London upon a certain day;
As they were riding along the road as fast as they could ride—
'Oh, stop your horse', said Johnson, 'for I heard a woman cry'.

'I will not stop', said Wilson, 'I will not stop', said he;
'I will not stop', says Wilson, 'for robbèd we shall be.'
Then Johnson he got off his horse and searched the woods
   around,
He found a naked woman with her hair pinned to the ground.

'How came you here?' said Johnson. 'How came you here fast
   bound?
How came you here stark naked with your hair pinned to the
   ground?'
'They whippèd me, they strippèd me, my legs and arms they
   bound,
They left me here stark naked with my hair pinned to the
   ground.'

Then Johnson being a valiant man, and a man of courage bold,
He took the coat all off his back to keep her from the cold;
Then Johnson being a valiant man and a man of valiant mind,
He wrapped his coat around her and he took her up behind.

As they were a-riding along the road, as fast as they could ride,
She put her fingers to her lips and gave three dreadful cries;
Then up stepped three young swaggering blades, with staffs all in
    their hand,
A-riding up to Johnson and bidding him to stand.

'I'll stand, I'll stand', said Johnson, 'I'll stand, I'll stand', said he,
'For I never was in all my life afraid of any three.'
Then one of them he quickly slew, and the woman he did not
    mind,
But she drew a knife all from his side and ripped him up
    behind.

'I must fall, I must fall', said Johnson, 'I must fall upon the
    ground,
It was this wicked woman that gave me my death-wound;
And she shall be hung in iron chains for what she has done,
For she's murdered the finest butcher that ever the sun shined
    on.'

There were certainly other songs that dealt with non-historical highway-man figures in terms of the outlaw hero tradition.[35] The selection provided here gives a good indication of the nature and persistence of this particular tradition in Anglophone folk culture. Implicitly drawing on the existing traditions associated with Robin Hood and, to a lesser extent, other medieval outlaws factual or fictional, these ballads reflect the stability and coherence of the outlaw hero tradition over time and space. This diffusion and continual recreation and reworking of the various elements of the outlaw hero tradition also reinforced and maintained cultural knowledge of the tradition, providing a reservoir of appropriate stereotypes that could be drawn upon to articulate attitudes towards historical outlaws, highwaymen, badmen and bushrangers.

CHAPTER THREE

British Highwaymen

The outlaw hero traditions of many cultures have already been briefly mentioned. The similarities and parallels between the various national, ethnic and linguistic manifestations of the robber hero are marked and have frequently been noted and discussed. While such similarities are apparently significant, it is difficult to know exactly what such expressions may signify in each of the diverse circumstances in which they operate without quite detailed linguistic, historical and cultural studies. With regard to the Anglophone permutations of the tradition, we are fortunate in being able to trace it over three major English-speaking nations, each with related but distinctive characteristics and cultural heritages. The historical circumstances of the British highwayman outlaw hero differ from those involved in the frontier, pioneer and migration experiences of the United States and Australia. Yet essentially the same tradition articulates social and political discontent in these diverse situations. As the linguistic and cultural cradle of the dominant cultural forms and preoccupations of both American and Australian culture, Britain is the appropriate starting point for an examination of the English-speaking tradition of the outlaw hero.[1]

In the case of the medieval outlaws and the highwaymen, there is a considerable literature of manuscript and early print materials, particularly in chapbook and broadside ballad form. Examination of any collection of these materials confirms the enormous interest of the public in ballads and prose treatments of the lives and deeds of Robin Hood and the later highwaymen.[2] Their ballads and chapbooks are continually reprinted, revised and reworked from the time of the outlaw's death until the effective demise of the broadside industry in the nineteenth century. All the major and minor broadside and other popular publishers printed versions of highwayman and Robin Hood ballads; it is clear that such pieces were a staple of the trade, indicating a large popular demand. Generally, these productions are careful to maintain a degree of respectability and morality in their treatments of highwaymen. Along with any outlaw hero characteristics that might be included in the ballads is an appropriately moralising ending, cautioning others to beware of taking up a life of crime. This moral warning is part of the genre of the literary and popular treatments of outlaw heroes of all kinds, right up to the present day, when film-makers and others, wary of censorship and possible community criticism, are usually careful to convey their 'proper' position, even while they glamorise their subject. Similar, and often overlapping, processes can be identified in the popular mythologising of American and Australian outlaw heroes, as will be seen in subsequent chapters.

While popular treatments were, and are, generally careful to draw the appropriate moral and sound the appropriate warnings about lives of crime, they are also clearly captivated by certain features of the outlaw hero—his courtesy, his strength and manliness (accentuated and underlined by his association with that ancient signifier of maleness, strength and virility, the horse), his cleverness, his sympathy for the underdog. All these features are positive and are shown in various balances against the criminal activities of the hero, depending upon the aims of the writer, whether wishing to point a moral, pander to popular sensationalism, or give a judicious account of a notable, if notorious, life.

These popular presentations are the official, formal antipodes of the folkloric tradition. At some points they intersect; at other points they overlap; elsewhere they throw up contradictions and ambivalences. But regardless of the particular balance of these interactions, there is a complex and ongoing intertextuality between the formal and the informal ends of the tradition that provides mutual reinforcement and provides the vehicle for the persistence of the tradition and its transmission through time and over distance. It is this dynamic relationship between the formal and the informal that constitutes the cultural tradition of the outlaw hero. The folkloric—that is, local, small-scale, face-to-face, primarily oral—intertwines with the popular—national or international, large-scale or mass produced, formal, commercial. This intertextual dynamic is the outlaw hero tradition, a coherent set of cultural rules or moral guidelines that has operated since at least the late medieval period and which underpins the celebration of selected British highwaymen.

HIGHWAYMEN HEROES

William Nevison

Called William Nevison in the contemporaneous chapbooks and broadsides concerning his life and death, 'Swift Nicks', as he was popularly known, is referred to as John Nevison by later writers, including the author of his biography in the *Dictionary of National Biography*. The confusion seems to stem from a later highwayman by the name of John Nevison and the habit of highwaymen—or their balladists—to dub themselves after famous criminals of earlier generations. There were a number of Swift Nicks before and after Nevison, so-called because he was said to have made the famous one-day ride from London to York usually attributed to Richard 'Dick' Turpin. Prodigious feats of speed are a common motif of hero lore.

The historical Nevison to whom the following texts refer was born in 1639 and hanged at York on 15 March 1684. Active in and around York, Derby, Nottingham and Lincoln, Nevison had quite a long career of highway robbery. A reward of 20 pounds was offered for his arrest on a charge of murder by the *London Gazette* as early as October 1681. The size of the reward indicates that Nevison was considered a serious nuisance. However, it seems that no-one was willing or able to apprehend him. A female member of Nevison's gang apparently informed against the highwayman, and he was taken near Wakefield, imprisoned, tried and hanged at York.

Nevison's longevity in folklore and popular memory is something of a mystery, though it is at least partly related to literary romanticisations of the highwaymen of the nineteenth and early twentieth centuries. In popular literature, Nevison has the basic outlaw hero requirements. He was 'a person of quick understanding, tall in stature, every way proportionable, exceeding valiant, having also the air and carriage of a gentleman', according to his chapbook. Nevison's ballads also endow him with the fundamental attributes of the outlaw hero—he robs only the rich to benefit the poor, offers no unjustified violence, and is self-righteously defiant of the forces of authority when captured.

'Bold Nevison' is a broadside of Nevison's exploits. It is a disappointment as an example of its genre, having no swashbuckling feats of defiance or cunning and showing the celebrated highwayman rather meekly surrendering to 'Captain Milton' (actually a Captain Hardcastle). Nevertheless, Nevison is presented as a hero of the outlaw code, being good to the poor, claiming never to have murdered and being politely defiant of the judge and jury. A number of other highwaymen preceding Dick Turpin also claimed or were granted outlaw hero traits.[3]

BOLD NEVISON[4]

Did you ever hear tell of that hero,
   Bold Nevison it was his name?
He rode about like a great hero,
   And by that he gained a great fame.

He maintained himself like a gentleman,
   Besides he was good to the poor;
He rode about like a bold hero,
   And gained himself favour therefore.

Oh the twenty-first day of the month
   It proved an unfortunate day,
Captain Milton was riding to London
   And by mischance rode out of his way.

He called at a house by the roadside,
   It was the sign of the Magpie,
Where Nevison he sat a-drinking,
   And the Captain soon did him espy.

A constable soon then was sent for,
   And a constable very soon came
With three or four more in attendance
   With pistols charged in the King's name.

They demanded the name of this hero:
   'My name it is Johnson', said he,
When the Captain laid hold of his shoulder,
   Saying, 'Nevison, come thou with me.'

'Tis now before my lord the judge,
   'Oh, guilty or not do you plead?'

He smiled at the judge and the jury,
  And these were the words that he said:

'I have now robbed a gentleman of tuppence,
  But I've never done murder nor killed.
But guilty I've been all my lifetime,
  So gentlemen do as you will.'

'Now when I rode on the highway
  I always had money in store,
And whatever I took from the rich,
  Why, I freely gave it to the poor.'

An oral version of the Nevison ballad was collected from Mr Joseph Taylor of Brigg, Lincolnshire, by Australian composer and folklorist Percy Grainger. It is a masterpiece of economy, condensing the essentials of the broadside into three verses that emphasise Nevison's outlaw hero characteristics and conveniently ignore the rather less heroic circumstances of his capture.

BOLD NEVISON[5]

Did you ever hear tell of that hero,
  Bold Nevison it was his name,
And he rode about like a brave hero,
  And by that he gained a great fame.

Now when I rode on the highway
  I always had money in store,
And whatever I took from the rich
  Why I freely gave it to the poor.

I have never robbed no man of tuppence,
  And I've never done murder nor killed,
Though guilty I've been all my lifetime,
  So gentlemen do as you please.

The presence of the highwaymen in popular literature is strong from around the end of the sixteenth century, with chapbooks and broadside ballads about their lives, exploits and deaths being produced and reprinted in great numbers. By itself such busy publishing activity might be no more than an indicator of public interest in the more lurid and sensational aspects of criminality. But there was more to it than this. A powerful, subterranean relationship between this best-selling literature and actual deeds, between artifice and actuality can be briefly glimpsed in such apparently trivial events as the highwayman who went to the gallows clutching a copy of the defiant ballad, 'Chevy Chase'.[6] The concomitant importance of the ballad and the chapbook in spreading and perpetuating the code of the highwayman hero is indicated by the concern that many highwaymen expressed for the ballad-mongers to present the highwaymen as these criminal heroes wished to be seen.

With the rise of the novel as a commercial genre, serious prose writers also turned their attention to outlaw heroes: Scott treats Rob Roy; Turpin is featured in W. A. Harrison's *Rookwood: A Romance* (1834); Robin Hood is a continual subject for writers of all kinds. In the Victorian era, the highwayman becomes part of the staple fare of the 'penny dreadful'. Claude Duval (often Du Val), largely forgotten by folklore, except in the Australian ballad of 'The Death of Ben Hall', becomes 'the dashing knight of the road'. A little later Duval continues as a hero of *Boys' Own* historical adventures, gallantly saluting his victims in his fine brocade and three-cornered hat while astride a magnificent steed. This is also the image of the highwayman represented in Alfred Noyes' nineteenth-century poem 'The Highwayman', with its moonlit night, moor, old inn door and other accoutrements of romance. The romantic highwayman has continued to interest producers and purveyors of popular fictions in the twentieth century. A number of feature films based on the highwayman as hero have been released, and the highwayman has featured strongly in certain genres of juvenile literature.[7] None more so than Dick Turpin.

Richard Turpin

We have seen that the defining characteristic of Robin Hood's image is the fact that he robs the rich to help the poor. While it has been pointed out that this is only rarely explicit in Robin Hood balladry[8] (and appears to be a later development), the notion is inherited in the popular and folkloric treatments of the highwaymen who prowled the roads and forests of Britain between the sixteenth and eighteenth centuries. But not all highwaymen. Only a select few of these men were celebrated as popular heroes of their day and as folk heroes through successive generations. To depict these individuals as 'highwaymen', with the attendant picture of masked and caped figures galloping gallantly across the moors on moonlit nights, is to deal only partially with the range of their activities and their significance as symbols of popular discontent and protest. The major focus of such treatment has been Richard 'Dick' Turpin.

Born in either 1705 or 1706 (sources differ on the date, as on much else), Turpin was the son of an Essex innkeeper or farmer. He became a butcher, and when his business declined he took to stealing cattle to stock his shop. Discovered in this illegal sideline, Turpin joined a gang of smugglers and deer-poachers, taking part in some particularly unpleasant crimes of violence, rape and robbery. A reward of 100 guineas was eventually offered for members of the gang, who were soon betrayed and mostly captured. Turpin escaped, the first of many times. From early 1735 he embarked on a career as a highwayman, mostly in and around Epping Forest, often in company with Tom King whom, by accident it seems, Turpin later mortally wounded. Turpin was named as 'wanted' in the *London Gazette* in early 1735 and a proclamation for his apprehension was issued in June 1737, with a 200 pound reward for his capture.[9]

It is from this period that the Turpin legend originates. While his previous activities had been largely submerged in the relative anonymity of the criminal gang, his appearance in official records of various kinds as a notorious individual established a basis for his later heroisation. The interaction of the official and the unofficial that characterises the creation and continuation of folk legends can be seen operating here, as it can in the generation of all outlaw hero traditions.

After shooting his accomplice, Turpin was obliged to escape from the London area, King having given information against him before dying. Turpin eventually travelled to Yorkshire, going under the maiden name of his mother, Palmer, and living as a horse-stealer and dealer. Turpin's sudden disappearance was no doubt the cause of popular and official speculation, a fact that further contributed towards the development of his legend, particularly allied as it was with his 'betrayal' by the unfortunate Tom King.

Turpin's popularity and his growth as folk legend at this time is attested in the writings of Abbé le Blanc, who tells us that in 1737 stories about Turpin's valour, generosity and general good bearing were being told wherever he went while living in England. Le Blanc also provides evidence of the ineffectiveness of law and order at this period and the resultant *de facto* rule of robbers:

> It is usual in travelling to put ten or a dozen guineas in a separate
> pocket, as a tribute to the first [robber] that comes to demand
> them; the right of passport which custom has established here in
> favour of the robbers, who are almost the only highway surveyors
> in England, has made this necessary; and accordingly the English
> call these fellows the 'Gentlemen of the Road', the government
> letting them exercise their jurisdiction upon travellers without
> giving them any great molestation.[10]

The Abbé goes on to say that anyone foolish enough to resist this impost
is likely to be handled very roughly indeed. He also relates that during
the 1720s the robbers were audacious: they were so unencumbered by
law that they fixed notices to the doors of the London rich forbidding
them to venture out of the town without ten guineas and a watch—on
pain of death. While Turpin was not one of these robbers, much the
same conditions persisted in his day, making it possible for him to carry
out his real crimes and those exploits popularly attributed to him even
before he was caught and hanged.

In 1739 Palmer alias Turpin was arrested, according to tradition
after shooting a publican's game-cock following an argument. Palmer's
true identity was discovered when he wrote from gaol to his friends and
relations in Essex. His handwriting was recognised and he was informed
on, eventually being tried and convicted to hang for the stealing of a
mare and foal. He paid five men to follow the cart transporting him to
the York gallows on 7 April 1739, and died bravely in proper outlaw
hero fashion. The 'mob', as the gawping, jibing crowds that habitually
attended executions were called, rescued Turpin's body from the officials
in order to save it from the humiliation of dissection by the surgeons.
They buried the highwayman in a proper grave filled with quicklime to
foil any attempt at exhumation. Immediately the belief arose that Turpin
had been restored to life and, in accordance with tradition, lived on.[11]

As was the custom of the period, the chapbook publishers had their
wares already printed and on sale even before the unfortunate suffered.
Turpin was commemorated immediately in *The Trial of Turpin*, an often
reprinted account, and in many subsequent works, remaining a stock
character of popular literature.[12]

Dated c. 1737 by Barlow,[13] 'Dick Turpin' is probably the earliest
Turpin ballad. It contains the essentials of Turpin's outlaw hero legend,
including the incident where he supposedly robs back the poor tenant's
rent from the unsympathetic landlord. By 1817 the refrain of this ballad

had become 'When a-robbing he doth go, doth go' and was later noted
by Thomas Seccombe in *A Collection of Diverting Songs*. (Seccombe wrote
two articles on Turpin in the *Essex Review*, January and April 1902, and
also composed Turpin's entry in the *Dictionary of National Biography*.)
In the same pamphlet as 'Dick Turpin' is found the song that eventually
became 'Turnpin's [sic] Valour', also known as 'Dick Turpin and the
Lawyer', or 'Rare Turpin-O' (on page 57).

DICK TURPIN[14]

Of all the famous robbers
    that does in England dwell,
The noted Richard Turpin
    does all the rest excel
        Tho' to Ireland he did go, go, go, etc.

He is a butcher by his trade
    and lived in Stanford town
And eight men did at Leicester rob
    as it is full well known
        Now to Ireland he is gone, gone, gone, etc.

He only taketh from the rich
    what they well can spare
And after he hath served himself,
    he gives the poor a share,
        Tho' to Ireland, etc.

He met with a poor tenant
    upon a certain day;
Whose landlord would seize on his goods
    'cause his rents he could not pay
        Tho' to Ireland, etc.

Then Turpin he does lend him
    directly fifty pounds
That when the landlord called for's rent
    he might pay the money down
        Now to Ireland, etc.

The landlord came and got his rent
    but was met upon the day

By Turpin who did take it all
  and then run quite away
    Now to Ireland, etc.

The very next day that he did meet
  at the highway side
Was a gentleman and lady fine
  who in a coach did ride
    But to Ireland, etc.

He soon made the gentleman
  deliver all his money
But the madam she did put her watch
  into her hairy c. . .y [*sic*]
    Tho' to Ireland, etc.

But Turpin quickly found it out
  which made the lady cry
Because he handled her twat
  and stroked her plump soft thigh
    But to Ireland, etc.

Then he killed the keeper's man
  on Epping Forest wide
For which if ever he is caught
  he must to Tyburn ride
    Tho' to Ireland, etc.

But if ever he returns again
  unto the English shore
They'll hang him up on Tyburn Tree
  where he can rob no more
    Tho' to Ireland, etc.

Other Turpin ballads painted a similar picture. A version of 'Turpin's Appeal to the Judge', collected by the industrious Alfred Williams, contains the lines 'The Poor I fed, the Rich likewise / I empty sent away.'[15] This broadside version of the song usually known as 'Dick Turpin and the Lawyer' was published in 1803 by J. M Robertson of Saltmarket, Glasgow. It seems to be a collation of a number of eighteenth-century Turpin broadsides, and tells the story of Turpin outwitting the lawyer, and robbing an excise-man (an appropriate victim, given Turpin's smuggling past), a judge, and a palmer. The last section of the song, bemoaning Turpin's fate, mentions his betrayal and his boldness. Although the song makes no direct reference to Turpin being a friend of the poor, his victims are all people who have benefited or might conceivably benefit from the misfortunes of others. The sympathies of the writer, and presumably of the readers and singers of the song, are clearly on the side of the highwayman hero.

TURNPIN'S VALOUR[16]

On Hounslow-Heath, as I rode o'er
I spied a lawyer riding before
Kind Sir, said I, are you not afraid
Of Turpin that mischievous blade.
    O Rare Turpin hero
    O Rare Turpin-O.

Says Turpin I've been most secure
My gold I hid in the heels of my shoe.
O says the lawyer there's none can find
My gold, for it lies in my cap behind.

As they rod[e] by the Poultry-mill
Turpin demands him to stand still
Said he, your cap I must cut off
For my mare she wants a saddle-cloth.

This caused the lawyer for to fret
To think he was so fairly hit
For soon he robbed him of his store
Because he knew how to lie for more.

As Turpin rode in search of prey
He met an exciseman on the way
He boldly bid him for to stand
Your gold, said he, I do demand.

With that the exciseman he replied
Your proud demands must be denied.
Before my money you receive
One of us two will cease to live.

Turnpin then without remorse
He knocked him quite from off his horse
And left him on the ground to sprawl
So off he rode with his gold and all.

As he rode over Salisbury Plain
He met Lord Judge with all his train
Then hero and like he did approach
And robbed the Judge as he sat in coach.

An Usurer as I am told
Who had in charge a sum of gold
With a clock clouted from side to side
Just like a Palmer he did ride.

And as he jigged along the way
He met with Turnpin that famed day
With hat in hand most courteously
He askèd him for charity.

If that be true thou tells to me
I'll freely give thee charity,
But I made a vow, and it I'll keep
To search all Palmers that I meet.

He reached his bags wherein he found
Upwards of 800 pound
In ready gold and white money
Which made him to laugh heartily.

This begging is a curious trade
For on the way thou art well sped.
These prize I count it found money
Because thou made an arrant lie.

For shooting of a dunghil-cock [*sic*][17]
Poor Turnpin he at last was took
And carried straight into a jail
Where his misfortunes he does bewail.

Now some do say that he will hang
Turnpin the last of all the gang.

I wish this cock had ne'er been hatched
For like a fish in the net he's catched.

But if I had my liberty
And were upon yon mountain high
There's not a man in Old England
Durst bid bold Turnpin for to stand.

I ventured bold at young and old
And fairly fought them for their gold
Of no mankind was I afraid
But now, alas, I am betrayed.

Now Turnpin he's condemned to die
To hang upon yon gallows high
Whose legacy is a strong rope
For stealing of a Dunhil-Cock [*sic*].

An oral version of the Turpin and the lawyer theme was collected from Mr John Gartell of Somerset by Cecil Sharp in 1907.[18] Here we are given the single story of Turpin and the lawyer, with few explicit outlaw hero characteristics other than Turpin's general valour. Although this singer has assembled a text with few specific outlaw hero motifs, Turpin is still a hero, fitting into the singer's personal conception of the highwayman, a conception that dovetails with the traditional view.

TURPIN HERO

As Turpin was riding across the moor
He spied a lawyer on before
He rode up to him and thus did say:
Have you seen Turpin ride this way?
　　Hero, Turpin hero, I am the valiant Dick Turpin O.

No, I've not seen Turpin for many a long day
Nor do I wish to see him ride this way
For if I did I'd have no doubt
He'd turn my pockets inside out.

They rode till they came to a powder mill
When he told the lawyer to stand still

Saying: The tails of your coat they must now come off
For my mare she's in want of a new saddle cloth.

Now I've robbed you all your store
You can go and blow for more
The very next town that you ride in
Tell them you've been robbed by Dick Turpin.

Turpin was caught and his trial was passed
And for a game cock he died at last
Five hundred pounds he gave so free
All to Jack Ketch as a small legacy.

A nineteenth-century addition to the Turpin legend was the story
of the faithful, powerful and, in folk tradition magical, steed Black Bess.
On this mount Turpin was supposed to have made the famous one-day
ride to York. This sentimental tear-jerker was issued by Henry Such
around 1865 and is a good example of subsequent media romanticisation
of Turpin. The song was very popular in the United States in oral versions mostly derived from the broadside reproduced here.

POOR BLACK BESS[19]

When fortune, blind goddess, she fled my abode,
And friends proved ungrateful I took to the road,
To plunder the wealthy, to relieve all distress,
I bought thee to aid me, my poor Black Bess.

No vile whip or spur did thy sides ever gall,
For none did'st thou need, thou would'st bound at my call,
For each act of kindness thou didst me caress,
Thou wert never ungrateful, my poor Black Bess.

When dark sable midnight its mantle had thrown,
O'er the bright face of nature how oft have we gone,
To famed Hounslow-heath tho' an unwelcome guest,
To the minions of fortune, my poor Black Bess.

How silent thou'st stood when a carriage I've stopt,
And their gold and their jewels its inmates have dropt,
No poor man I plundered, or e'er did oppress
The widow or orphan, my poor Black Bess.

When Argus-eyed justice did me hotly pursue,
From London to York like lightning we flew.
No toll bar could stop thee, thou the river did breast,
And in twelve hours reached it, my poor Black Bess.

But fate darkens o'er me, despair is my lot,
The law does pursue me through a cock that I shot;
To save me, poor brute, thou didst do thy best,
Thou art worn out and weary, my poor Black Bess.

Hark! the bloodhounds approach, but they never shall have,
A beast like thee noble, so faithful and brave;
Thou must die, my dumb friend, tho' it does me distress,
There! there! I have shot thee, my poor Black Bess.

And in after ages when I'm dead and gone,
This tale will be hand[ed] from father to son;
My fate some may pity, but all will confess,
'Twas in kindness I killed thee, my poor Black Bess.

No one can say that ingratitude dwelt
In the bosom of Turpin, 'twas a vice he ne'er felt;
I shall die like a man, and soon be at rest,
Then farewell forever, my poor Black Bess.

Black Bess appears again in an oral tradition collected from Mrs
May Bradley by Fred Hamer.[20] Mrs Bradley also sang a one-verse version
of 'My Bonny Black Bess', providing evidence of the continuation of
Turpin in oral as well as commercial traditions.

My grandfather told me Dick Turpin used to rob the rich to give
to the poor. Well he reared this pony—she was coal black, he
reared her and saddled her and used to go and rob the rich and
give to the poor. When the police catched Dick Turpin and
Black Bess, they couldn't keep him in jail, ne'er her. She used to
fly over. Well this one particular morning the man at the jail
asked Dick Turpin if he'd put the bridle on for him to ride
round the prison wall. He said 'Yes, but I'll have to put the
bridle on myself.' So when he put it on he whispered summat in
her ears and God she threw him off. He couldn't ride her.
Well, he said, 'Now Dick, you go and see if her'll go for you.'
And my God she did go for Dick. Poor Dick whispered in her

ear and she went—whizz-over she went. The last time they caught him they made a song about it.

IMMORTAL TURPIN

Turpin's popularity,[21] and even if less-markedly, that of other highwayman heroes was not restricted to the ballad-mongers, the tellers of tales and those forced to the depths and margins of society, like the Gypsies who frequently honoured their childen with Turpin's name. Richard Turpin's doings, real and imagined, were exploited in respectable forums like Harrison Ainsworth's *Rookwood*, a work that moulded the highwayman hero into the figure of romance that is still the central representation of Turpin in popular fictions of all kinds. For the folk traditions about Turpin, Ainsworth's importance was to introduce, or at least refine, the notions of the famous ride to York and the gallant steed, Black Bess. These motifs were readily incorporated into the existing Turpin traditions in the British Isles and were also influential in America.[22]

Turpin's extreme longevity as a figure of popular and folk mythology is in some ways puzzling. As far as folklore is concerned, Turpin acted, or at least could reasonably be seen to have acted, in accordance with some of the central elements of the outlaw hero tradition. He was an escaper and disguiser, was betrayed by accomplices on two occasions and mostly conducted himself with proper highwayman aplomb and dignity up to and including his public execution. He died 'game', behaving

> in an undaunted Manner; as he mounted the ladder, feeling his
> right Leg tremble, he stamp'd it down, and looking round about
> him with an unconcerned Air, he spoke a few Words to the
> Topsman, then threw himself off, and expir'd in five Minutes.

Thus *The Gentleman's Magazine* of 7 April 1739 described the highwayman's final performance. Since this appropriate death, or at least its appropriate reporting, the usual folkloric manifestations have proliferated, in place-names, local legends and beliefs. However, there is no suggestion of Turpin's being oppressed or wronged in any way, or having the support of his own community—indeed it was a member of that community, albeit a more educated one, who provided the authorities with proof of Turpin's true identity in an early example of forensic handwriting analysis.

In printed celebrations of highwaymen, we find any number of individuals who might with as much justification as Turpin be represented as outlaw heroes. These include James MacLean, the 'Gentleman Highwayman', executed only eleven years after Turpin, and Dennis Neale, the 'Second Turpin', executed 1754; and one of the various criminals called the 'Flying Highwayman'—William Hawke, executed 1774, and Thomas Boulter, executed 1778. An even more likely candidate for immortalisation would have been John Rann, alias 'Sixteen-String Jack' due to the breeches with eight strings at each knee that he habitually wore. When he was 'topped' at Tyburn in 1774 he wore a pea-green coat and an oversize nosegay, to the great delight of the gallows mob. Attempts were even made to romanticise this colourful character in Leman Rede's play about the highwayman, performed at the Olympic Theatre in 1841 and including a number of songs.[23]

Another outstanding candidate was the housebreaker, master escapologist and paradigmatic stylist of the eighteenth-century underclasses, Jack Sheppard. So famous was Sheppard that the James gang and the Kellys, among others, were continually compared with him. The James gang even penned letters to a newspaper signing themselves 'Jack Sheppard'. Sheppard's uncanny ability to escape, use disguise, avoid recapture and his penultimate and highly public 15-day progress of robbery and debauchery around London before his last arrest and inevitable hanging in 1724, were long remembered. At least they were in the popular media and theatre, where Sheppard often appeared.

But Sheppard has left few folkloric traces. Why? Sheppard's story was that of the audacious, colourful urban criminal who thumbs his nose at the law, delighting his peers and unsettling the comfortable. Certainly he was a heroic figure, but not one representing the same hatreds and desire for vengeance as the armed highwayman. Sheppard is instead the forerunner of the Al Capones of the twentieth century. These figures are celebrated as defiant resisters of the law, but they are not seen as representatives and redressers of the grievances of a particular and well-defined social group or groups. So they leave no folkloric manifestations, no surviving songs, ballads, tales or other items. Their memories are carried in the popular media and not in the folkloric consciousness. Although there is an ongoing cross-fertilisation between these cultural domains, each has its own rules, its own genres and its own imperatives.

Few of the innumerable other candidates for outlaw heroism that could be named are remembered either in folklore or in popular representations. Only a very select few became outlaw heroes. As Peter Linebaugh's account of Turpin makes clear, he was a typical product of the eighteenth-century metropolitan underworld.[24] What, then, is different about Turpin, and can we realistically view him as an authentic articulator of political and economic discontents? The answer to these questions seems to be that, while Turpin himself may have had few of the virtues of the outlaw hero, these were sufficient to attract the approbation of contemporaries and of subsequent romancers. Even such a stern moral policeman as Francis Place was not above retailing his unreformed youth by recalling snatches of a ballad he called 'Jack Chance', in which a highwayman states: 'It's from the rich I rob, and it's to the poor I give.'[25] To ask whether or not Turpin was a deserving representative of the outlaw hero tradition is as pointless as trying to establish the historicity of Robin Hood. However, like the real or imaginary Robin Hood, it does seem that Turpin was a figure of cultural necessity at the time of his execution and since. The intersection of the folkloric and the popular has provided a convenient figure to inhabit this necessary cultural category of 'highwayman hero', of which category Dick Turpin is the pre-eminent British example.

However, there were also certain contemporaneous resonances to Turpin's career that provided an appropriate context for his transmutation to outlaw hero. Dick Turpin initially belonged to a group of smugglers and poachers whose activities went beyond the simply criminal. For the communities from which Turpin and his accomplices sprang, as for those who cheered him on to the gallows, outwitting the customs and excise officers and the gamekeepers of the aristocracy was a reaffirmation of traditional attitudes and customary beliefs in certain aspects of common law. Such attitudes underlay a great range of social protest and struggle over the long period of subjugating common law to more convenient legal systems that favoured the development of rational rural capitalism. The end result of this process was the entrenchment of a legal, economic and moral system that shifted access to common resources from the poor to the rich, from the landless labourer and peasant to the rising middle classes. Under common law, the poor had access to a wide variety of fish, meat, flora, land and other perquisites. These rights were increasingly eroded between the sixteenth and eighteenth centuries through a variety of measures, in particular through the enclosure of the commons, which was essentially complete in England by the nineteenth century.[26]

While this economic transformation was taking place, popular attitudes did not alter, particularly among communities that had vested economic interests in maintaining certain common rights. Typically these were rights of access to game and livestock[27]—hence the prevalence of poaching, a practice widely held to be legal, even today. Smuggling communities along the coast held similar views about their right to import goods for their own use and resale, resenting the imposition of customs duties and the activities of excisemen not simply because these were representative of the law, but because they undermined what was a means of economic survival or improvement for those who smuggled. Turpin's activities in this regard would have fitted him well for his subsequent elevation to the status of 'gentleman highwayman' and friend of the poor.[28] It was not by any means a status that Turpin had invented, but one that he inherited. Arthur Hayward's *Lives of the Most Remarkable Criminals*, first published in 1735, tells of the highwayman James Wright, executed in 1721, who 'valued himself not a little that he had never injured any poor man'. Another highwayman, John Levee, gave back a poor man's horse and money, while John Turner, alias Civil John, was renowned for his courtesy to his victims, often giving back a portion of what he had robbed from them, a continuing characteristic of outlaw heroes. His generosity, however, did not save him from the gallows in 1727.

These examples (by no means the only ones) of courteous highwayman behaviour mean little by themselves. It is only when they are considered in light of the outlaw hero tradition that their significance is apparent. There was a tradition, an expectation, an unspoken assumption that certain kinds of behaviour were appropriate when breaking the law. Of course most highwaymen were simply thugs, but there were also those who, for whatever reasons, wished to appear in a different light; they took pains to treat their victims decently and to rob the rich rather than the poor, in accordance with the code of the outlaw hero. None of the unfortunates just mentioned have been celebrated in folk or popular expressions, though they might well have been, given their philosophies. Their dying words or reported speeches on these themes in court, no doubt often a last grasp at mitigation, nevertheless helped to fuel the continuation of the outlaw hero tradition and contributed to the production of ballads about fictional or anonymous highwaymen.

There are occasional hints that such highwaymen may have had motives other than straightforward illicit gain. The 1656 Edinburgh-printed chapbook on Gilder Roy provides a succinct account of his life and depredations:

> The Wonderful Life of Gilder Roy, a noted murderer, ravisher, incendiary and highwayman. A native of the Highlands of Perthshire, who was executed, at Edinburgh, about the year 1656, and hung in chains on a gibbet forty feet high, on Leith Walk.

The reference to incendiarism indicates that Roy's activities were not solely criminal but may have had a political element related to Scots national aspirations. Although the connection between the criminal and the political is somewhat murky in Gilder Roy's case, as it is in the case of another Scots figure, Rob Roy MacGregor, it is definitely present. It is particularly marked in some of the actions and expressions of later outlaw heroes in Ireland, America and Australia.

A number of other highwaymen are known to have had political affiliations of various kinds related to their activities and to their significance as symbols of popular discontent and protest. Dick Turpin, as already mentioned, belonged to a group of smugglers and poachers whose activities went beyond the simply criminal. Further proof of the danger that certain nominally criminal activities posed to the social order can be found in the considerable unease with which the authorities viewed highway robbery. This was not simply because such activities were an affront to law and order, not to mention private property, but also because of the tremendous appeal of certain highwaymen and the potential power that such popularity contained.

In the turbulent seventeenth and eighteenth centuries the English 'mob' was a political force to be reckoned with: it was apparently unreasoning, unpredictable and could certainly be devastating in its effects upon citizens, private property and public order. The term 'mob', a contraction of the earlier 'mobile' (from the Latin *mobile vulgus*, an excitable crowd), came into general use towards the end of the seventeenth century to describe the rampaging masses that frequently took the law into their own hands and asserted various forms of common law or rough justice in defiance of the often ineffectual representatives of properly constituted authority. The mob was highly dangerous to persons and property, and represented a potential, if inarticulate, political threat. Not surprisingly, the authorities were extremely wary of any individual, group or force that attracted the interest of the mob, and therefore potentially wielded the possibility of unleashing, perhaps even of directing, its awesome powers. The admiration of the populace for great thieves and criminals was most powerfully and therefore most dangerously focused upon the deeds, real and imagined, historical and folkloric, of highwaymen, nominally, if rarely legally, outlaws. Ballads and chapbooks celebrating highwaymen were therefore viewed with concern by the authorities, because they represented a potential, if rarely realised, threat to social stability in their implicit refutation or dismissal of the legal system and its hegemony.

Particularly dangerous were the public executions of such criminals, which routinely attracted large numbers of spectators. These events were designed by the authorities as spectacles of judicial terror. The mob turned Tyburn and other gallows into carnivals of death, in which the condemned highwayman was treated as a hero, balladised, dressed in fine clothes, often having finely dressed mourners following the cart taking him to the 'tree' and being ogled by the ladies, high and low. The hero was expected to perform his part in this festival, just as he was expected to perform according to the outlaw hero code in life. Before facing the final drop, the hero was required to mount the scaffold bravely, make a dying speech (if his nerve failed him, the ballad and chapbook writers had already composed it) and be 'turned off', 'behaving in an undaunted manner'. The obscene screeches and cheering of the mob as the hero danced the Tyburn jig were the voice of the unofficial, the informal, the folkloric—unbound and triumphant in this moment of domination in which the roles and the rules were temporarily reversed. Such demotic moments were situations in which the unleashed power of the people might conceivably be directed against the state and those who benefited from its stability. Rarely did this occur, though in the rescuing of Turpin's body from the surgeons by the York gallows mob we can glimpse the possibilities for subversion and insurrection that the powerful admitted only in their darkest moments, preferring to think of the Tyburn excesses as either salutary or as a useful safety valve—possibly both. As Frank McLynn points out in his study of eighteenth-century crime: 'There could be little question but that the Tyburn hangings had become, not an awestruck acceptance of the ruthless majesty of the Law, but a ritual defiance of that very Law.'[29] Peter Linebaugh discusses the economic imperatives behind highway robbery during the eighteenth century and reinforces McLynn's observation:

'The Idle 'Prentice Executed at Tyburn, 1747'—the final act for many highwaymen.
(Engraving by William Hogarth. Copyright British Museum.)

> In aspiring to that proud, if temporary, status of 'Gentlemen of
> the Road', they [highwaymen] did not question the inegalitarian
> hierarchy of their society. Yet their boldness of act and deed, in
> putting them outside the law as rebellious fugitives, revivified the
> 'animal spirits' of capitalism and became an essential part of the
> oppositional culture of working-class London, a serious obstacle
> to the formation of a tractable, obedient labour force. Therefore,
> it was not enough to hang them—the values they espoused or
> represented had to be challenged.[30]

It was the persistence of such dangerous possibilities in both the
reality and the legendry of the British highwaymen that ensured the later
utilisation of the tradition in decidedly political circumstances on the
frontiers of Australia and America. That tradition was given its essential
form and meaning through the popular and folkloric representations of
the British highwaymen.

IRISH OUTLAW HEROES

While standing out as the pre-eminent example of the legend of the English highwayman, the historical Turpin was a typical product of his time and place. In Ireland a different set of circumstances nevertheless gave rise to markedly similar manifestations of the outlaw hero, notably in the persons of James Freney, William Brennan and Jeremiah Grant. Without exception, the activities and the folklorisation of those figures possessed a strong political element.

The history of Irish resistance to domination generated a strong tradition of noble robbers, combining everyday criminality with real or romanticised resistance to the English. The guerilla warfare of the seventeenth-century 'tories' and 'rapparees' provided a tradition and a social background of nationalistic defiance which the later agrarian protest movements, variously known as Whiteboys, Ribbonmen and other group pseudonyms, inherited and incorporated into their political mythologies. As George-Denis Zimmerman points out in his *Songs of Irish Rebellion*:

> There was probably nothing chivalrous in the highwaymen and robbers who replaced them [the tories and rapparees]. These were no longer trying to redress a wrong or to recover the heritage of which they had been despoiled, but they enjoyed some of the sympathy which had been bestowed on their predecessors.[31]

That residue of support and sympathy made the figures of highwaymen James Freney and the later William Brennan into popular heroes.

James Freney

Active in the mid-eighteenth century, 'Captain' Freney is one outlaw whose heroism does not appear to have lasted well outside Irish folk tradition.[32] This is despite—or perhaps because of—his surrender and the subsequent publication of his extremely popular autobiography in the 1750s. The only clue to his importance is contained in some versions of 'The Wild Colonial Boy' where he is mentioned along with Brennan as a noble precursor. That he was considered in outlaw hero terms during and after his lifetime is confirmed in observations by the Irish folklorist J. Healy. According to Healy,[33] Freney was 'reputed to have been endowed with a sense of chivalry. He spared the purse of the poor man; and even gave back sufficient to the rich to carry them to the end of their journey.' Zimmerman also provides evidence of Freney's fame amongst the Irish.[34] It is likely that Freney's failure to 'die game' in the appropriate outlaw hero style has been the cause of his relatively short-lived popularity as a noble robber. However, he lives on in the annals of Australian bushranging, appearing as 'Freincy' in some versions of 'Bold Jack Donohoe' (see Chapter 5).

The following song has Freney playing a variant of the same trick on the Quaker as Turpin played on the lawyer and also disdaining to rob a tailor of the tools of his trade. Structurally, the song is very similar to broadside versions of 'Dick Turpin and the Lawyer' or 'Turpin Hero', as it is often known, probably deriving from that source.

Percy French celebrated Freney in a stage musical of the 1890s. It included a song that portrays Freney in classic outlaw hero terms,[35] though the song does not appear to have passed into oral tradition. The texts of both songs are reproduced below to allow comparison of the folkloric and the popular manipulation of the motifs that make up the morphology of the outlaw hero tradition.

BOLD CAPTAIN FRENEY[36]

One morning as, being free from care,
I rode abroad to take the air,
'Twas my fortune for to spy
A jolly Quaker riding by;
        And it's oh, bold Captain Freney!
        Oh, bold Freney, oh!

Said the Quaker—'I'm very glad
That I have met with such a lad;
There is a robber on the way,
Bold Captain Freney, I hear them say.'
        And it's oh, bold Captain Freney, etc.

'Captain Freney I disregard,
Although about me I carry my charge;
Because I being so cunning and cute,
It's where I hide it within my boot.'
        And it's oh, bold Captain Freney, etc.

Says the Quaker—'It is a friend
His secret unto me would lend;
I'll tell you now where my gold does lie—

I have it sewed beneath my thigh.'
    And it's oh, bold Captain Freney, etc.

As we rode down towards Thomastown,
Bold Freney bid me to 'light down.
'Kind sir, your breeches you must resign;
Come, quick, strip off, and put on mine,
    For I am bold Captain Freney,' etc.

Says the Quaker, 'I did not think
That you'd play me such a roguish trick
As my breeches I must resign,
I think you are no friend of mine.'
    And it's oh, bold Captain Freney, etc.

As we rode a little on the way,
We met a tailor dressed most gay;
I boldly bid him for to stand,
Thinking he was some gentleman.
    And it's oh, bold Captain Freney, etc.

Upon his pockets I laid hold—
The first thing I got was a purse of gold;
The next thing I found, which did me surprise,
Was a needle, thimble and chalk likewise.
    And it's oh, bold Captain Freney, etc.

'Your dirty trifle I disdain.'
With that I return'd him his gold again.
'I'll rob no tailor if I can—
I'd rather ten times rob a man.'
    And it's oh, bold Captain Freney, etc.

It's time for me to look about;
There's a proclamation just gone out;
There's fifty pounds bid on my head,
To bring me in alive or dead.
    And it's oh, bold Captain Freney!
    Oh, bold Freney, oh!

STREET BALLAD[37]

Come all ye fine ladies and gentlemen, too,
Attend to me singin' and I'll tell ye true
About a brave boy who lived out in the cold,
And the name that he went by was 'Freny the Bold.'
    Tur-in-ah, tur-in-ah, tur-in-an-the-dan-day.

Now Jack was a robber upon the highway,
And stopped the mail-coaches be night and be day:
What he took from the rich he would give to the poor,
So of Poverty's blessin' he always was sure.
    Tur-in-ah, tur-in-ah, tur-in-an-the-dan-day.

One day when the coach had set off for the fair,
It was met by Jack Freny bestriding his mare:
Some called for the soldiers, some called for the watch
And one lady called for two-penn'orth of Scotch.
    Tur-in-ah, tur-in-ah, tur-in-an-the-dan-day.

The guard held his blunderbuss out on full cock,
Sez he, 'Jack, clear out, or you'll know what's o'clock.'
Jack flattened him out wid the butt of his gun,
Sez he, 'What's o'clock? Well, it's just strikin' one.'
    Tur-in-ah, tur-in-ah, tur-in-an-the-dan-day.

So the gentlemen pulled out their purses of gold,
And handed them over to Freny the bold:
Sez Freny, 'Me boys, ye got off mighty well,
I'd ha' fleeced ye far more if I'd kept an hotel.'
    Tur-in-ah, tur-in-ah, tur-in-an-the-dan-day.

Now, all ye fine ladies and gintlemen, too
Ye've heard from my singin'—and I've told ye true,
All about the brave boy who lived out in the cold,
And the name that he went be was 'Freny the Bold.'
    Tur-in-ah, tur-in-ah, tur-in-an-the-dan-day.

William Brennan

Also known as Captain Brennan, William Brennan was hanged in Cork
in 1804. He was a farm labourer who, according to tradition, was forced
to take to the road after a hoax on a British officer backfired. Healy also

tells us that Brennan robbed a widow's rent back from a greedy landlord, just as Jesse James and other outlaw heroes are said to have done. As well, and again in common with other outlaw legends, after Brennan's execution 'a tradition persisted for many years afterwards of a treasure trove which he had concealed, but this was never found'.[38]

An English version of Brennan's song, 'Brennan on the Moor', shows Willie to be appropriately fearless, to rob only the wealthy and to divide his spoils with the poor, in this instance represented by 'widows in distress'. Brennan's capture occurs only after a fierce fight in which he is severely wounded. Although this version is not specific as to Brennan's execution, we can hardly be in any doubt that such a classic example of the outlaw hero will remain 'bold and undaunted' unto the very end.

Brennan's encounter with the packman, or itinerant pedlar, is a loud echo of the ballad 'Robin Hood and the Pedlar'. As with the Robin Hood mythology, the incident is here designed to show the fairness and generosity of spirit attributed to Brennan and, of course, his solidarity with 'the common man'.

The reference to Turpin, by the time of this ballad more than sixty years dead, is an indication of the longevity of the outlaw hero's popular image. From around this time, such references to the deeds of earlier outlaw heroes become a frequent stylistic element of the tradition, as will be seen in the following texts. The reference to Black Bess shows how fully the popular romanticisation of the highwayman had permeated his folklore by this time and provides yet another example of the interaction between the folkloric and the popular.

BRENNAN ON THE MOOR[39]

It's of a fearless highwayman a story I will tell,
His name was William Brennan and in Ireland he did dwell
And up on the Libbery mountains he commenced his wild career
Where many a wealthy gentleman before him shook with fear.

CHORUS
Bold and undaunted stood bold Brennan on the moor,
   Brennan on the moor,
   Brennan on the moor,
Bold and undaunted stood Brennan on the moor.

A brace of loaded pistols he carried night and day,
He never robbed a poor man all on the King's highway,
But what he'd taken from the rich, like Turpin and Black Bess,
He always did divide between the widows in distress.

One day he robbed a packman and his name was Pedlar Bawn,
They travelled on together till the day began to dawn.
The pedlar found his money gone, likewise his watch and chain,
He at once surrounded Brennan and he robbed him back again.

When Brennan saw the pedlar was as good a man as he,
He took him on the highway his companion to be.
The pedlar threw away his pack without any more delay,
And proved a faithful comrade until his dying day.

One day upon the highway as Willie he sat down,
He met the Mayor of Cashel a mile outside the town;
The mayor knew his features, I think you're my man, said he,
I think you're William Brennan, you must come along o' me.

Willie's wife had been to town provisions for to buy.
When she saw her Willie she began to sob and cry.
He said: Give me tenpence. As quick as Willie spoke,
She handed him a blunderbuss from underneath her cloak.

Now with this loaded blunderbuss, the truth I will unfold,
He made the mayor to tremble and robbed him of his gold.
A hundred pounds was offered for his apprehension there,
But with his horse and saddle to the mountains did repair.

He lay among the fern all day, it was thick upon the field,
And nine wounds he had received before that he would yield.
He was captured and found guilty and the judge made his reply:
For robbing on the King's highway you're both condemned to
    die.

The narrative 'Willie Brennan' is essentially a prose rendition of the events described in 'Brennan on the Moor', namely the encounter with the Bold Pedlar Bawn, and the incident of robbing back the poor woman's rent, which is also attached to a white South African outlaw hero named Scotty Smith, active during the 1870s and 80s, to the Scots Jacobite Rob Roy MacGregor (1671–1734) and many other outlaw heroes. One of the Robin Hood ballads also features a similar encounter between Robin and a 'pedlar'. The story is also told of Captain James Hind (1616–52), a highwayman who was hanged and quartered for treason due to his political activities. Contemporary accounts and treatments of Hind, including a play and some verse, cast him very much in the mould of the noble robber, courteous to all and kind to the poor:

> He made our wealth one common store,
> He robbed the rich to feed the poor:
> What did immortal Caesar more?

But Hind did not persist as a folk hero, perhaps because he seems to have been more of a political hero and because his feats were celebrated in rather higher-flown literary genres than was usual for the common highwayman. Brennan has been a much longer-lasting and evocative figure, as the following story, collected from Thomas O'Riordan, Cork, by Sean O'Sullivan in 1934,[40] indicates.

> Brennan was born in Kilmurry, near Kilworth. He listed in the army and then he deserted out of it. They were hunting him around the country day and night.
> One day outside at Leary's Bridge, Brennan met the Pedlar Bawn. I never heard him called by any other name. The Pedlar was travelling for a firm in Cork, going about the country selling different kinds of things. Brennan put the blunderbuss up to him and made him hand out what he had, watch and chain and all. Then the Pedlar asked him to give him some token to show to the people of the firm in Cork that he had met him.
> 'Tell them that you met Brennan the Highwayman.'
> 'Give me some token that you met me, or I'll be put to jail,' said the Pedlar.
> 'What have I to do for you?' asked Brennan.
> 'Fire a shot through this side of my old coat,' said the Pedlar.
> He did.
> 'Fire another through this side now,' said the Pedlar.
> So he did.
> 'Here!' said the Pedlar. 'Fire another through my old hat.'
> Brennan did.
> 'Come!' said the Pedlar. 'Fire another through my old cravat.'

'I have no ammunition,' said Brennan.

The Pedlar then drew a pistol, wherever he had it hid.

'Come!' said he, 'Deliver!'

Brennan had to deliver, quick and lively too!

'You're a smarter man than me,' said he. 'All I ever went through, I robbed army, men and lords, and you beat me. Will you make a comrade for me?'

The Pedlar only flung his pack over the ditch.

'I will,' said he. 'I'll stand a loyal comrade until my dying day.'

And he was, a loyal comrade.

'We'll go along to County Tipperary,' said Brennan. ''Tis a wealthy county. There's agents and landlords there going around the country gathering the rent in the houses, and we'll whip them going back in the evening.'

So the two of them went along to the County Tipperary. Brennan went in to a widow there one morning. The poor woman was crying and lamenting. He asked her what was the matter with her.

'What good is it for me to tell you, my good man?' said she.

She didn't know but he was a tramp.

'How do you know?' said he.

'The agent is coming here by and by, and I haven't a halfpenny to give him for a rent,' said she.

'Well, what would you say to the man who'd give it to you?' said Brennan.

He asked her how much it was, and she told him—five or six pounds, I suppose. He counted it out to her.

'Tell me now,' said he, 'the road he goes home in the evening.'

She told him the road he'd take after giving the day gathering around. He made her go down on her knees then and swear to God and to him that she would never tell anyone that she saw him, or mention that anyone gave her the money. Himself and the Pedlar met the agent going home with the money and whipped the whole lot that he had gathered that day.

Brennan is buried over in Kilcrumper near the old church wall.

Jeremiah Grant

Jeremiah Grant, low-born in Queen's County in the late eighteenth century, joined one of the bands of patriotic outlaws known as Whiteboys or Ribbonmen. He was particularly adept at highway robbery and at maintaining the loyalty and affection of 'the lower orders' through the combination of liberality and terror often employed by outlaws. Like a number of other outlaw heroes and mythical leaders of agrarian insurrections, Grant styled himself 'Captain', as in his ballad reproduced below. He was captured through the activities of an informer but, in true highwayman style, escaped from Maryborough gaol, only to be recaptured, tried, and hanged in August 1816, aged about twenty years old.

The text of 'Captain Grant' reproduced here, like most of the English versions of this song, has shifted the scene of Grant's activities from Ireland to Scotland. However, it shows the essential outlaw hero characteristics of robbing the rich and helping the poor, bravery, courteousness, escapology and betrayal.

CAPTAIN GRANT[41]

My name is Captain Grant, I'll be bound for to say,
I'm one of those bold heroes all on the king's highway.
With my brace of loaded pistols and my steady broad sword.
O stand and deliver it, it's always the word.

To do a dirty action I always did scorn,
In robbing from the rich I thought it no harm.
With my gold and my jewels I always did secure,
One half I kept myself and the other gave the poor.

If I meets with the traveller that's hungry and dry,
I'll take him to some ale-house and his wants I will supply.
With good ale, wine and brandy, boys, till I spent all my store
When my money is all gone I'll boldly rob for more.

To Edinburgh gaol they marched me away
And there I did remain till my trial it did come on.
For shooting at the King I was then condemned to die,
But I never had no hand in the same robbery.

Out of Edinburgh gaol then I made my way out
And those that did oppose me I put them to the rout.
With my bars and iron bolts I knocked the sentry down
And I made my escape out of Edinburgh town.

Out of Edinburgh gaol then I made my way good
And I took up my lodgings in the centre of a wood,
Until some wicked woman she did me betray
And she had me surrounded as sleeping I did lay.

I flew to my arms, but my powder was wet
And to my sad misfortune I found that I was beat,
And to my sad misfortune I gave myself up
To the . . . young hero called the man takes up.

To Edinburgh gaol then they marched me again,
And there I did remain through sorrow, grief and pain.
God bless my wife and family and may they never want,
And the Lord have mercy on my soul, cries bold Captain Grant.

Like Turpin in England, Freney, Brennan and one or two others were not only balladised, they also featured in popular literature and were widely known and loved by the Irish.[42] The primarily criminal activities of these men were nevertheless interpreted by many Irish people, not only the peasantry, in terms of the continuing resistance to English domination. The outlaw hero tradition was a convenient and appropriate structure for the expression of such emotions and aspirations. Irish highwaymen therefore came to mediate the ambivalent categories of crime and protest in a particularly compelling manner. While the relationship between criminality and social action is generally a murky one in the case of the English highwaymen, it is generally explicit in the case of their Irish counterparts. This is particularly so in relation to the antagonistic attitudes towards the government and the monarchy that are expressed in Irish outlaw hero traditions. These attitudes imparted to the Irish inflection of the outlaw hero a distinctive aura that would condition the representation of the outlaw hero in Australia, though they played little part in the legendry of the American badmen.

CHAPTER FOUR

American Badmen

I n the vast social and economic experiment being undertaken in nineteenth-century America, tensions and conflicts between various groups were endemic. The most serious of these ultimately produced the Civil War, whose aftermath was a continuing legacy of bitterness between the industrialising north and the primarily agrarian south. This situation was the kind of rupture in the fabric of order that revealed underlying conflicts and generated outlaw heroes like Jesse James, the Younger brothers and, a little earlier, Quantrill. Other conflicts and power struggles along the frontier between various vested and developing interests generated the gunslinging figures of popular mythology, such as John Wesley Hardin, the Youngers and, most notably, William 'Billy the Kid' Bonney.

The outlaw hero tradition migrated to America through the formal and the informal traditions of Robin Hood and the highwaymen. British migrants carried their cultural baggage with them, as evidenced by the versions of Robin Hood and highwaymen ballads and narratives collected in America. There was thus available an existing stereotype into which indigenous outlaws might be placed, should the appropriate combination of social, political and economic circumstances come about. It seems that these circumstances did emerge on the American frontier, particularly after the Civil War ended in 1865 and much of the country moved into an unsettled period of reconstruction and shifting patterns of social and economic power. The James brothers, Quantrill, Billy the Kid, Sam Bass and others were among the very few badmen whose activities were deemed worthy of celebration in terms of the outlaw hero tradition.

A good deal of scholarly and popular attention has been paid to the American outlaw. Historians of the west have been particularly interested in the conflicts between competing groups of farmers, cattle-men, sheep-farmers and so on, particularly in the border states of Mis-souri and Mississippi, home to the James gang, and also in the Lincoln Range wars in the Arizona Territory during the 1870s. Folklorists have been no less assiduous in their investigations of the traditions of the western heroes and their presence in various folkloric genres. This work has made available a substantial body of research material for investi-gating both the facts and the folklore behind the outlaw heroes of the American frontier.

An even greater interest has been taken in the outlaw and the history of the western frontier by popular media. This began while the frontier was still moving westwards, particularly after the Civil War when an immense popular fiction and 'faction' publishing industry developed around the images of the cowboy, the outlaw and other aspects, real and imagined, of frontier life. Generally known as dime novels, such cheap publications were printed and sold in great numbers and, it seems, eagerly devoured by a wide readership. Subsidiary publishing industries in old-time anecdotes, tales of the west and autobiographical recollections have also been influential carriers of information, factual and otherwise, concerning outlaw heroes and their deeds. Popular interest continued in the form of extravagant spectacles like Buffalo Bill Cody's immensely successful Wild West Show and the less spectacular, but no less influ-ential, stage melodramas concerning outlaws and other related western themes. The Hollywood movie industry inherited this interest and much of the existing audience, creating that quintessentially American con-sumer product 'the western', which has depended significantly on real and created outlaw figures for much of its existence as a film genre, including its recent revival.

As with the literature and folklore of the British highwayman and of the Australian bushranger, there has been significant cross-fertilisation for long periods of time. Such interaction between the informal, largely oral tradition and the more formal print and other media traditions of the outlaw hero has provided the impetus for the continued potency of the outlaw hero as a cultural figure. Some of the more important folkloric articulations of the American outlaw hero give an indication of the inter-play between the folkloric and the popular, especially in relation to the continuing images of Jesse James and Billy the Kid.

LINKS IN THE CHAIN OF TRADITION

The image of the British highwayman was not lost in the migration of British culture to America. Not only were highwayman and Robin Hood ballads sung there: the notion of the 'highwayman' persisted in American folk culture and was applied to those figures of myth and history known to latter-day audiences as 'outlaws' or 'badmen'. Cole Younger was called a 'bandit highwayman' in one of his ballads, and the term 'highwayman' is often used in American folksongs to describe outlaw heroes. It was not only the terminology of the British outlaw hero that was transmitted to the New World, but also the concept of the noble robber, contained particularly in British ballads that crossed the Atlantic. These songs included 'Turpin Hero' and 'The Yorkshire Bite' (see Chapters 3 and 2), and a song from the later accretions to the Turpin legend, 'My Bonnie Black Bess' (also called 'My Poor Black Bess'). This American version of the nineteenth-century British broadside was traditional in Carolina. It presents a sentimentalised version of the outlaw hero and his gallant steed, retaining the essential elements of robbing the rich and the need to 'die like a man'.

MY BONNIE BLACK BESS[1]

When Fortune, vain goddess, she fled from my bode,
And friends proved unkindly, I took to the road.
A-robbing the rich to relieve my distress,
I brought you to aid me, my bonnie black Bess.

No vile whip or spurs did on your side fall,
No need for to use them, you'd bound at my call.
For each act of kindness, you did me caress;
You ever proved faithful, my bonnie black Bess.

When dark sable midnight her mantle had drawn
O'er the bright scenes of nature, how oft have we gone
To the famed house of wealth, though an unwelcome guest,
To the minions of Fortune, my bonnie black Bess.

How silent you stood when the carriage I'd stop,
And the inmates their gold and bright jewels did drop.
No poor man we robbed, nor did we oppress
The widows or orphans, my bonnie black Bess.

When august Justice did me now pursue,
From London to York like lightning we flew.
No tall bars could stop you, the river you'd breast,
And in twelve hours we reached it, my bonnie black Bess.

Now despair gathers o'er me, and dark is my lot.
For the law doth pursue me through the man that I shot.
But to save me, poor brute, you did do your best,
Though worn out and weary, my bonnie black Bess.

Hark, the bloodhounds approach! No, they never shall have
A beast like thee—noble, so handsome and brave.
You must die, my dumb friend, though it does me distress.
There, I have shot you, my bonnie black Bess.

No one can e'er say that ingratitude dwelt
In the bosom of Turpin; 'twas a vice he ne'er felt.
I shall die like a man and soon be at rest—
Then farewell forever, my bonnie black Bess.

In years to come, when I'm dead and gone,
This tale will be handed from father to son.
Some will take pity, while all will confess
'Twas through kindness I shot you, my bonnie black Bess.

While not strictly an outlaw hero ballad, the song usually known as 'Johnny Troy' is especially interesting as an example of an Australian song that has a busy life in American tradition, while having apparently dropped from Australian folklore altogether. The text refers to various bushranger heroes that would date its composition at c. 1830 and it is likely that its hero—whoever he may have been—would have made a fine example of the heroic bushranger. Troy is brave, defiant, and altogether a fine specimen of the noble convict. Why his ballad has not taken hold in Australia while retaining a hold in America is a mystery that is as intriguing as it was when Kenneth Porter first drew attention to it many years ago.

JOHNNY TROY[2]

Come all ye daring bushrangers
And outlaws of the land,

82

Who scorn to live in slavery
   Or wear the convict's band.

I'll tell to you the story
   Of the most heroic boy:
All the country knew him
   By the name of Johnny Troy.

Troy was born in Dublin
   That city of great fame,
Brought up by honest parents;
   The world knows the same.

For the robbing of a widow
   He was sent o'er the main,
For seven years in New South Wales
   To wear a convict's chain.

There were a hundred and forty
   Serving out their times,
Some of them for murder,
   And some for smaller crimes.

Johnny Troy was one among them
   And solemnly he swore:
'This very night I'll free you all,
   Or I shall be no more.'

There were six well-armed policemen
   All seated in the bow;
And they were none [much] surprised
   When John commenced his row.

And they were none [much] surprised
   When Troy he made a rush;
And six more as brave heroes
   Rushed bravely in the bush.

'And it's now we've gained our liberty,
   Our escape we will make sure;
We'll smash and break those handcuffs
   When once we reach the shore.

'When once we reach the shore, brave boys,
    We'll shout and sing for joy;
We'll hiss and stone those horse police
    And sing "Bold Johnny Troy".'

There were Troy, Bill Harrington,
    Tim Jackson, and Jack Dun,
Four of the bravest heroes
    Who ever handled gun.

They chanced to meet an old man
    All on the king's highway,
And Troy rode up to him
    While these words he did say,

'Your gold watch and your money
    I quickly do demand,
Or I'll blow out your brains instantly
    If you refuse to stand.'

'I've neither watch or money,'
    The old man then replied;
'But for a wife and family
    I daily do provide.'

'I've been cast out of the Shamrock Isle
    For being a reckless boy,
But if that's so, you shan't be robbed,'
    Cried gallant Johnny Troy.

Troy then mounted on his steed,
    And before he rode away,
He said, 'Here's fifty pounds, old man,
    'Twill help you on your way.'

'The poor I'll serve both night and day,
    The rich I will annoy;
The people round know me right well;
    They call me "Johnny Troy".'

Said Troy to Bill Harrington,
    'Load every man his piece;
For this very night I intend to fight
    Against the horse police.'

Now Johnny Troy was captured
And sentenced then to die
Upon the tenth of April
Upon the scaffold high.

His friends and all that knew him,
Wept for this fearless boy:
'There goes our brave young hero
By the name of Johnny Troy!'

As it is sung in Canada, Ireland, England and elsewhere, the Australian bushranger ballad of 'The Wild Colonial Boy' is also widely known in American tradition—another link in the chain of the outlaw hero tradition.[3]

HOMEGROWN BADMEN

A number of folkloric studies of the outlaw hero in America have been produced. These include Klapp on the folk hero (1949),[4] Simeone on the links between Robin Hood and the American outlaw (1958),[5] Steckmesser's investigations of various outlaw heroes (1965, 1966),[6] Meyer's study of James, Bass, Bonney and Floyd (1980)[7] and Roberts' application of Meyer to railroad balladry (1981).[8] Paul Kooistra wrote a substantial sociological insight into the American criminal hero, *Criminals as Heroes: Structure, Power and Identity* (1989). As well, a number of primarily historical works have appeared that deal with aspects of outlawry relevant to the present work, and there have also been studies of the continued presence of outlaw heroes in popular cultural manifestations.[9] Drawing on these works, it is possible to indicate the relationships between some of the most noted outlaws, their socio-cultural circumstances and the continuation of their images over time.

William Clarke Quantrill

A man with a diverse career, including school-teaching, gambling and farming, Quantrill was born in Ohio in 1837, the first of eight children. From 1860 he attracted official attention through an accusation of murder and the classic outlaw's crime of horse-stealing. He was eventually arrested on this latter charge in Kansas, but escaped to Missouri. Quantrill fought with the Confederate forces at Lexington and then became the leader of an irregular guerilla force known as Quantrill's Raiders that depredated Missouri and Kansas, nominally on the side of the Confederacy. Quantrill and his men were formally declared outlaws by the Union in 1862, took part in the capture of Independence, Missouri, in August that year, and thereafter became part of the regular Confederate forces, with Quantrill having the rank of Captain.

In August 1863, Quantrill led a large group of men on a raid on the town of Lawrence, Kansas, during which many civilians were butchered and much of the town burned. This was a revenge raid for what the supporters of the Confederacy believed to be the effective murder of female supporters of their cause, arrested by the Union and imprisoned in what was probably an unsafe building. In retaliation, Union forces ransacked and burned the properties of all those living beyond the towns in Jackson, Bates, Cass and Vernon counties. This 'burnt district', one of the numberless vengeance grievances of the Civil War, was to become the home area of the James gang. Quantrill also appears to have been responsible for the murder of a number of Federal non-combatants. In May 1865 the guerilla leader was fatally wounded in an encounter with Federal forces in Kentucky.

As with many other outlaw heroes, the facts of Quantrill's life do not appear to be of a kind deserving or attracting celebration. However, in the heightened tensions of the Civil War, it was quite possible for Quantrill to appear as a Confederate hero of some stature. His relative youth and his employment of terrorism contributed to this, as did the subsequent careers of a number of the men who rode with him at various times, including the James brothers. Quantrill's legend appears to have benefited from the reflected glory of these longer-lived badmen. As with these and other outlaw heroes, ambivalence has not only been a defining feature of Quantrill's legend but is in fact essential to its existence.

In the version of Quantrill's ballad reprinted here (with the common mis-spelling/mis-pronunciation of his name), he is described as a hero in relation to his attack on Lawrence, responsibility for which is partially elided through the arresting statement that 'The boys were so drunken with powder and wine.' Quantrill is also described in generally celebratory terms, and specifically as 'a fighter, a bold-hearted boy' who would 'take from the wealthy and give to the poor'.

QUANTRELL[10]

Come all you bold robbers and open your ears;
Of Quantrell the lion heart you quickly shall hear.

With his band of bold raiders in double quick time,
He came to lay Lawrence low, over the line.

CHORUS
All routing and shouting and giving the yell,
Like so many demons raised up from hell,
The boys were so drunken with powder and wine,
And come to burn Lawrence just over the line.

They came to burn Lawrence; they came not to stay.
They rode in one morning at breaking of day
With guns all a-waving and horses all foam,
And Quantrell a-riding his famous big roan.

They came to burn Lawrence; they came not to stay.
Jim Lane he was up at the break of the day;
He saw them a-coming and got in a fright,
Then crawled in a corn crib to get out of sight.

Oh, Quantrell's a fighter, a brave-hearted boy:
A brave man or woman he'd never annoy.
He'd take from the wealthy and give to the poor,
For brave men there's never a bolt to his door.

Jesse James

Jesse Woodson James was born in 1847 into relatively comfortable circumstances. His Baptist minister father owned a 275-acre farm, while his stepfather was a physician. Other family members were also well-off, as were many of the supporters of the James–Younger gang in the years following the Civil War. As already mentioned, during that conflict, Jesse, along with other family members and friends, rode with Quantrill's Raiders. Members of such irregular forces were generally recruited from the better-off classes of the south, in particular the elder sons of established slave-owning families.[11]

Jesse James and family, friends and peers were clearly not 'poor' in the conventional sense of the term. However, the outcome of the Civil War meant a great change in economic and social status for many supporters of the defeated Confederacy, particularly those who had been involved with the controversial wartime, and post-war, activities of guerrilla bands. Members of the James and Younger families, not unrealistically, felt that their lives were endangered by the post-war tensions within the Kansas–Missouri region and no doubt these tensions also adversely affected their business and occupational lives. However, as Richard White points out, to see the Jesse James saga simply in terms of North–South rivalry is inadequate, particularly as the James–Younger gang was not supported by all ex-Confederates in the region.

Nevertheless, the Civil War and its aftermath were the formative events of the lives and legends of Jesse James and the other outlaw heroes of the period. Jesse rode with Quantrill's Raiders as a youth, experiencing both the horrors and the camaraderie of war. Upon returning to Missouri at the end of hostilities in 1865, he became disillusioned with the nature of society, politics and economics in western Missouri. Probably from 1866, in league with other family members and the related Younger family, he began a career of outlawry rarely equalled either for its duration or its ability to focus the tensions and conflicts endemic in the post-war border states.

The James–Younger confederation initially came to public notice in February 1866 with the raid on the bank at Liberty, Missouri. At the time, Jesse James was probably too ill to participate in this raid, but it is widely thought that he planned the details of the robbery, during which an innocent bystander was killed. Three further Missouri banks were robbed by the gang in the period 1866–67, and in March 1868 the bank in the Kentucky town of Russellville was emptied of $14,000.

Neither Jesse nor his brother, Frank, were in good health. They appear to have travelled to California for medical reasons, reappearing in December 1869 when they robbed the bank at Gallatin, Missouri. Jesse, apparently in cold blood, shot down the cashier (a Union supporter who had been involved in the killing of one of the James boys' wartime leaders) in this raid. After that the gang disappeared again until June 1871, when at Corydon, Iowa, they took almost $40,000 from the bank. They apparently lived off this until robbing the bank at Columbia, Kentucky, in April 1872, shooting the bank clerk in the process. In September that year they are credited—or blamed—with robbing the cash box of the Kansas City Fair, returning to public view again only in May 1873 when they plundered the bank at Ste Genevieve.

In July of 1873 the gang derailed a train on the Chicago, Rock Island and Pacific Railway, mistakenly expecting it to be laden with gold. Two men were killed in the derailment, which heralded the entry of the James gang into the highly specialised and modern form of highway thieving known as train robbing. Perhaps disillusioned by the paltry

Jesse James
(Still from 'JESSE JAMES' © 1939 Courtesy of Twentieth Century Fox Film Corporation.

takings of this train robbery, the gang next attacked a stagecoach on the way to Hot Springs, Arkansas, in January 1874. Later in the month the gang successfully robbed the train from St Louis at Gads Hill, and followed this with a stagecoach robbery in April. On 24 April, Jesse James married his cousin, Zerelda Mimms. He effectively removed himself from the attention of the authorities and the travelling public for almost nine months, until December when a gold shipment worth approximately $40,000 was stolen from a train at Muncie, Kansas.

Throughout this period, however, Missouri was in election mode. During the campaign, outlaws in general and the James gang in particular became political issues, with Republicans accusing Democrats of sympathising with one-time Confederate guerillas. According to Kooistra, the election attracted a good deal of interest from newspapers elsewhere in the country, thus spreading the notoriety of Jesse James from the local and state levels to the national level.[12]

On 25 January, 1875, agents of the Pinkerton detective agency working for the Federal government surrounded the home of Jesse's mother and stepfather, Mrs and Dr Samuels, in the erroneous belief that Jesse was inside. The agents put an incendiary device through the window of the house, killing Jesse's eight-year-old half-brother and severing his mother's right arm. This inept and malicious incident, widely reported and condemned, contributed greatly to the notion that the James family were the victims of injustice, always an important element of outlaw hero legends.

The activities of the Pinkerton detective agency during the Civil War had involved spying for the Union. The agency's operatives were therefore not popular in the South. When the Pinkerton's agents began working in Clay County as part of the effort to capture or kill the James brothers, a number of them were murdered, probably through the actions of James supporters and sympathisers. In the afterglow of public sympathy for the bombing outrage, the issue of granting an amnesty to the outlaws arose. The amnesty resolution presented to the Missouri house of representatives refers to the James gang in classic outlaw hero terms. They were said to have been driven into banditry by the oppressive actions of the government, to be brave, generous, gallant and honourable, mostly innocent of the crimes levelled against them, and generally persecuted for political reasons. The resolution was defeated by a few Republican votes.

Huntington, West Virginia, was the scene of the the gang's next bank robbery, probably followed in July by the Rocky Cut train robbery near Otterville, Missouri. In September the James gang disastrously mismanaged a raid on the bank in Northfield, Minnesota. Jesse murdered the bank clerk who refused to hand over the safe keys, and the outlaws themselves were badly shot-up in the ensuing gunfight with some of the citizens of Northfield who were enraged at this attempt on their savings. The gang split up, with the three Younger brothers, Cole, Jim and Bob, being captured near Madelia a few weeks later, all badly wounded. They all stood trial in due course and were imprisoned, Bob dying of tuberculosis after thirteen years, while Cole and Jim were paroled in 1901.

The Northfield raid marks the start of the decline of Jesse James and his gang. During the depression years of the 1870s, the banks and the railroads were popularly viewed as the agents of the wealthy and the exploitative. Repossessions by banks and barely controlled financial exploitation by the railroad companies, with consequent economic hardship for many ordinary families, contributed to this negative public image. Those who attacked these interests, for whatever motives, were therefore seen by many as vicarious avengers of their own disenchantments and difficulties. These attitudes found expression in popular sympathy and active support for the outlaws and was even manifested in newspapers such as the *Kansas City Times* of 23 August 1876: 'The bold highwayman who does not molest the poor or the ordinary traveller, but levies tribute on banks and railroad corporations and express monopolies, is not generally such an object of popular detestation that he cannot secure a fair trial in our courts.'[13] In his laudatory *Noted Guerillas*, the indefatigable Edwards fleshed out the outlaw hero characteristics of the James boys in general and of Jesse in particular. They were persecuted for their wartime activities and so driven to their crimes. To Edwards, and probably to many other Southerners, the James gang could be seen as a continuation of the Civil War, an attitude implicit in passages describing Jesse James as 'an outlaw, but he is not a criminal'.[14]

After the Northfield fiasco, the James brothers could not be found at all. They remained in hiding until October 1879 when, with a new gang, Jesse robbed a train at Glendale, Missouri. The outlaws were widely criticised for this action, even by the Democrat press and supporters, popular sentiment regarding railroad companies having softened somewhat. In 1880 William Crittenden was elected Governor of Missouri. Sympathetic to railroad interests, Crittenden was to engineer the demise of the James gang. But before that happened, the James gang committed a number of further, uncharacteristically brutal, crimes. Two railway employees were killed during the gang's next train robbery at Winston in July 1881 and they made only a small haul from the train they robbed at Blue Cut, Missouri, in September, although their once-impeccable outlaw hero target of the ill-gotten bullion of banks and corporations had degenerated to common pilfering of the personal belongings of train passengers.

During this period, the gang was in its final decay. Perhaps because there were fewer ties of kinship in the new James gang, dissension became a problem, resulting in a lack of security. One member of the gang was arrested in March 1881 near Nashville, where Jesse had been living. The outlaw leader moved to Kansas City and then to St Joseph, Missouri, where he lived quietly and respectably as Mr Thomas Howard. Rewards for Jesse James were now totalling many thousands of dollars, tempting two of the gang's accomplices, Charles and Bob Ford, to plot Jesse's betrayal and death, apparently in complicity with Governor Crittenden.[15] Their chance came on 3 April 1882, when James removed his guns to attend to a household chore and was immediately shot in the back of the head by Bob Ford, who wasted no time in claiming the reward from the state governor. Ford (pardoned for the murder of James by the governor) was nevertheless widely reviled for his action. Ten years later he was shot dead in Colorado by a relation of the Youngers, another indication of the potency of kinship networks in such situations. This event is celebrated in the song 'Jesse James'.

The lyrics concentrate on the heroic attributes of James, his murder by Ford and the killer's subsequent—and righteous—end: 'as you do you'll git according'.

JESSE JAMES[16]

Jesse James was one of his names, another it was Howard.
He robbed the rich of every stitch. You bet, he was no coward.

His mother she was elderly, his father was a preacher,
Though some do say, I can't gainsay, his mother was his teacher.

Her strong right arm, it came to harm. Detectives blew it off, sir,
And killed her son, the youngest one. No wonder such she'd
scoff, sir.

My Jesse dear, your mother here has taught more than she ought
ter,
For Robert Ford, I pledge my word, has marked you for his
slaughter.

For robbing trains Bob had no brains, unless Jess plainly showed
him.
Our governor for peace or war explained this for to goad him.

So Robert Ford he scratched his gourd, and then he said 'I'll go
you,
Give me a price that's something nice, and then, by gee, I'll
show you!'

92

Then Governor C. [i.e. Crittenden] he laughed with glee and
 fixed a price to suit him,
And Bob agreed, with ready speed, to find Jess James and shoot
 him.

And then he did as he was bid and shot Jess in the back, sir,
Then ran away on that same day, for cash he did not lack, sir.

He did his best to live out west, but no-one was his friend there.
'You've killed your cousin', they went buzzin', however free he'd
 spend there.

And then one day, the papers say, Bob Ford got his rewarding:
A cowboy drunk his heart did plunk. As you do you'll git
 according.

With Jesse James dead, the folkloric processes were able to continue
weaving the strands of his legend. The betrayal was provided by history,
while Jesse's hero status was confirmed by rumours and claims that he
was not really dead at all, despite the body of Mr Howard being identified as that of James by his mother and others who knew him. The
most common Jesse James ballad seems to have been composed quite
soon after James' death and to have achieved instant sanction and wide
circulation, if the reminiscences of Robert Kennedy published in the
Missouri *Springfield Leader* on 18 October 1933, with the folkloric
conclusion, can be relied upon:

> Soon after the killing of James a ten-foot poem, set to music,
> came out and was sung on the streets of Springfield quite
> frequently. It told how Jesse James had a wife who warned him
> all her life and the children they were brave and the dirty little
> coward who shot Mr Howard and they laid poor Jesse in the
> grave. It caused tears to be shed; it was the Mark Antony eulogy
> at the bier of Caesar. An old blind woman used to stand in front
> of the court house in Springfield and sing it by the hour;
> mourners would drop coins in her tin can. She went up to
> Richmond, Mo., and was singing her sad song with tears in her
> voice when she found herself slapped and kicked into the middle
> of the street. Bob Ford's sister happened to be passing that way.[17]

This song and the legends of the James gang also motivated the
activities of a later group of train and bank robbers. The Daltons of

Jesse James in death, 1882

Oklahoma Territory were distantly related to the James family. The Daltons were not particularly good at their chosen criminal profession, it seems, and their activities lasted only from February 1891 to October 1892, when they set out to eclipse the doings of the James–Younger gang by robbing two banks at once in Coffeyville. This misconceived escapade resulted in the end of the gang, though a considerable body of outlaw hero folklore accreted around them.[18] This came mainly, it seems, from the reflected glory of their relations and mentors of the James–Younger collaboration, whose folklore has been both more potent and widespread.

The folkloric version of the James gang's motivations and activities has been succinctly described by Steckmesser:

> Jesse and Frank James return from Confederate guerilla service in the Civil War to find their home state of Missouri overrun with carpetbaggers, Radicals and other vindictive Unionists. In the folklore version these persecutors attack Jesse's father, put his mother in jail, and savagely beat him with rope ends. The law itself has become a weapon of the Yankee oppressors. To secure justice for himself and his friends, Jesse must live outside the law.[19]

Here are two of the persistent strands of the outlaw hero tradition, particularly in its American and Australian manifestations of the late nineteenth century. The importance of the family as the focus of injustice is clear, as it is in the James ballads and other folklore. Less clearly articulated in the folk expressions, but implicit in their tradition, is the failure of the law, together with its blatant subversion. That the James family was not subjected to such treatment, apart from the ill-judged Pinkerton bombing in 1875, a fact that fitted well with the already-established folklore, is of no matter. Once the outlaw hero tradition was motivated, history was invented or distorted within the controlling framework of the tradition.

Nor was this legend-building restricted to the folkloric processes. The popular media and literature industries, sensitive to the currents of hearsay and rumour that flow beneath the surface of society, soon initiated their own stereotyping and representations. As Steckmesser and others[20] have pointed out, journalists frequently praised or at least adverted to the Robin Hood characteristics of the James gang. One particular editor, the Missouran John Newman Edwards, began to celebrate the gang in explicit Robin Hood and British highwayman terms after the Kansas City Fair event, and continued in like vein for seventeen years.[21] Newspapers have also been more than willing to provide outlaws with a forum to express their point of view, as did a member of the James gang in the Kansas City *Times* of 15 October 1872. The letter, signed 'Jack Shepherd, Dick Turpin, Claude Duval', claimed that 'we rob the rich and give it to the poor' and that they killed only in self-defence. The authenticity of this letter (probably fabricated by Edwards, or at his instigation) matters not at all as far as folklore is concerned. What it provides is firm evidence for the continuation of the ideals of the British highwaymen heroes and of the general currency of essential elements of the outlaw hero tradition.

Nor was this the first published letter purporting to be from the James gang. After the first robbery blamed on Jesse James (the bank at Gallatin, Missouri, in December 1869), Jesse wrote to the state governor, claiming innocence and suggesting that he was being persecuted for wartime grievances. Published in *The Liberty Tribune* of 24 June 1870, this letter was only the first of many penned by James in defence and explanation of his actions.[22] The written defence was a recurring element of nineteenth-century outlawry, and was also used extensively by the Australian bushrangers. As well as being posted to newspapers and civil or political figures, such defences could be left at the scene of the crime. This technique was used with considerable effect by the James gang, as in an 1874 train robbery, during which the outlaws also took pains to avoid robbing workingmen or women. On another occasion, the gang returned the money and belongings of an ex-Confederate soldier, an action that has numerous historical and folkloric parallels in the legendry of the outlaw hero.[23]

The extent of support and sympathy for the James–Younger gang in and around their native regions has been well documented.[24] Again, kinship ties were of crucial importance here; as with the Kellys and other bushrangers, they provided the outlaws with a sustaining network of informers, providers of food, ammunition, shelter and transport. Unrelated but tied to the James family through community loyalties and obligations were numerous friends and acquaintances who could be relied on for aid and support. In addition to such active supporters, the James gang had many more passive sympathisers for whom the folkloric version of events and motivations had a compelling resonance. They were not averse to proclaiming their sympathy, even in towns which had recently been robbed by the gang.[25] Of particular importance was the fact that the James gang was supported by the ex-Confederate wing of the Dem-ocrats in Missouri, still smarting from the grievances of the Civil War and the perceived inequities of its aftermath. Consciously or otherwise, Jesse James and his fellow outlaws represented a powerful political network, and in spite of (and sometimes because of) their violence, expressed the antagonisms that ran deep in Missouri during the 1860s and 1870s.[26]

THE CONTINUING IMAGE OF JESSE JAMES

After Jesse's death at the hands of Robert Ford, history and folklore again intertwined. Ford's membership of the gang, a result of his relationship to an existing gang member, meant that his gunning down of its leader was easily interpreted as treachery and betrayal, thus completing the requirements of the outlaw hero tradition. The most common version of the James ballad originated at this time and has had a varied and energetic existence ever since. Oral traditions about Jesse, such as the widow and the landlord story,[27] among others, persisted and spread. They were aided as ever by the media of the day, for whom the murder of the country's most wanted criminal was news indeed. The press has had a continuing interest in, and influence upon, the persistence of the James legend, with features and discussions about the pros and cons of the story providing a reliable standby. The effect of such treatments was to continually reinforce the image—negative, positive or 'balanced'—of the outlaw, and to recycle the various elements of the outlaw hero tra-dition in the manner peculiar to the types of convenient fictions purveyed by sections of the press.

A quotation concluding W. A. Settle Jnr's examination of the lit-erary and media representations of Jesse James provides an appropriate preface to the best-known James ballad presented below:

> Although there have been a few attempts ... to destroy the
> Robin Hood aspect of the James legend, it is apparent that it is
> too well rooted in American folklore to suffer serious damage.
> The forces that sustain it are far greater than any that would
> destroy it. Hence the Jesse James legend will live on and continue
> to excite Americans with the exploits of their native Robin Hood.[28]

In this ballad, James is manly, brave, smart, an unambiguous friend and benefactor to the poor and a unique figure who 'came of a solitary race'.

He is betrayed by the 'thief in the night', Robert Ford, who is also execrated as 'that dirty little coward that shot Mr Howard' (Howard was James' alias at the time when Ford shot him). James is a caring figure with 'a hand and a heart and a brain' who would 'never see a man suffer pain'. His victims are the impersonal, corporate targets of the banks and the railroads.

The duality and ambivalence typical of outlaw hero figures is apparent here. On the one hand we are invited to sympathise with Jesse and his wife and children, yet he is also a murderer 'who killed many a man'. The outlaw 'went to his rest with hand on his breast' but 'The devil will be upon his knee.' Even though he is outside the law, he is greater than the law. He represents a more fundamental imperative of justice and revenge than that provided within the legal framework, as implied in the lines 'no man with the law in his hand / Could take Jesse James when alive'.

The theme of the family, very much an element of the American and Australian manifestations of the outlaw hero, forcefully reappears here. Brother Frank is in evidence, as are Jesse's wife and children. The family theme is conflated with that of betrayal in verse 5, where the vicious Pinkerton attack on the home of Jesse's parents, resulting in the death of Jesse's half-brother and the maiming of his mother, is combined with Jesse's treacherous murder. While this is historically wildly inaccurate, it is perfectly logical and correct within the framework of the outlaw hero tradition, another example of the interpenetration of history and folklore. Internally, this combination of two of the central elements within the American manifestation of the outlaw hero tradition operates to give the song considerable emotional potency, explaining the popularity and the longevity of this particular song and its representation of the James legend.

BALLAD OF JESSE JAMES[29]

Jesse James was a lad who killed many a man.
    He robbed the Glendale train
He stole from the rich and he gave to the poor
    He'd a hand and a heart and a brain.

CHORUS
Jesse had a wife to mourn for his life
    Three children, they were brave

But that dirty little coward that shot Mister Howard
    Has laid Jesse James in his grave

It was Robert Ford, that dirty little coward
    I wonder how he does feel,
For he ate of Jesse's bread and he slept in Jesse's bed,
    Then he laid Jesse James in his grave.

Jesse was a man, a friend to the poor
    He'd never see a man suffer pain,
And with his brother Frank he robbed the Chicago bank,
    And stopped the Glendale train.

It was on a Wednesday night, the moon was shining bright,
    He stopped the Glendale train
And the people all did say for many miles away,
    It was robbed by Frank and Jesse James.

It was on a Saturday night, Jesse was at home,
    Talking to his family brave,
Robert Ford came along like a thief in the night,
    And laid Jesse James in his grave.

The people held their breath when they heard of Jesse's death,
    And wondered how he ever came to die,
It was one of the gang called little Robert Ford,
    That shot Jesse James on the sly.

Jesse went to his rest with hand on his breast,
    The devil will be upon his knee,
He was born one day in the county of Shea
    And he came of a solitary race.

This song was made by Billy Gashade,
    As soon as the news did arrive,
He said there was no man with the law in his hand
    Could take Jesse James when alive.

Jesse had a wife to mourn for his life,
    Three children, they were brave,
But that dirty little coward that shot Mister Howard,
    Has laid Jesse James in his grave.

Other forms and genres of cultural production have been no less fascinated by the James saga. W. A. Settle Jnr has followed the traces of Jesse James in various forms of popular representation, including those on the stage:

> Dramatizations of events in the life of Jesse James and of
> incidents pertaining to members of his band, including the Fords,
> date from immediately after the day Bob Ford shot Jesse. They
> continued to be stand-bys for travelling stock companies until
> competition from motion pictures and other factors brought the
> decline of such groups.[30]

Settle goes on to discuss different stage dramatisations, including a particularly popular one, *The James Boys in Missouri.* It was the subject of attempted suppression by an outraged and now respectable Frank James when it played in Kansas City in 1902. The same play, despite Frank's complaints and legal actions, was still drawing large audiences in St Louis as late as 1911. In 1938, these theatrical versions of Jesse James the noble robber and outlaw hero reached Broadway in the form of Elizabeth Beall Ginty's *Missouri Legend.* It it had a reasonably successful run though, more importantly for the continued diffusion of the James legend, it was widely staged by amateur theatrical groups.

The James family were investors in the first of many feature films to be made about the outlaw. Released in 1921, *Under the Black Flag* not surprisingly presented a partisan account of Jesse's activities, though it did little business outside western Missouri. The numerous Hollywood treatments began in 1927 with Paramount's *Jesse James,* a sympathetic portrayal. Tyrone Power played the outlaw hero in the Twentieth Century Fox production, *Jesse James,* of 1939. The film was hugely successful, firmly establishing the Jesse James persona as a Hollywood hero and leading man, and ensuring the continued circulation of the popular representation of the outlaw hero. A sequel, *The Return of Frank James,* appeared in the 1940s, followed by two treatments during the 1950s. In 1965 a television series dealing with James was broadcast by ABC television, and the subject has also been treated in radio broadcasts and as a sub-plot in numerous other movies and television shows.

Beginning with publication in 1875 of *The Guerillas of the West; or the Life, Character, and Daring Exploits of the Younger Brothers* by Augustus C. Appler, Jesse James has been the subject of a very great number of books, whether serious, fictional, absurd, opportunistic or simply

The Outlaw. *(© 1941 RKO Pictures, Inc. Used by permission Turner Entertainment Co.*
All rights reserved.)

entertaining. Appler's work was followed in 1877 by John N. Edwards' *Noted Guerillas, or the Warfare of the Border.* Both books were partisan accounts and so added to the favourable aspects of the James legend. Settle notes numerous other 'serious' accounts of the Jameses in the years before Jesse's death, and over thirty other such titles published since. Some of these accounts have attempted a balanced assessment of the James life and legend, though these are in the minority. A few others attempt to debunk the legend in various ways, but most, as Settle notes, 'present the gang as both bad men and Robin Hoods'.[31] While some of the titles discussed by Settle achieved print runs of only a few thousand copies, many were widely distributed and reprinted in various editions.

Another widespread and influential form of popular or ephemeral literature in which the James legend was generally celebrated were dime novels and other forms of pulp fiction. Settle notes hundreds of titles dealing exclusively, substantially or tangentially with the characters and events of the James saga. Titles such as *The James Boys and the Mad Sheriff* and *The James Boys at Bay* were capped by other pulp writers anxious to find new twists to an evergreen narrative; they produced works titled *Jesse James Among the Mormons* and *Jesse James at Coney Island.* Absurd though such titles now sound, they had circulations throughout the country in the tens, even hundreds, of thousands. According to Settle,

> in spite of the strange mixture of ingredients that make up the characters of the Frank and Jesse James of the dime novel, this portrayal is not greatly unlike the popular conception of them.[32]

The tone and approach of this material is in accord with the vast majority of popular representations of the outlaw hero, an ambivalent combination of respect, romance and moralising, as in this advertisement for the first paperback history of the gang published anonymously as No. 2 of the Police Gazette Library series in 1881: 'The career of those daring highwaymen, whose cruel murders and many crimes have made the mere mention of their names a terror to law-abiding citizens, is full of romance.'[33] Although the times, the names and the places had changed, James and his comrades were being treated by the popular media in exactly the same manner as their British highwaymen predecessors had been portrayed in the chapbook and the broadside ballad. The popular representation of the outlaw hero was as alive as it always had been, as was his folkloric representation. The interaction of those two modes of cultural representation was as essential to the creation and continued celebration of Jesse James as an outlaw hero as it was to that of William Bonney.

Flowing on from these confluences, and contributing to them, is the relatively recent discourse of tourism. Not far from Kansas City, Missouri, Jesse James and his legend still ride along the tourist trail. Jesse's birthplace at Kearney is the site of a museum, gift shop and audio-visual presentation in the authentically restored James family farmhouse. Jesse's grave can be viewed here (though his body has been moved to the Clay County cemetery to dissuade souvenir hunters from chipping bits off the headstone). And there are the usual accoutrements of outlaw heritage—guns, boots, spurs, remains of his casket, some furniture, and the very table on which his body was embalmed. One of the many James books has been dramatised and performed at the farm as an outdoor spectacle of family theatre, involving a cast of twenty actors. In Liberty there is a Jesse James Bank Museum where the curious can see the bank that the James gang robbed restored to its former glory, together with re-enactments of the event. The outlaw and his legend cannot be allowed to die.

WILLIAM 'BILLY THE KID' BONNEY

Known to legend as Billy the Kid, William Bonney also went by a number of other names in his short life. Born probably in New York City on 23 November 1859, he was known as Henry McCarty and Henry Antrim at various times. There was nothing to distinguish him from many other young thugs and thieves until he lost an argument with a blacksmith at Fort Grant, Arizona Territory, in August 1877. Bonney shot the man dead. On the run, he was hired by an English rancher, John Tunstall, becoming deeply involved in the Lincoln County range war in the New Mexico of the late 1870s. Bonney was either responsible for or deeply implicated in the killing of numerous men working for the Santa Fe Ring. This was a group of ranchers and traders, who were apparently colluding with the authorities and were desperate to protect their interests against the threat from the ambitious Tunstall. While the Lincoln range war was fundamentally a struggle for control of economic resources and power in the area between two competing commercial-criminal combines, it could easily be seen from below as a struggle of the weaker, and apparently eminently respectable, English rancher, against the vested interests of a group of venal and corrupt officials and businessmen. The Tunstall faction, then, had the sympathy of the smaller landholders and workers, including Mexican-Americans. This is a classic set of circumstances for the motivation of the outlaw hero tradition. That so unlikely a candidate as William Bonney eventually surfaced as the main player is testimony to the strength of that tradition and of the social and cultural needs that impel it.

In 1878 the Lincoln range war subsided somewhat. After the killing of Tunstall, the now-secure business-official combine took their revenge on the losers. Bonney became a fugitive, an outlaw instead of a hired gun, and a bit-player in a large-scale political and economic drama that had national and even international repercussions. When it became clear that law and order had totally broken down in Lincoln County, the sitting governor was removed from office and replaced by Lew Wallace. Further bloodshed followed and, perceptively reading the signs of the times, Bonney negotiated an amnesty with the new governor that saw him taken into protective custody. Due to further political machinations, Bonney decided, after a few months of custody, that he would be safer outside gaol. He escaped but was recaptured by the new sheriff, Pat Garrett, an old acquaintance, late in 1880. In April 1881, Bonney was found guilty of murder and sentenced to death. But Billy the Kid, probably with the aid of a sympathiser, escaped again, killing two prison guards, and disappearing. After some delay, Garrett formed a posse and pursued him to Fort Sumner where, on 14 July 1881, Garrett shot him dead.

Ostensibly unsuitable as Bonney was for outlaw heroisation, there were some facets of his life that, in the circumstances outlined, could be transmuted into legend. He was young, about twenty-five, when he died. His killings, while hardly brave, were at least in line with the implicit machismo of the outlaw hero. He did perform a sensational, if bloody, gaol-break, and the man who killed him was a one-time friend, so Billy the Kid could be seen as the victim of treachery. He has been referred to as 'the darling of the common people' and his popularity among Mexican-Americans is well-documented, though little evidence exists to show that he did perform a Robin Hood role for this particular group. More likely he was seen as something of an avenging demon, spreading blood and terror among the hated Americans, rather as Mexican bandit heroes like Murieta and Gregorio Cortez were admired by their peers.[34] In common with the tradition of other outlaw heroes, many people refused to believe that Billy the Kid was dead: stories about his survival or even resurrection were rife in New Mexico and elsewhere as late as 1926, according to Botkin. He also retails traditions that Billy was driven to crime by persecution, and first paid a poor widow's mortgage and then robbed it back again, along with further accounts of the outlaw hero lore already mentioned.[35]

Billy the Kid's ballad is a particularly good example of the balancing of tradition and history to produce an outlaw hero out of an unlikely set of events and personalities. It should be noted that Bonney's ambivalent status as an outlaw hero has also generated an 'anti-heroic' ballad.[36]

SONG OF BILLY THE KID[37]

I'll sing you a true song of Billy the Kid,
I'll sing of the desperate deeds that he did
Way out in New Mexico long, long ago,
When a man's only chance was his own forty-four.

When Billy the Kid was a very young lad,
In old Silver City he went to the bad;
Way out in the West with a gun in his hand
At the age of twelve years he first killed his man.

Fair Mexican maidens play guitars and sing
A song about Billy, their boy bandit king,
How ere his young manhood had reached its dead end
He'd a notch on his pistol for twenty-one men.

'Twas on the same night when poor Billy died
He said to his friends: 'I am not satisfied;
There are twenty-one men I have put bullets through
And sheriff Pat Garrett must make twenty-two.'

Now, this is how Billy the Kid met his fate:
The bright moon was shining, the hour was late.
Shot down by Pat Garrett, who once was his friend,
The young outlaw's life had now come to its end.

There's many a man with a face fine and fair
Who starts out in life with a chance to be square,
But just like poor Billy he wanders astray
And loses his life in the very same way.

In his song, Billy is represented primarily in terms of the sentimental strand of his legend. However, the 'satanic' side of the legend is acknowledged through the twenty-one notches on his gun, a reflection of the difficulty that the tradition has in balancing the positive elements of folklore and the rather awkwardly murderous facts of Bonney's life. This accounts for the slightly muted outlaw hero tone of the text. It refrains from an explicit statement of the Kid's Robin Hood stature, though this is implicit in the first two lines of verse 3, where the Mexican maidens sing songs about 'their boy bandit king'.

Other outlaw hero traits are clearly present. Billy's criminality is justified through the suggestion that law and order was in short supply 'Way out in New Mexico long, long ago' and that the Kid was only doing what was necessary to survive in killing his first man at twelve years of age—a persistent element of his legend. The folkloric notches on his gun, paralleling his equally folkloric age, again acknowledge the violent elements of the legend, but are quickly elided through the outlaw hero manner of his death: 'Shot down by Pat Garrett who once was his friend'. Finally, again recognising the fact that 'poor Billy wanders astray', the song suggests that such unfortunate circumstances have happened to many others.

This song is clearly not a product of local New Mexico legends of Billy the Kid. It draws on a range of elements manipulated and, in the case of the Mexican maidens, introduced by the subsequent popular mythologisation of the Kid. The text therefore is an excellent example of the manner in which the folkloric traditions of the outlaw hero interact with the imperatives and convenience of the popular media. It takes the basic elements of the local manifestation, or *oicotype*, of the outlaw hero tradition and merges these with the sentimental imperatives of the popular media, producing a text that simultaneously acknowledges and mediates some blatant contradictions and ambivalences of folklore and history. As a convenient fiction in the outlaw hero tradition, 'Song of Billy the Kid' is an unqualified success.

In folklore, then, a short, buck-toothed gunslinger passed into local legend and lore as a classic outlaw hero. Beyond that, his image was rapidly appropriated by the popular media of the day. His real and imagined deeds were widely reported (and plagiarised) in newspapers, and given fictional representation in dime novels and 'factional' representation in dime 'biographies'. As with most outlaw heroes, there was a folkloric reluctance to accept that the man was really dead.[38] The man

William Bonney—'Billy the Kid', c. 1880.

who killed Bonney was one of the first to establish his legendary characteristics. Pat Garrett published a ghost-written book in 1882 titled *The
Authentic Life of Billy the Kid*, in which he described the outlaw as brave,
loyal, generous, resourceful and gallant as well as being the equal of 'any
fabled brigand'.[39]

There were—and continue to be—many popular treatments of the
life and legend of Billy the Kid. Steckmesser has perceptively tracked
these representations of the Kid, which generally portray him as a
'satanic' type, and has also identified an equally powerful strand of
popular treatment that represents the Kid as a 'saint'. This positive image
is particularly associated with stage and filmic treatments, beginning with
the 1903 melodrama *Billy the Kid* by Walter Woods and continuing
through Hollywood adaptations of inaccurate but best-selling journalistic
treatments of the story that began to appear in the mid-1920s. The first
of these was W. Burns' *Saga of Billy the Kid* (1926), upon which the
first Hollywood feature film, *Billy the Kid* (MGM) was based. This
appeared in 1930 and has been followed by at least thirty other feature
films about Billy the Kid, as well as a 1960s television series, *The Tall
Man*. In most of these representations, the Kid appears as the wronged,
often innocent, youth of somewhat ambivalent morality who nevertheless
displays virtues, being manly, generous and likeable. All are fundamental
outlaw hero characteristics, and are frequently bolstered by an emphasis
on the Kid's celebration by Mexican-Americans and his explicit or
implicit Robin Hood activities on their behalf.

A second filmic treatment of the Kid's saga, *The Gamblin' Man*,
was released in 1934 and Aaron Copland created a ballet based on the
Kid in 1938. It is perhaps not surprising that this sentimental Robin
Hood image of Billy the Kid should take hold of American popular
consciousness during the 1930s, when the depressed economic circumstances of the period threw many out of work and created large groups
of dispossessed and discontented individuals for whom a robber of the
rich would have a particular resonance. A similar process occurs with
the activities of 'Pretty Boy' Floyd, and in Australia in relation to the
image of the bushranger Ned Kelly. It is not surprising, then, that we
should find the ballad of Billy the Kid being sung in New York state
in 1934.

Stephen Tatum has provided us with an investigation of the varying
cultural representations of the Kid over time, together with their signif-
icance(s). Tatum discerns the figure of this particular outlaw in relation

to the classic tragic hero of literature. After tracking the Kid's representation in dime novels, stage melodramas, film, ballet, literature and other
high and not so high cultural niches, including the later frontier search
for order, the Prohibition period of the depression, the Cold War and
Watergate, Tatum describes the Kid's perennial appeal in these terms:

> he objectifies not only the human desire to abolish any obstacles
> to the free self but also the human acceptance of the limitations
> imposed on the free self by time and the environment. If the
> outlaw hero is successful only as a defeated delivering hero in
> legend, not as a successful hero in history, there is ultimately
> safety in his defeat, for this subversive figure's challenge to our
> perhaps too easy acceptance of life as it is becomes removed safely
> into the legendary past.
>
> If the Kid's perennial appeal can thus be explained in part
> by the manner in which certain basic psychological needs are
> fulfilled through his role as a conventional heroic outlaw, it is
> equally clear that he has endured because he has been a timely
> invented outlaw, because he has been an outlaw whose meaning
> has changed along with the changing preoccupations of his
> creators and their cultural context.[40]

This could apply as much to the images of Robin Hood, Jesse James,
Dick Turpin and Ned Kelly.

Most recently, Bonney has featured in the *Young Guns* movies,
mostly though not totally in accord with the romantic aspects of his
legend. As well, numerous persons have claimed to be Billy the Kid, and
there is also a thriving Kid tourist industry in the region where he was
active.[41] Like those of a select few other badmen, Billy the Kid's legend
lives on.

OTHER BADMEN HEROES

Sam Bass

'Desperado' is the description of Sam Bass given by one of his biog-
raphers. True though it may be, Bass does not seem to have been any
more desperate than many of the American outlaws and badmen, even
less so than most. Born in Indiana in 1851, Bass was one of ten children on a small but comfortable farm. His parents died before he
reached his teens, and he was raised by an uncle until 1869, when he
left home to make his own way in the world. After various jobs in a

mill, a hotel and as a cowboy, Bass suddenly, it seems, in 1875 took to gambling and fast living, followed by horse-stealing. Various crimes, including stealing, stagecoach holdups and train robberies occupied Bass and his companions in Nebraska and Texas. Closely pursued, Bass escaped to rob a number of trains in the Dallas and Fort Worth area in 1878. Some of Bass's companions were killed and captured by Texas Rangers, and one of the survivors was persuaded to return to the gang and inform on their movements. This was done and in July 1878, Bass's attempt to rob the Round Rock bank was foiled by the informer. In the ensuing gunfight, Bass was wounded, dying two days later on his twenty-seventh birthday.

Again, there seems little in the bare facts of Bass's brief life to justify his distinction as an outlaw hero. His unfortunate orphaning could be seen as perhaps a partial reason, if not a justification, for his later criminal activities, though there is no suggestion that his foster-home was particularly unhappy or oppressive. Bass managed to avoid killing anyone until the end of his career; he seems to have been regarded—in Texas, at least—as something of a mild-mannered hero, or so his folklore asserts.

Additional to the ballad printed below, Sam Bass folk narrative and belief presents him in outlaw hero guise. Sam was kind-hearted and generous: he tips the porters and brakemen on the trains he robs; he gives cripples silver dollars; he pays for simple country generosity and sustenance with two twenty-dollar gold pieces; and he forgoes robbing a naive young store-clerk, warning him of the dangers of leaving too much cash in view. He performs feats of pistol-shooting, such as tattooing his initials into a tree; he fools, hoaxes and escapes a deputy sheriff; and he is almost everyone's popular hero. The story of Sam paying the mortgage of a poor widow and then robbing it back from the landlord is also told of numerous other outlaw heroes. He is, of course, betrayed as he was in reality and there is at least one legend that Sam Bass is not the man inside the grave bearing his headstone (which, incidentally, bears the inscription 'A brave man reposes in death here. Why was he not true?'). Finally, his lost treasure can still be found in the Round Rock country. The outlaw hero tradition is here displayed in almost its full array. All that is missing is the motive for outlawry. It is clear that this can be satisfactorily replaced by the other motifs of the tradition to present a perfectly satisfactory outlaw hero fiction convenient to the tellers of the tales and singers of the songs of Sam Bass.

SAM BASS[42]

Sam Bass was born in Indiana—it was his native home—
And at the age of seventeen, young Sam began to roam.
He first went down to Texas, a cowboy bold to be;
A kinder-hearted fellow, you'd scarcely ever see.

Sam used to deal in race stock, had one called the Denton mare.
He watched her in scrub races, took her to the County Fair.
She always won the money, however she might be.
He always drank good liquor, and spent his money free.

Sam left the Collins ranch in the merry month of May
With a herd of Texas cattle, the Black Hills to see;
Sold out in Custer City and all got on a spree—
A harder lot of cowboys you'd scarcely ever see.

On the way back to Texas, they robbed the U.P. Train,
All split up in couples and started out again.
Joe Collins and his partner were overtaken soon;
With all their hard-earned money they had to meet their doom.

Sam made it back to Texas all right side up with care,
Rode into the town of Denton, his gold with friends to share.
Sam's life was short in Texas 'count of robberies he'd do.
He'd rob the passengers' coaches, the mail and express, too.

Sam had four bold companions, four bold and daring lads:
Underwood and Joe Jackson, Bill Collins and Old Dad.
They were four of the hardest cowboys that Texas ever knew;
They whipped the Texas Rangers and ran the boys in blue.

Jonis borrowed of Sam's money and didn't want to pay;
The only way he saw to win was to give poor Sam away.
He turned traitor to his comrades; they were caught one early
    morn.
Oh what a scorching Jonis will get when Gabriel blows his horn.

Sam met his fate in Round Rock, July the twenty-first.
They pierced poor Sam with rifle balls and emptied out his
    purse.
So Sam is a corpse in Round Rock, Jonis is under the clay,
And Joe Jackson in the bushes trying to get away.

Jim Fisk

A particularly unlikely candidate for outlaw hero status was James Fisk, entrepreneurial capitalist and scorner of convention. Fisk began his working life as a pedlar, graduated to trading, and earned enough money from Civil War trading to start his own business. After various business ups and downs, Fisk teamed up with Jay Gould in the Erie Railroad venture in 1868; the two men conducted numerous unscrupulous but mostly profitable business and financial deals. Such was Gould and Fisk's control of the American business world that the eventual collapse of their schemes in September 1869 ruined hundreds of businesses and adversely affected the entire American economy. Fisk died in 1872, shot by Edward Stokes in New York City. The two men were both vying for the attention of a famous actress of the day, Josie Mansfield.

Fisk was an exhibitionist of excessive appetites who was either reviled or adored by the general public, it seems. The ballad that appears here portrays Fisk as a friend to the poor and an enemy of the rich. The ballad shows that it was not necessary to ride a horse and wield a pistol to attain at least some of the attributes of the outlaw hero, in this case a capitalist outlaw. By no stretch of the imagination could Fisk be seen to have represented any oppressed or discontented social group. Nevertheless, his well-known attitude towards the financial establishment and his brief control of that system as, if not an outlaw, then certainly as an outsider, promoted him in the popular media and the folk perception as an individual to be celebrated within the framework of the outlaw hero tradition. In these respects he anticipates to some extent the usually brief popularity of 'gangster heroes', like Capone, Dillinger and others who colourfully thumbed their noses at the law and the financial system during the years of the Great Depression. Fisk's ability to manipulate the financial and communication systems of his time also makes him a possible precursor of the electronic outlaws of the Internet discussed later.

JIM FISK[43]

If you will listen a while I will sing you a song
    Of this glorious land of the free,
The difference I will show 'twixt the rich and the poor
    In a trial by jury, you see.

If you have plenty of cash you can hold up your head
    And walk from your own prison door;

But they will hang you up high if you have neither friend or
　　gold,
　　Let the rich go, but hang up the poor.

In a trial of murder we have now,
　　And the rich ones get off slow but sure;
With their thousands to buy both the jury and judge
　　You can bet they'll go back on the poor.

Let me speak of a man who is dead in his grave,
　　As good a man as ever was born.
Jim Fisk he was called, and his money he gave
　　To outcast [sic], the poor and forlorn.

If a man was in trouble Jim Fisk would help him along
　　To drive the grim wolf from his door;
He strove to do right, though he might of [sic] done wrong,
　　But he never went back on the poor.

Jim Fisk was a man who wore his heart in [sic] his sleeve;
　　No matter what people may say,
He done all his deeds, both the good and the bad,
　　In the broad open light of the day.

With his grand six-in-hand on the beach of Long Branch
　　He cut a big dash, to be sure;
But Chicago's great fire showed the world that Jim Fisk
　　With his wealth still remembered the poor.

When the telegram came of the homeless that night,
　　They were starving to death, slow but sure,
With his lightning express nobly minded Jim Fisk
　　Flew to feed all the hungry and poor.

Now what do you think of this trial of Stokes,
　　Who murdered this friend of the poor?
If such men get free is anyone safe
　　To step outside their own door?

Is there one law for rich, is there one law for poor?
　　It seems so, at least so they say.
If they hang up the poor, why oughtn't the rich
　　To be hung up the very same way?

Now don't show no favour to friend or to foe,
    To prince or to beggar at your door,
But the millionaire you must hang up also;
    But never go back on the poor.

LAW AND LAWLESSNESS

The relationship between incidents of outlawry and the state of law and order is important in understanding why a very few outlaws became heroes and very many more did not. The debate among American historians and social scientists on the nature and extent of frontier violence has produced differing views of this relationship. It has been argued that the image of the west as a lawless, violent place of near anarchy is a product of western mythmaking, tall stories and the sensationalism of the popular press and other media. Eugene Hollon's *Frontier Violence—Another Look*, is a book that effectively puts forward a case for this point of view.[44] Others have argued as compellingly that there was an absence of law and order on the frontier that led to citizens frequently taking the law into their own hands, usually in the form of vigilantism. While both points of view have validity, it is not necessary to take up the cudgels for either position in considering the outlaw hero tradition.

As with all forms of folklore, we are dealing with belief, with perception, and with myth when considering the nature of the problem. It does not matter whether the frontier was lawless or not, simply that certain groups in certain circumstances *believed* that adequate law was absent or that what law did exist was being used against their interests by other groups. It is not necessary, or desirable, to take a moral position on these conflicting interests, merely to acknowledge their existence and to understand them in relation to a fundamental reality underlying the specific experience of outlawry and the more general question of social order. That reality, as pointed out elsewhere in this study, is that the 'folk imperative' residing in notions of common law, custom and tradition is commonly regarded as giving groups of people the right to sustain themselves and to protect themselves when and if the official apparatus is unable or unwilling to ensure the continuation of life and order. This imperative transcends the law, substituting various kinds of folk justice, including, in the context of the American west, the institution of vigilantism.

Vigilantism, of course, has its own set of rules that are agreed on by those who organise such activities in the absence or ineffectiveness of official law and order. The same observation applies to the tradition of the outlaw hero which, as we have seen, also has its own code or set of rules that provide well-delineated boundaries of acceptable behaviour. In both cases the law is perceived to be—and may actually, though not necessarily, be—failing, absent, slow, or otherwise unacceptable to a significant group within the community. In both cases, actions outside the law are executed with the approbation of those involved—excepting of course, the unfortunate victims of vigilantism. But then they have been categorised as villains, while the noble outlaw is categorised as a hero.[45]

THE LAST OUTLAWS?

The lives and legends of other badmen of the west could be examined much as those of James and Bonney have been here. Similar patterns can be discerned in the traditions surrounding the Youngers, Clay Allison and Butch Cassidy. There are also distinct traces in the stories surrounding some rural–urban outlaws of the 1930s, such as Bonny Parker and Clyde Barrow, better known as Bonny and Clyde. Perhaps the most notorious of these was a man named by the FBI as 'Public Enemy Number 1'—John Dillinger. Dillinger in particular attracted—and encouraged—outlaw hero celebrity. Said to have been the recipient of an unjustly harsh prison sentence in his youth, he repeatedly avoided the law, escaped from an 'escape-proof' Indiana gaol in 1934, and was noted as someone who only wanted to rob the banks, not the poor. He was widely compared—favourably—with Robin Hood, Dick Turpin and Jesse James as he successfully robbed bank after bank during the depression. After he was betrayed by a whorehouse madam and shot by FBI agents in Chicago in July 1934, thousands came to the death scene, soaking up his blood in their garments. Later, thousands viewed Dillinger's coffin, and outlaw hero legends began circulating. According to these legends, Dillinger's penis was unusually large; perhaps this was an allusion to his superhuman abilities? More closely aligned with the outlaw hero of tradition, there was a general refusal to believe that Dillinger was dead and, like other outlaw heroes, he was sighted by many people at many places in the years following his death.[46]

While these gangsters of the depression period attracted certain aspects of the outlaw hero tradition to their popular images, only one has any real claims to outlaw hero celebrity and those claims rest largely on the ballad written by an artist steeped in Anglophone folkways. Charles Arthur 'Pretty Boy' Floyd, born in 1901, was killed by FBI agents in October 1934, after a career of bank-robbery and violence that made him 'Public Enemy Number 1'. His status as a folk hero to the depression-hit working class of Oklahoma is well known, impelled by Woody Guthrie's ballad. Guthrie was himself an Oklahoman; he based his song on what he was told by sympathisers of Floyd, and was clearly well versed in the essentials of the outlaw hero tradition.[47] Like the bushranger Ned Kelly, Floyd is frequently said to have burned the mortgages he found in the safes of banks he robbed.[48] And, as with a number of other American outlaws and gangsters, it was said that Floyd was not the man killed by police. They made a mistake and tried to cover up their incompetence.[49]

Woody Guthrie's justly famous song about Floyd adroitly manipulates the essential elements of the outlaw hero tradition in its American permutation. Floyd's wife is abused by a representative of the forces of law and order. Floyd's defence of her honour results in his victory but also in his having to flee 'to the trees and timbers', where he is unjustly blamed for all manner of crimes. In true outlaw hero style, however, Floyd has friends and supporters among the poor whom he aids by leaving gifts of money and paying their mortgages. There is a distinct echo of the outlaw hero paying the mortgage only to rob it back from the landlord here. Floyd also helps those on relief:

> 'You say that I'm an outlaw.
>   You say that I'm a thief.
> Here's a Christmas dinner
>   For the families on relief.'

The song also points out that one is as likely to be robbed by a fountain-pen, that is, by a fast-talking professional or con artist, as by someone like himself carrying a gun. In the end, Floyd would never drive a family from their home as this is not the kind of behaviour expected of an outlaw. The theme of the family is here very strong, as is often the case in American and Australian outlaw traditions. The final lines of the song are:

> You won't never see an outlaw
> Drive a family from his home.[50]

116

With Floyd and his balladising, the American celebration of the outlaw hero reaches a natural conclusion as what was left of the frontier became absorbed by suburban sprawl, improved transport and communications. Certain criminals continue to be glorified and glamourised, but their motives are no longer those of Robin Hood. In an age that likes to think of itself as sophisticated, such crude depictions of social distress have long been passé, even for underprivileged groups well aware of their own oppression and poverty. Our sophistication is heavily loaded with a world-weary cynicism. The altruistic notion of someone robbing the rich to help the poor is greeted with sneering disbelief. We know, and have known for some time, that everyone is out for whatever they can wrest from the system. Those individuals who visibly succeed in this by criminal means may be accorded some degree of respect. Those who fail spectacularly and usually bloodily may attain brief media notoriety. But none of these are outlaw heroes—with the possible exception of certain 'virtual' outlaws who range the postmodern frontier of the Internet, as discussed in the final chapter.

CHAPTER FIVE

Australian Bushrangers

The initial settled European presence on Australian soil was a gaol. In 1788 the First Fleet arrived off the east coast near the present-day site of Sydney. From its eleven ships was disgorged a cargo of convicted British thieves, fences, swindlers, forgers and at least seventy-one highway robbers,[1] along with the military force that was to guard them all. Together, at the end of the world, the gaolers and the gaoled were to build and maintain a prison for holding the overflow of Britain's creaking judicial and penal system. Even without the isolation and incomprehensibility of the Australian environment, the experiences of the gaoled were clearly not to be happy ones. It was only a short time before the first convicts escaped into the bush in doomed hope of reaching China or some other impossible haven. These men (few women attempted such escapes) were generally referred to as 'bolters', though by the end of the 1790s it seems that the term 'bushranger' was being generally applied to such individuals. Most of the bushrangers perished in the harsh climate, disappeared or were recaptured; not infrequently, they gave themselves up, preferring the lash over starvation in the bush. Many bolters took to 'highway' robbery (though there were no such roads at that time, only tracks) and to raiding the stores of settlers and convict shepherds. A few became outlaw heroes.

The penal colonies of New South Wales and its offshoot, Van Diemen's Land, provided an often brutal cradle for the antipodean extension of the outlaw hero. A society stripped to its essentials of the powerful and the powerless—gaoler and gaoled—provided a fertile bed for a tradition that revolved around the righting of wrongs, the vicarious revenge of the weak against the strong, and the celebration of male prowess in

119

wilderness locations at the periphery of law and settlement. There were outlaw heroes in Van Diemen's Land as early as 1818, just two years after Captain Grant met his inevitable end in Ireland. The first of the bolters to attain lasting heroic status were Michael Howe, Martin Brady and Martin Cash, all of whom were considered by the authorities to be a serious threat to the fragile web of law and order that supposedly applied to the island gaol off the south-east tip of the Australian mainland. An early traveller, Richard Howitt, wrote in his *Impressions of Australia Felix &c* (1845) of the popularity of these bushrangers, describing them as:

> outlaws, run-away convicts. The more gentlemanly of them in Van Diemen's Land are there what Robin Hood and Rob Roy were in Britain. . . . Of these famous robbers, none are so much talked of for their generosity, their invariable respect and tenderness for women and children as Mike Howe, and more especially Brady . . .

A few years later, in 1856, an early historian of the Van Diemen's Land bushrangers wrote in flowery prose:

> the bushranger was, in general, looked upon as a sort of martyr to convictism. It was he who had experienced the shame, the lash, the brutal taunt, from which they had suffered. It was he who rose against the tyranny of their prison despot and the dread consequences of their criminal law. He was the bold Robin Hood of their morning songs, and he was now the unfortunate victim of legal oppression, the captured of the chase. Without denying the atrocities of his career, they would discover many extenuations for his crimes. His reckless daring would be the noblest chivalry; and the jovial freedom of his manners, the frankest generosity. His immoral jests would be cherished for posterity, and the *éclat* of his life and death would stimulate the worthy ambition of sympathising souls. The very gallows had a charm.[2]

Such accounts show how these men and their activities were celebrated and balladised by their numerous sympathisers and supporters within the convict community, with the obvious tensions and conflicts between the gaoled and their gaolers providing an ideal setting for the genesis of avenging outlaw heroes. In these extreme and basic circumstances, the relationship between the oppressed and the oppressors that is fundamental to the outlaw hero tradition was starkly present. That fundamental relationship, increasingly obscured by the developing social and economic diversity of south-east Australia, nevertheless continued to fuel bushranging outbreaks and the heroisation of selected[3] outlaw figures throughout most of the nineteenth century.

Despite the notoriety of the Van Diemen's Land bolters and the various attempts to romanticise them in terms of the English rhetoric of Robin Hood and highwaymen evident in the above quotation, the first bushranger hero of enduring folkloric fame was in New South Wales. His name was Jack Donohoe, and his Irish origins imparted what was to be a lasting element of political bitterness to the Australian extensions of the outlaw hero tradition.[4]

JACK DONOHOE

Jack Donohoe was transported to New South Wales for life in 1824– 25, found guilty of intent to commit an unspecified felony. Escaping in 1827, Donohoe was credited by the ballads and some witnesses with many of the attributes of the outlaw hero: he was courteous to women; he never robbed 'the poor', in this case the convict and ex-convict population; he was heroically daring; and he died game. He enjoyed the sympathy and the support of convict society, many of whose members provided Donohoe and his gang with information about trooper movements, food and shelter. This assistance kept Donohoe alive until 1830, when he was killed in a shoot-out with the troopers near Sydney.[5]

A number of ballads were composed about Donohoe, though the one that has survived is undoubtedly the best. This presents the bushranger in unabashed outlaw hero terms, drawing explicit comparisons with earlier outlaw heroes from Robin Hood, and the Irishmen Willie Brennan, Captain Freney and Jeremiah Grant. As well, the ballad introduces a strong note of anti-authoritarianism, expressed as antagonism towards the representatives of the English government and Crown. This element recurs often in subsequent Australian manifestations of the outlaw hero tradition, and it has also ensured the popularity of the ballad, in various versions, in Ireland.[6]

Other versions of this song tell essentially the same tale in the same sympathetic manner, and Donohoe is generally acknowledged as the likely progenitor for the later but much more widely distributed ballad 'The Wild Colonial Boy'—though the only evidence for this is a book published in 1847 that refers to a version of the Donohoe ballad that

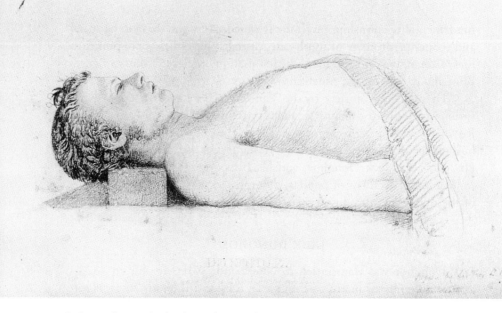

Jack Donohoe in death, drawn by Sir Thomas Mitchell, 1830. (Mitchell Library, State Library of NSW.)

may be related to 'The Wild Colonial Boy'.[7] The historical Jack Donohoe, like the mythical Wild Colonial Boy, was Irish, was transported, became a bushranger, and was gunned down in a battle with the trooper (effectively military) police. But so did any number of other unfortunates who were not celebrated in song, at least as far as we know. The rather different style and tone of the two songs also suggests that they are related only through genre.

BOLD JACK DONAHOE[8]

'Twas of a valiant highwayman and outlaw of disdain
Who'd scorn to live in slavery or wear a convict's chain;
His name it was Jack Donahoe of courage and renown—
He'd scorn to live in slavery or humble to the Crown.

This bold, undaunted highwayman, as you may understand,
Was banished for his natural life from Erin's happy land.
In Dublin city of renown, where his first breath he drew,
It's there they titled him the brave and bold Jack Donahoe.

He scarce had been a twelve-month on the Australian shore,
When he took to the highway, as oft he had before.
Brave MacNamara, Underwood, Webber and Walmsley too,
These were the four associates of bold Jack Donahoe.

As Jack and his companions roved out one afternoon,
Not thinking that the pains of death would overcome so soon,
To their surprise five horse police appeared all in their view,
And in quick time they did advance to take Jack Donahoe.

'Come, come, you cowardly rascals, oh, do not run away!
We'll fight them man to man, my boys, their number's only
   three;
For I'd rather range the bush around, like dingo or kangaroo,
Than work one hour for Government,' said bold Jack Donahoe.

'Oh, no,' said cowardly Walmsley, 'to that I won't agree;
I see they're still advancing us—their number's more than three.
And if we wait we'll be too late, the battle we will rue.'
'Then begone from me, you cowardly dog,' replied Jack Donahoe.

The Sergeant of the horse police discharged his car-a-bine,
And called aloud to Donahoe, 'Will you fight or resign?'
'Resign, no, no! I never will, until your cowardly crew,
For today I'll fight with all my might,' cried bold Jack Donahoe.

The Sergeant then, in a hurry his party to divide,
Placed one to fire in front of him, and another on each side;
The Sergeant and the Corporal, they both fired too,
Till the fatal ball had pierced the heart of bold Jack Donahoe.

Six rounds he fought those horse police before the fatal ball,
Which pierced his heart with cruel smart, caused Donahoe to
   fall;
And as he closed his mournful eyes he bade this world adieu,
Saying, 'Good people all, pray for the soul of poor Jack Donahoe.'

There were Freincy, Grant, bold Robin Hood, Brennan and
   O'Hare:
With Donahoe this highwayman none of them could compare.
But now he's gone to Heaven, I hope, with saints and angels too—
   May the Lord have mercy on the soul of Brave Jack Donahoe.

In Australia the outlaw hero code conditioned the attitudes and the actions of a variety of outlaw heroes and their supporters from the earliest penal days of settlement until 1880. The first bushrangers were escaped convicts. Most notable, from a folkloric point of view, was Donohoe, whose position in regard to the primarily military policing of the colony was easily transformed into that of defiant and rebellious robber of the rich and powerful (almost anyone other than a convict). In the aftermath of various colonial government efforts to 'unlock the lands' and disperse the rapidly growing and largely disappointed population after the eastern coast gold rushes of the 1850s and 60s, a large social group was created: landholders—mainly renters of Crown land—with small to medium-sized farms. These 'free selectors', as they may be generically termed here, were allowed to lease Crown lands in order to create a yeomanry of peasant landholders supporting themselves from the fruits of their labours. Unfortunately, a previously powerful group directly descended from the earliest settlers and including some ex-convicts controlled large tracts of the better land, either by grant or by lease from the Crown, often amassing even more through their prosperity. These 'squatters' saw their dominance and their security threatened by the selectors and went to great lengths, both legal and otherwise, to ensure that they held on to the best land near water and transportation. Consequently, the new selectors were usually left only the poorer and more remote tracts for their use. Tensions between squatters and selectors were generally intense: they proved a fertile bed for the genesis of a number of notable outlaw heroes during the 1860s and were especially important in the Kelly out-break of 1878–80. These pressures were exacerbated by the ongoing gold discoveries in eastern Australia during the 1850s and 1860s, events which encouraged the influx of large numbers of new settlers and some disruption of civic society occasioned by the temptation to get rich quickly and easily.

Of the bushrangers that arose during the 1860s, a handful was selected by the processes of the outlaw hero tradition for celebration and commemoration. There were hundreds, perhaps thousands, of other highway robbers who have left little trace at all outside court records. Why Hall, Gardiner, Morgan, Thunderbolt and a very few others were thought worthy representatives of the outlaw hero was directly related to the social and economic circumstances of their time. In a period of serious economic and social tension and dislocation, such figures were rapidly appropriated as worthy symbols of revenge and justice by those who felt themselves dispossessed or discriminated against. The ballads and traditions surrounding these men show the persistence of the outlaw hero and his fundamental connection with certain types of recurring social and economic turmoil.

Related to such turmoil was the manner in which expressions and actions of protest and disaffection were dealt with by the duly constituted authorities. The history of bushranging legislation amply demonstrates the inability of government to deal with movements of popular protest and resistance within the usual framework of English law. From the early convict bolters like Jack Donahue to the wild colonial boys of the 1860s, those in power frequently found it necessary to suspend the normal rights and guarantees provided by law, and to impose restrictions similar to those of a police state.[9] By 1830 bushrangers, particularly Donohoe, had become so troublesome in New South Wales that the Legislative Council introduced what came to be unpopularly known as the Bushranging Act. The official title of this legislation was *An Act to Suppress Robbery and Housebreaking and the Harbouring of Robbers and Housebreakers*.[10] It proclaimed that anyone having reasonable suspicion that a person was carrying firearms to be used for robbery could apprehend that person, without a warrant, and take him before a Justice of the Peace where the person apprehended then had to prove his innocence. If unable to satisfy the Justice of either his identity or innocence, or both, the suspect could be taken to Sydney for closer examination.

Useful though such legislation was in apprehending escaped convicts, many innocent people, both native-born and newly arrived immigrants, most of whom had no formal identification, were continually apprehended without warrants, often dragged to Sydney and held in gaol for long periods without trial until they or someone else could establish their innocence and identity. Not surprisingly, this Act was widely resented and its legality was strongly questioned by both Governor Bourke and Mr Justice Burton.[11] The governor thought the act 'contrary to the spirit of English law' and Burton stated that it was 'repugnant to the laws of England' in almost all of its provisions. Despite these misgivings, the legislation was re-enacted in various forms almost continuously up to 1853.

Those charged with carrying out the responsibilities of this legislation were even more unpopular than the law itself. The New South Wales Police Force originated as a predominantly military organisation. In 1824–5 a mounted police was formed to patrol the outer areas of settlement. The members of this force were military personnel serving under army officers, wearing military uniforms, and subject to military rather than civil authority. Despite attempts to render this force liable to civil authority, the trooper police remained a firmly military organisation until the Police Act reforms of 1862 which introduced less militaristic uniforms and equipment. The culture of the police, though, could not be so easily reformed and in any case the generally antagonistic attitudes of many colonists towards the trooper police, conditioned by the penal years, were ineradicably established.

Where the law did impinge on the lives of many colonists, it appeared as a coercive and oppressive force. The militaristic policing of the Bushranging Acts contributed to a strong current of resentment against the state and its protectors that is still evident in Australian society today. It was not simply that the police and many civil authorities, such as magistrates, were inefficient and corrupt—that was expected and could even be useful. Rather it was that for the first seventy years of Australia's European history the police were seen to be given the powers, and assumed the character, of something akin to an army of occupation. With a significant section of the convict and ex-convict population antagonistic towards the police and the law in general, deep resentment could rapidly become passive, and active, resistance by the primarily rural working-class populations who supported certain bushranger heroes.[12]

Among these groups, attitudes towards private property diverged considerably from those of the law. From the 1820s the rapid spread of settlement in New South Wales rapidly outpaced administrative and judicial control. Squatting was the norm; fencing was non-existent, with boundaries being recognised by prominent natural features and oral testimony.[13] Unless squatters brought stock with them, or could afford to purchase it at market prices, they were likely to purchase it illegally at around half the legitimate market price.[14] Sheep and cattle could be obtained even more cheaply 'on the cross'. There were many methods of stock-stealing or 'duffing' (also referred to as 'gully-raking' and 'poddy-dodging') throughout the developing grazing districts.[15] Judge Therry pointed out in his reminiscences that, during the 1830s, 1840s and 1850s, 'This species of crime formed the staple business of our criminal sessions and was reduced to a sort of science by the criminal class in the colony'.[16] These activities and the attitudes that underlay them provided a fertile ground for the genesis of bushrangers, much as the poaching trade intersected with the development of the English highwayman.

The population and economic expansion generated by the gold rushes of the 1850s and 1860s led to a new group of bushrangers. Following in the tradition established by Donohoe and the Van Diemen's Land bolters, Frank Gardiner, Ben Hall, Mad Dog Morgan and Thunderbolt, were among those who became celebrated as folk heroes.

FRANCIS CHRISTIE (FRANK GARDINER)

Also going by the surname of Clarke and the nickname Darkie, Frank Gardiner is the name by which this unusual bushranger is known to folklore and history. Gardiner was born near Goulburn, New South Wales, in 1830, his father was a Scots migrant and his mother an Irish-Aboriginal named Clarke. Imprisoned for three years' hard labour for cattle-duffing in 1850, Gardiner escaped. He probably conducted a butchery business on the Bendigo, Victoria, goldfields, thus continuing the long and strong connection between stock-stealing of one form or another, butchering and highway robbery that can be traced back to at least the highwaymen of the eighteenth century. By 1852 Gardiner had returned to New South Wales and to duffing, being arrested again in February 1854. He received fourteen years' hard labour, but was released on a ticket-of-leave to the Carcoar district in December 1854. He absconded in 1860, hiding around Kiandra in the Snowy Mountains, but had returned to the Abercrombie region to resume duffing and butchering by early 1861. In April he was arrested for these activities but absconded from bail and rode off into bushranging legend.

Gardiner then masterminded the century's most spectacular robbery at Eugowra Rocks in 1862. With eleven others (one of whom was probably Ben Hall), Gardiner robbed the Forbes gold escort of 4000 pounds in cash, over 200 ounces of gold and the Royal Mail. Most of the loot was recovered fairly soon after the robbery. In 1864 Gardiner was captured in Queensland, where he was living under an assumed identity with Ben Hall's sister-in-law, Kitty Brown. Gardiner was spared the gallows because he had not (as far as could be proven) killed anyone, and was instead sentenced to thirty-two years' hard labour. After ten years of constant lobbying by his family, Gardiner was released and exiled (a most unusual and intriguing occurrence). Eventually he went to America, where he is said to have opened a saloon on the San Francisco waterfront and to have been killed there in a gun-fight during the 1890s.

Despite these notably unheroic events, Gardiner has survived in Australian folklore as yet another example of the outlaw hero. This is largely due to his association with the much more folklorically famous Ben Hall and the interconnected group of bushrangers of the Forbes district of New South Wales, who enjoyed extensive support and sympathy from the local population during the 1860s. Hall and his accomplices, who at different times included John Gilbert, John Vane, John O'Meally, John Burke and others, were definitely treated by the ex-convicts, small settlers and itinerant workers of their region as latter-day Robin Hoods. The more intelligent of the bushrangers, notably Hall and Gardiner, went to some trouble to foster this image, Gardiner even writing to a local newspaper to defend himself against a rumour of ungallant behaviour during one of his lesser highway robberies. He signed the letter 'Prince of Tobymen, Francis Gardner [sic], the Highwayman'.[17]

Other incidents of Gardiner's bushranging career also show him adhering to the moral code of the outlaw hero, at pains to demonstrate chivalry, courtesy and general bonhomie. Gardiner was reported to be in the habit of returning money to some of his victims for their expenses along the road, an old outlaw hero tradition. He was also reported shouting drinks for all present and even sharing out confectionery stolen from one of a group of men.[18] These incidents, along with Gardiner's naming of at least one of his numerous horses Black Bess, after Dick Turpin's legendary steed, soon earned him an appropriate oulaw hero reputation. As the editor of the colony's main newspaper, the *Sydney Morning Herald*, wrote in 1863, some people saw Gardiner and his accomplices as ' . . . avengers of the poor and only the robbers of the rich'.[19] As well, Gardiner's courtesy to women was renowned, a fact commented on by Chief Justice Stephens in his otherwise comprehensive execration of Gardiner at the bushranger's final trial in July 1864.[20]

The reflected glory of all this activity and Gardiner's illustrious associates is evident in his ballad, one version of which refers to the bushranger as 'the poor man's friend'. As well, Gardiner is usually said to have been betrayed by a woman and mention is usually made of the last stand of Johnny Gilbert,[21] which is retold in terms reminiscent of the last fight of Jack Donohoe and the Wild Colonial Boy. Although it is not mentioned in this ballad, Gardiner, like most outlaw heroes, was noted for his escapes from custody—a feat he even managed after his final sentence, though it took a decade and was legal.

FRANK GARDINER[22]

Frank Gardiner he is caught at last and now in Sydney gaol,
For wounding Sergeant Middleton and robbing the Mudgee
    Mail;
For plundering of the gold escort, the Cargo [i.e. Carcoar] Mail
    also;
It was for gold he made so bold, and not so long ago.

His daring deeds surprised them all throughout the Sydney land,
He gave a call onto his friends and quickly raised a band,
Fortune always favoured him until the time of late,
There were Bourke, the brave O'Meally too, met with a dreadful
    fate.

Young Vane he surrendered, Ben Hall got some wounds,
As for Johnny Gilbert, at Binalong was found;
Alone he was, he lost his horse, three troopers hove in sight,
He fought the three most manfully, got slaughtered in the fight.

When lives you take, a warning, boys, a woman never trust;
She will turn round, I will be bound, Queen's evidence the first.
Two and thirty years he's doomed to slave all for the Crown,
And well may he say he cursed the day he met Old Mother
    Brown.

Day after day they remanded him, escorted to the bar;
Fresh charges brought against him from neighbours near and far.
But now it is all over, his sentence is brought down,
He's doing two and thirty years, he's doomed to serve the
    Crown.

Farewell, adieu to outlawed Frank, he was the poor man's friend;
The government has secured him, the laws he did offend.
He boldly stood his trial and answered in a breath:
'Do what you will, you can but kill, I have no fear of death.'

Gardiner's initial success as a bushranger, capitalised on by the
Lachlan bushrangers who succeeded him—John Gilbert, John Dunn,
John O'Meally and Ben Hall—was dependent on the efficiency of his
'bush telegraph' system. Sometimes called the 'mulga telegraph', this was
the colloquial term for the network of relatives, friends and sympathisers

Frank Gardiner (left) and, possibly, John Gilbert. (Mitchell Library, State Library of NSW.)

who provided bushrangers with information, supplies and shelter, as well as often misleading the police by providing false details of the bushrangers' movements. In Gardiner's case, the nucleus of the bush telegraph was the Walsh family of Wheogo. Patriarch of the Walsh clan was an Irish Catholic ex-convict, John Walsh. His daughter Bridget married Ben Hall. Another daughter, Helen, married John McGuire and a third daughter, Catherine, eventually became Frank Gardiner's mistress, the Kitty Brown (her married name) who, in folklore, betrayed Frank to the New South Wales Police. The Walshes were aided by the O'Meally family and many other local farmers, graziers, stockmen, and publicans. As a correspondent to the *Yass Courier* put it:

> Of all the numerous settlers on the Fish River, Abercrombie
> ranges, or the Levels (Bland Plains), scarcely half are true subjects;
> only five settlers on the Levels are considered by the police to be
> free from taint of harbouring and, directly or indirectly,
> encouraging bushranging.[23]

When the remains of Hall, Burke, O'Meally and other bushrangers were returned to their communities for burial, they were invariably honoured as martyred heroes.[24]

Accusations of disloyalty, sedition and treason were frequently levelled against bushrangers and their supporters by the press, the public, the police, the government and the judiciary. In August 1864 the *Sydney Morning Herald* complained of a 'robber union [that] embraces a very large proportion of the inhabitants of a certain condition and occupation in life. Many are connected by family relations. They have hereditary traditions of violence and outrage. Their moral sense, if it ever existed, is imbrued and destroyed.'[25] The ruling classes of the colony were deeply concerned that what they were looking at from the top down was, like the London mob, a potentially lethal force that might sweep them all to perdition if it were not put down with the utmost ferocity. Where the British rulers of the eighteenth century had the theatrical terror of Tyburn at their disposal for social control of the mob, in the new society of New South Wales the only means available were the essentially military police, and perversion of British law. The police were given the power to burn properties and arrest those suspected of harbouring bushrangers and, through the Felons Apprehension Act, the old medieval form of outlawry was applied in the antipodes so that an outlawed bushranger could be legally shot on sight by any citizen. Much of this repression came into effect only after Frank Gardiner, accused by his judge as 'being the head, the front, the parent of all this',[26] had been safely locked away. But the spirit, if not the provisions, of the Felons Apprehension Act was put into enthusiastic effect by the police pursuing Gardiner's most notable successor, Ben Hall.

BENJAMIN HALL

Known generally as Ben Hall, this man is the protagonist of a series of powerful ballads and related traditions that portray him as a friend of the poor, driven to bushranging through official persecution. Hall was born at Breeza, New South Wales, in 1837; his parents had both been transported. They moved with Ben to the Forbes area in 1847, settling in an area noted for the prevalence of 'gully-raking' and the lack of moral stigma attached to such activities by those who perpetrated them.[27] As we have seen, he married Bridget Walsh in 1856. Hall's co-lease with his brother-in-law John McGuire of Sandy Creek Station was a success and Hall was well on the way to a modest but respectable future as a local grazier.

But Hall was arrested in 1862 on suspicion of having participated in a minor highway robbery led by Frank Gardiner. After spending a month in gaol, Hall was acquitted and returned home, only to find that his wife had deserted him, taking their baby son with her. The story goes that Hall then fell in with the Gardiner gang. He was arrested after the Eugowra Rocks gold escort robbery, gaoled for two months and finally released for lack of evidence. On again returning to his property, Hall found that the police had burned his house and left his cattle to die, penned in the mustering yard.[28] From this time Hall seems to have turned to bushranging, joining the large numbers of active outlaws operating in this part of the colony. His activities were varied, including highway robbery, raids on wealthy properties, arson, attempted abduction, and raids on towns, including the regional centre of Bathurst.

In February 1865, Hall in company with John Dunn and John Gilbert attempted to kidnap the four sons of wealthy squatter W. Faithfull. Unexpectedly, the bushrangers were resisted effectively by the gunfire of the two older boys. The battle became a life-or-death struggle in which the boys managed to escape, the only casualty being Gilbert's horse, which he accidentally shot himself. However, three armed bushrangers attacking what they assumed were easy prey was hardly the stuff of the outlaw hero tradition. No matter what the intentions of Hall and his companions, this was by any measure an act of criminal cowardice. Tellingly, the Ben Hall ballads are all silent on this incident. By this time, though, Hall's outlaw hero image was well enough established for this awkward escapade to be ignored, especially as he was shot to death in his sleep by police only three months later.

However, it was probably the celebrity accorded Hall by his most daring act that assured his folkloric image. On 3 October 1863, Hall's gang raided Bathurst, the major town of the district. Financially the raid was a failure, but the fact that these outlaws could attack a major town with impunity panicked the population and also the government of the colony. Unrealistic fears were raised about a raid on Sydney, expressed humorously but uneasily in another ballad of the time:

> And next to Sydney city we mean to pay a call
> For we're going to take the country, says Dunn, Gilbert and Ben Hall.

The *Sydney Morning Herald* called for strong and extraordinary remedies to suppress bushranging and the threat it posed to the lawful

Ben Hall. (Reproduced with kind permission of the Justice and Police Museum, NSW.)

stability of New South Wales. If these remedies required the suspension of the customary framework of British law and justice, that was unfortunate but necessary. Free selection was blamed for creating a class of criminals scourging the community, even though few if any of the Forbes district bushrangers were free selectors, most having been farming long before the Free Selection Acts of the 1860s.[29] Bushrangers and those who sympathised with them were spoken of in the press, through both articles and letters, as disloyal, disaffected and dangerous, while those who opposed them were loyal subjects and patriots.[30] Methods of control suggested ranged from those used in the disturbed areas of Ireland to lynch law, the lash, and the formation of a civilian militia.[31]

By the end of 1864, the failure of the New South Wales police to capture bushrangers protected by strong local support and sympathy, as were Ben Hall, John Gilbert and John Dunn, resulted in public pressure from the respectable classes for 'extreme measures'. On 18 January 1865, the *Sydney Morning Herald* published Chief Justice Stephens' considered suggestions for effective bushranging legislation. This lengthy piece of legalese basically advocated the outlawry of selected bushrangers, rendering them liable to be shot on sight by police or civilians. Sympathisers were to be apprehended only on the accusation of a policeman or citizen.

On 8 April 1865, as we have seen, these suggestions were given official sanction under the title of the Felons Apprehension Act and became effective from 10 May. Gilbert and Dunn were liable to be shot by anyone. Persons suspected of harbouring could be arrested and presumed guilty on the most flimsy evidence, and liable to forfeit all their goods and land as well as serving up to fifteen years in gaol with hard labour. A Justice of the Peace or police officer could enter, without a warrant, any dwelling suspected of harbouring bushrangers. Finally the police, if they were pursuing bushrangers, were empowered to commandeer horses, equipment or supplies. As a *Sydney Morning Herald* editorial put it: 'The Felons Apprehension Act ... has shown that the general public is resolved to re-establish order and security, even at the risk of temporarily impairing the liberty of the subject.'[32]

Hall had been killed two days before this proclamation of outlawry, while his surviving companions Gilbert and Dunn were liable to be shot on sight by any person.[33] This suspension of the fundamental guarantees of British law was entirely consistent with the previous history of bushranging legislation in New South Wales and, indeed, of the history of the legal concept of outlawry. The Felons Apprehension Act reflected the fragile nature of colonial society, together with the extent to which fear of subversion had permeated the 'respectable classes' of both town and country. The ballads made and passed on by those who sympathised with and harboured the bushrangers tell a different tale.

In 'My Name is Ben Hall', Hall is the victim of injustice on the part of 'the Crown'; he is courteous to women, even-handed and kind. He robs a squatter, a wealthy landowner, but in proper outlaw hero style returns him five pounds to see him to the end of his journey. Unusually for outlaw heroes, Hall resolves to 'preserve the last shot for myself', either a brave or a cowardly action, depending upon your point of view. In another version of this ballad, there is a suggestion that the bushranger is betrayed by his 'false wife' and also shares the results of his robberies in Robin Hood style— 'With my friends in the bush I'll distribute this wealth.'[34] This ballad appears to date from the period before Hall's death in 1865.

MY NAME IS BEN HALL[35]

My name is Ben Hall from Urunga I came,
The cause of my turn out you all know the same;
I was sent to the gaol my cattle turned to the Crown,
I was forced to the bush my sorrow to drown.

I was always well-mounted with a gun in my hand,
And I always spoke kindly when I bid them to stand;
I always acted fair to the female kind,
When I thought of the dear girl I left behind.

One day I met a squatter, I thought he had cash,
For the evening before he'd been cutting a dash;
With a hundred and fifty in notes and in gold,
And I thought he had more by what I'd been told.

With a pistol well loaded and a gun in my hand,
I boldly rode up and I bid him to stand,
He passed out his money without ever a word
And I gave him five pounds for his help on the road.

Here's a health to Frank Gardiner who's closely confined
Also young Jack Vane who is free from his time,
And I'll go to the bush and fare on this wealth,
And then I'll preserve my last shot for myself.

Like most of the Hall ballads, 'The Death of Ben Hall' deals with the circumstances of Hall's life through the focus of his death. It provides more detail than most of the other Hall songs, but again represents the bushranger as belonging firmly within the tradition of the outlaw hero. Hall is heroic, daring and manly; he is forced into bushranging, and scorns to offer unjustified violence, even preventing such actions by those associated with him. He robs the rich 'and scorned to rob the poor', and he is betrayed and murdered in a cowardly way by the police. In the last verse Hall's heroism is commended to future generations of Australians, linking with the initial verse and its unusual articulation of nationalist sentiment.

THE DEATH OF BEN HALL[36]

Come all young Australians, and every one besides,
I'll sing to you a ditty that will fill you with surprise,
Concerning of a 'ranger bold, whose name it was Ben Hall,
But cruelly murdered was this day, which proved his downfall.

An outcast from society, he was forced to take the road,
All through his false and treacherous wife, who sold off his abode,
He was hunted like a native dog from bush to hill and dale,
Till he turned upon his enemies and they could not find his
    trail.

All out with his companions, men's blood he scorned to shed,
He oft-times stayed their lifted hands, with vengeance on their
    heads,
No petty, mean or pilfering act he ever stooped to do,
But robbed the rich and hearty man, and scorned to rob the
    poor.

One night as he in ambush lay all on the Lachlan Plain,
When, thinking everything secure, to ease himself had lain,
When to his consternation and to his great surprise,
And without one moment's warning, a bullet past him flies.

And it was soon succeeded by a volley sharp and loud,
With twelve revolving rifles all pointed at his head.
'Where are you, Gilbert? Where is Dunn?' he loudly did call.
It was all in vain, they were not there to witness his downfall.

They riddled all his body as if they were afraid,
But in his dying moment he breathed curses on their heads.
That cowardly-hearted Condell, the sergeant of the police,
He crept and fired with fiendish glee till death did him release.

Although he had a lion's heart, more braver than the brave,
Those cowards shot him like a dog—no word of challenge gave.
Though many friends had poor Ben Hall, his enemies were few,
Like the emblems of his native land, his days were numbered
    too.

It's through Australia's sunny clime Ben Hall will roam no more.
His name is spread both near and far to every distant shore.
For generations after this parents will to their children call,
And rehearse to them the daring deeds committed by Ben Hall.

Apparently collected from oral tradition only once, the unusual
ballad known as 'The Streets of Forbes' (with an equally unusual modal
melody) is essentially a reworking of a poem (also reproduced below)
written by Ben Hall's brother-in-law, John McGuire, that was circulated
quite widely in New South Wales, it seems. Not surprisingly, given their
source, the poem and the song are partisan accounts of Hall's career and
death. Again, the heroic Hall is oppressed and 'hunted from his station',
or farm; he defies and outwits the 'traps', or mounted police; and he is
murdered in a reprehensible way by the police, his body thrown across
a horse and exhibited through the streets of the major local town.

THE STREETS OF FORBES[37]

Come all you Lachlan men and a sorrowful tale I'll tell,
Concerning of a hero bold who through misfortune fell;
His name it was Ben Hall, a man of good renown
Who was hunted from his station and like a dog shot down.

Three years he roamed the roads, and he showed the traps some
    fun,
A thousand pounds was on his head, with Gilbert and John
    Dunn.
Ben parted from his comrades, the outlaws did agree
To give away bushranging and to cross the briny sea.

137

Ben went to Goobang Creek and that was his downfall;
For riddled like a sieve was valiant Ben Hall.
'Twas early in the morning upon the fifth of May
When seven police surrounded him as fast asleep he lay.

Bill Dargin he was chosen to shoot the outlaw dead;
The troopers then fired madly, and filled him full of lead.
They rolled him in a blanket, and strapped him to his prad [i.e.
     horse]
And led him through the streets of Forbes to show the prize they
     had.

HOW HE DIED (McGuire's poem)[38]

Come all you highwaymen, a sorrowful tale I'll tell,
Concerning of a hero, who through misfortune fell;
His name it was Ben Hall, a chap of great renown,
He was hunted from his station, like a native dog shot down.

On the fifth of May, when parting from
His comrades all along the highway,
It was at the Wedding [sic] Mountains those three outlaws did
     agree
To give up bushranging, and cross the briny sea.

Then going to the billabong, which was his cruel downfall,
And riddled like a sieve was that hero, Ben Hall;
It was early in the morning, before the break of day,
The police they surrounded him as fast asleep he lay.

The tracker, he was chosen to fire the fatal shot,
The rest then they rounded him to secure the prize they got;
They threw him on his horse, and strapped him like a swag,
And led him through the streets of Forbes to show the prize they
     had.

The late Mrs Sally Sloane, a folksinger and musician of Irish ances-
try, was the bearer of a number of traditions concerning Ben Hall. She
sang 'The Death of Ben Hall' for John Meredith in the 1950s, and also
recounted to him local traditions about the bushranger. They contain

classic outlaw hero statements and also illustrate the persistence of the term and concept of the 'highwayman':

> Poor Ben Hall, he had a property of his own near Forbes, and all the bad deeds that used to be done were pinned onto poor Ben Hall. And he was yarding his cattle this day and they come onto him and took him into Forbes for trial for something that he didn't do, and all his cattle were left in the yard. Instead of the police pulling the sliprails down and letting them out, they was all left to perish.
>
> And when he come out after doing a month in jail they were just carcasses in the yard. They burned his place down. His wife had betrayed him and went off with another man . . . Ben took to the bush then, and turned out to be a highwayman. When he found out what had happened, his wife had gone, and his stock and everything destroyed and he became a bushranger.[39]

OTHER BUSHRANGER HEROES

Daniel 'Mad Dog' Morgan

Daniel Morgan operated in the Riverina area along the Victoria and New South Wales border between 1863 and 1865. Morgan carried out the usual bushranger's activities of horse and stock-stealing, highway robbery, raiding and occasionally occupying farms and stations. Evidence suggests that he may have been emotionally unbalanced, but he was not the pathological killer painted by the police and the press. In fact, Morgan had considerable support and sympathy, particularly in Victoria, where he was known as 'the traveller's friend'. The circumstances of Morgan's bushranging were brutal and tragic, ending in his death and disfigurement by police at Peechelba station, near Wangaratta, Victoria, in April 1865, as commemorated in 'The Death of Morgan'. This fiery ballad of outrage at the manner of Morgan's death is in stark contrast to the image of the bushranger projected in the media of the time, and in literary sources as well. Instead of being the heartless killer, almost an antipodean Frankenstein, Morgan is here represented in full outlaw hero appearance. His death and its grisly aftermath are claimed to be the result of treachery, and the blame is squarely laid with the authorities. The second-last verse describes Morgan as 'the traveller's friend' and the enemy of the squatters, as a 'highwayman' who was able to 'do the poor some good'. In the final verse Morgan is placed within the pantheon of the notorious New South Wales bushrangers, such as Gilbert, Hall, John Burke and

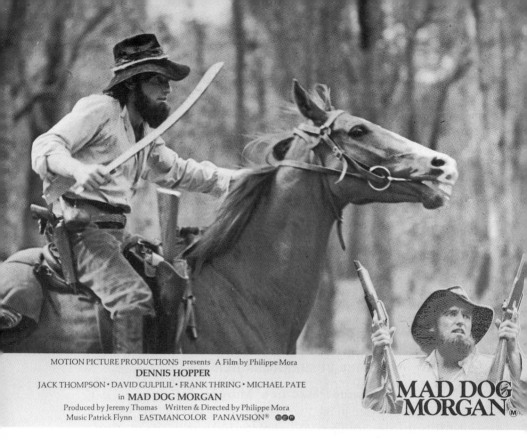

MOTION PICTURE PRODUCTIONS presents A Film by Philippe Mora
DENNIS HOPPER
JACK THOMPSON · DAVID GULPILIL · FRANK THRING · MICHAEL PATE
in **MAD DOG MORGAN**
Produced by Jeremy Thomas   Written & Directed by Philippe Mora
Music Patrick Flynn   EASTMANCOLOR PANAVISION® ⊕⊕⊕

MAD DOG MORGAN ⓜ

Mad Dog Morgan. *(Courtesy Philippe Mora.)*

John O'Meally. After such heroisation, the moralising end of the ballad comes as something of a surprise, probably indicating the journalistic origins of the text, as do a number of other stylistic elements, including vocabulary and syntax. Alternatively, it is possible that the song is a tidied-up version based on an earlier oral version.

The historian of Morgan, Margaret Carnegie, writes that flowers were placed on Morgan's grave on the day of his death each year until at least the mid-1970s.[40]

THE DEATH OF MORGAN[41]

Throughout Australian history no tongue or pen can tell
Of such preconcerted treachery—there is no parallel—
As the tragic deed of Morgan's death; without warning he was
    shot
On Peechelba station, it will never be forgot.

140

Daniel 'Mad Dog' Morgan in death, photography by Henry Pohl. (La Trobe Collection, State Library of Victoria.)

I have oft-time heard of murders in Australia's golden land,
But such an open daylight scene of thirty in a band,
Assembled at the dawn of day, and then to separate,
Behind the trees, some on their knees, awaiting Morgan's fate.

Too busy was the servant-maid; she trotted half the night
From MacPherson's down to Rutherford's tidings to recite
A messenger was sent away who for his neck had no regard,
He returned with a troop of traps in hopes of their reward.

But they were all disappointed; McQuinlan was the man
Who fired from his rifle and shot rebellious Dan
Concealed he stood behind a tree till his victim came in view,
And as Morgan passed his doom was cast—the unhappy man he
    slew.

There was a rush for trophies, soon as the man was dead;
They cut off his beard, his ears, and the hair from off his head.
In truth it was a hideous sight as he struggled on the ground,
They tore the clothes from off his back and exposed the fatal
    wound.

Oh, Morgan was the traveller's friend; the squatters all rejoice
That the outlaw's life is at an end, no more they'll hear his voice.
Success attend all highwaymen who do the poor some good;
But my curse attend a treacherous man who'd shed another's
    blood.

Farewell to Burke, O'Meally, young Gilbert and Ben Hall,
Likewise to Daniel Morgan, who fell by rifle-ball;
So all young men be warned and never take up arms,
Remember this, how true it is, bushranging hath no charms.

Captain Frederick 'Thunderbolt' Ward

Frederick Wordsworth Ward was born in Windsor, New South Wales,
around 1836. A bushman and stockman of high calibre, Ward was
imprisoned for horse-stealing in 1856 and sentenced to prison on Cockatoo Island. In July 1860, he was released on ticket-of-leave but was
arrested in September for failing to attend a 'muster' (the required condition of a ticket-of-leave) and for allegedly stealing a horse. Ward was
sent back to Cockatoo Island, the gaol from which no-one was able to

escape. In company with another inmate, highway robber Fred Britten (with whom Thunderbolt is often confused in folklore), Ward escaped from the island in September. The escapees stole clothing and headed north towards the New England area that Ward knew very well. They obtained horses, robbed a hut and eventually ran into a police party at Big Rock (since then known as Thunderbolt's Rock). In the ensuing exchange of shots, Ward was wounded in the leg, but the two men managed to escape, splitting up soon after. In December, Ward robbed a house at gunpoint in the Hunter Valley and officially began his career as a bushranger.

Between then and his eventual shooting down by a trooper Walker in May 1870, Thunderbolt, Captain Thunderbolt and Captain Ward as he was variously known, managed to pursue a career of intermittent robbery with a minimum of violence and no known murders. This, together with statements often made to victims and witnesses to the effect that he was driven to outlawry and that he would not prey on women, aided his celebration as an outlaw hero. He was said to have handed money back to those who needed it more than he did and, as his ballads indicate, was perceived by many to operate in a style and manner befitting the bushranging and highwaymen heroes of the past. One version of a toast or poetic introduction said to have been composed and used by Ward himself goes:

> My name is Frederick Ward, I am a native of this isle;
> I rob the rich to feed the poor and make the children smile.

Oral traditions regarding Thunderbolt are well in keeping with the general run of those attached to outlaw heroes. They include his alleged return of gold to a number of children at Moonbi, his hidden treasure and, most importantly, the belief that he was not really killed in 1870 (it was Fred Britten, his old mate) and that he lived on, either in Australia, New Zealand, America or Canada.[42]

'The Wild Colonial Boy'

Probably originating in the 1860s, this well-known song, quoted in Chapter 2, contains the essential elements of the Australian manifestations of the outlaw hero. The Wild Colonial Boy is, usually, transported from Ireland, is defiant, scornful of the Crown, robs only 'the rich' or at least the representative of that group, Judge MacEvoy, and finally dies game in a last defiant stand against the trooper police who outnumber him three to one. It is presumably these attributes that have ensured the song's continuing popularity in performance and in parody, not only in Australia, but throughout most of the English-speaking world.[43]

Joseph 'Moondyne Joe' Johns

Transported in 1853, Johns absconded, was captured and escaped repeatedly throughout the late 1880s, becoming a celebrated identity in the Swan River colony, later Western Australia. The problems of authority and control of land, resources and power that troubled New South Wales and Victoria were not so evident in the western third of the continent, or took different forms. Nevertheless, Johns' ability to escape was so marked that his figure has taken on the beginnings of an outlaw hero aura. While the only song text extant about Joe is a parody of the nursery rhyme 'Pop Goes the Weasel', in its brevity can be detected that set of tensions and conflicts between unpopular authority and those suffering beneath it that typically underlie outbreaks of social banditry and create outlaw heroes. Joe was able to survive well in the bush due to a network of sympathisers,[44] always a prerequisite for outlaw heroisation.

There are still stories about Moondyne Joe told in Western Australia—about his escapes, his cleverness, and his gold.[45] He fits the mould of the outlaw hero through his trickster characteristics, the fact that he did not murder anyone during his periods of depredation, and the fact that his irritating of the extremely unpopular governor of the colony was greeted with apparent joy by almost all its inhabitants.

MOONDYNE JOE[46]

The Governor's son has got the pip,
   The Governor's got the measles.
But Moondyne Joe has give 'em the slip
   Pop goes the weasel!

Australian tradition supports a considerable body of lore concerning bushrangers, real and fictional, other than those treated above. Songs about the exploits of 'Fred Lowry', Jack Lefroy and Jack Power have been collected and published, as has a song titled 'Taking His Chance' (derived from a Henry Lawson poem) which also deals with the romantic aspects of a mythical bushranger's life. There are a good number of Kelly ballads additional to those presented in the following chapter. As well, at least two versions of the British ballad concerning Dick Turpin and the lawyer have been collected (Chapter 3).[47] Examination of the lyrics of bushranger ballads indicates that their makers and singers were familiar with the legends of Robin Hood, Turpin, Duval, Brennan, and even relatively obscure figures, such as Freney, and that they saw these figures as representations of the ancient notion of the noble robber who robs the rich to benefit the poor. While space does not allow reproduction of the relevant texts here, they all treat their protagonists, to a greater or lesser degree, in terms of the outlaw hero tradition. Sometimes this treatment is sentimental, romantic, even moralistic, but essentially the outlaw is represented with sympathy and respect, with an implicit or explicit recognition of the duality of his position.

As well, there are strong local and occasionally national bushranging traditions expressed in narrative and belief, including elements of the outlaw hero tradition that have, over time, become attached to such leaders of Aboriginal resistance as Yagan, Pigeon and Pemulway. In the areas where historical bushrangers operated, their stories are still told, either by local inhabitants or, increasingly frequently, in the broader discourses of tourism and cultural heritage. The actions, real and imagined, of bushrangers, their supporters and their pursuers, can still spark stimulating exchanges of opinion in many parts of the country, particularly with regard to Ned Kelly. The most consistent feature of such exchanges is the absence of historical fact—they are based on what the participants 'know' or believe about their subjects of argument, whether positive or negative. In Australia this tradition reached its peak in the life and legend of Edward Kelly.

Pressures and tensions similar to those that generated the New South Wales bushrangers of the 1860s contributed a few years later to the Kelly outbreak in north-east Victoria. The history and subsequent legend of Edward 'Ned' Kelly is of particular interest. Not only is Ned Kelly's mythology a compelling example of the potency of the outlaw hero tradition, but the image of Kelly has transcended the folkloric and the popular. 'St Ned', as one writer has dubbed him,[48] is now the closest thing Australia has to a national hero. The processes through which this remarkable transformation have come about are directly relevant to the aims of this work. Ned Kelly's legend, in its historical manifestations, in its folklore and in its continuing appeal, is arguably the pinnacle of the

Anglophone outlaw hero tradition, in Australia and elsewhere. Other bushranger heroes, such as Ben Hall and Thunderbolt, have also been a continual focus of formal as well as folkloric interest, as have the notable outlaws of Britain and America already discussed. But none of these has achieved quite the same state of grace, and disgrace, as Ned Kelly.

CHAPTER SIX

Outlaw to National Hero: The Case of Ned Kelly

Edward 'Ned' Kelly is the logical culmination of the Anglo-phone outlaw hero tradition. His legend harks back, implicitly and explicitly, to the English and Irish highwaymen. The political nature of the Kelly outbreak links the bushranger strongly with Anglo-Celtic traditions of protest and struggle, and sees probably the last use of the medieval outlawry legislation. Kelly's activities and his folklorisation resonate closely with those of the American badmen, both being related to the rise of new technologies of transport and communication. Like the James gang, but unlike his Australian predecessors, Ned Kelly robbed banks. His attempt to attack a train resulted in his capture—a failure that symbolised the effective end of the social conditions necessary to sustain agrarian outlaw heroes in industrial societies. And, again like James and Billy the Kid in particular, Ned Kelly's image has been taken up by the mass media and that other central aspect of twentieth century life, tourism, as an appropriate icon of romance and adventure in the pioneering past. Kelly, James, Billy the Kid and Robin Hood have thus been given enhanced status as icons of heritage, anti-authoritarianism and resistance to real or perceived oppression and socio-economic dislocation. In the process they have transcended their status as local heroes, folk heroes and even national heroes to become internationally known images of the cinema and TV. Like James and Bonney, Ned Kelly is known in the international forums of high art through Sidney Nolan's paintings. He is also known through internationally oriented films such as the 1992 extravaganza, *Reckless Kelly*, by Yahoo Serious, clearly intended for an international as well as an Australian audience. His image, derived from his outlaw hero status, continues to provide related meanings in the modern world, well into the second century after his execution for the murder of a policeman in the damp bush at Stringybark Creek. In Australian culture, Ned Kelly is regarded by many as a national hero; this stature was confirmed in 1980, the centenary year of his death, when the Commonwealth government issued a postage stamp in his honour. The life and legend of bushranger Ned Kelly represent the full circle of the tradition that is the subject of this book—the individual who defies the state and is placed outside the law of the state achieves perhaps the ultimate symbolic representation of that state and its laws as a picture on a postage stamp.

THE KELLY SAGA

The Kelly family and their numerous relatives formed an extensive system of clan-like interdependence, based upon their common Irish heritage and their uneasy relationship with the forces of law and order. Ned Kelly's father, John 'Red' Kelly was transported to Van Diemen's Land (Tasmania) in 1841 for stealing two pigs in his native Tipperary, where he had been employed as a gamekeeper. Recent research has shown that Red Kelly was, in all likelihood, a police informer.[1] By 1848 he had served out his seven years' sentence and was freed, aged twenty-nine. By 1850 Red had met and married Ellen, daughter of James Quinn, originally an Irish 'bounty' immigrant, then living in Wallan Wallan, Victoria. After a number of relocations and incidents with the law, both the Kelly and the Quinn families settled in the same general area during the 1860s; the Quinns at Glenmore station on the King River, and the Kellys near Greta. By this time, 1867, Red Kelly had been dead for six months and Ned, at twelve years of age, was the oldest male of the Kelly household. Including his mother and himself, it numbered nine, the children ranging in age from two to fourteen. By the time he was in his teens, Ned Kelly had served a number of gaol terms for horse-stealing and robbery, including one of three years' hard labour.

After his release from this last sentence in February 1874, Ned broke away from the seemingly inevitable pattern of arrest, conviction, and imprisonment, and worked steadily as a bush labourer around northeastern Victoria and in the Riverina. In 1877 he was fined for being drunk and disorderly after a fight with four policemen, two of whom, Constables Fitzpatrick and Lonigan, were to play further roles in the Kelly tragedy. Other than this he appeared to be leading a blameless life,

Ned Kelly, c. 1875.

though from late 1876 Ned and his stepfather George King (an American prospector who had married Ellen Kelly in 1874) were probably engaged in a large-scale duffing operation in the King Valley and surrounding districts. They were never caught, though they might well have been if Ned Kelly's elevation to murderer and outlaw had not transcended such relatively minor infractions of the law.

Historians have pointed out that, although land settlement was important in Australia during the 1870s, the decisive developments were the growth of manufacturing industries in the cities so that business and administration were centralised in the colonial capitals. This, in Victoria, together with the influence of the railways in transforming many rural areas from a grazing to a farming economy, resulted in the economic success of people with farming skills, some capital, and reasonably fertile land close to the railways. Many people, like the Kellys and their relations, lacking these requisites, were unable to participate in this shift of economic emphasis and so were deprived of its benefits.[2]

During the same period, the increasing centralisation of administration widened the existing gap in co-ordination and comprehension between police headquarters in Melbourne and the practical problems of the local constabulary. In 1854–56, the Victoria Police in Melbourne was reorganised on the model of the London Metropolitan Police.[3] This was a reasonably satisfactory system for the rapidly expanding capital, but was not geared to handle the policing of rural areas like the north-eastern district, where a system similar to that of the New South Wales trooper police was used. Structured after the militaristic Royal Irish Constabulary, the Victorian version was no more popular than its predecessor across the border.[4] Nevertheless, the organisation and manning of the Victoria Police contributed to the inefficiency of the force and general disdain in which it was held in many quarters. Police administration of country districts was constantly hampered by changes of personnel that resulted in the removal of men familiar with the local terrain and population and their replacement by those lacking the experience and knowledge needed to handle the often refractory locals. This certainly appears to have been the case in the north-eastern district, which was a region notorious for stock-theft for at least thirty years before the Kelly outbreak.[5]

The problems of local policing were compounded by the crippling necessity to consult a higher authority before any significant action could be taken and having to requisition and document even the most trifling items. Horses, housing, and men were all inadequate, and there was strong antipathy between senior officers.[6] The shortcomings of the Victorian police contributed to the generally poor image of the force.[7] In addition, the small selectors of the north-eastern district generally believed the police to be on the side of the squatters, the banks, and shopkeepers.[8] This belief inflamed the strong feelings that already existed in the area, the endemic stock-stealing being a way of evening the score with the squatters for their apparent collusion with the police in impounding stray beasts. To regain an impounded horse or cow it was necessary to pay a fine to the impounder. This practice is one of the major grievances expressed in Ned Kelly's Cameron and Jerilderie Letters,[9] and underpins the elaboration of the bushranger as an outlaw hero.

At the Victorian Crown Lands Commission of 1878–79, evidence was given that selectors often had no means of physical survival other than stealing from the larger squatters, and that this practice was not only common but also viewed by struggling selectors as the accepted procedure.[10] Many small selectors considered the law allowing some men to impound stock was nothing more than legalised duffing, and that their own stock-stealing was certainly no more reprehensible.

Linked with this sort of grievance was the injustice that the Quinns, Kellys, and Lloyds reportedly felt about their difficulty in obtaining Crown land for selection. Rural discontent about the equity of the selection system was not restricted to the north-eastern district. The Victorian Crown Lands Commission was one response to the general dissatisfaction. The actions of the Kellys and their sympathisers were a very different response to the same fundamental problems.[11] Those actions were initiated by a trooper policeman.

In March of 1878, Constable Fitzpatrick was sent to take charge of the Greta police station for a few days. He had seen a police notice of the issue of a warrant for Dan Kelly, Ned's younger brother, in relation to a case of horse-stealing. After refreshing himself at one hotel, at least, Fitzpatrick decided, against orders and without a copy of the warrant, to bring in Dan Kelly. When he was heard from again, Fitzpatrick said that he had tried to arrest Dan but was attacked by Mrs Kelly, Dan, Bill Skillion (husband of Margaret Kelly) and 'Bricky' Williamson—and that he had been shot in the wrist by Ned Kelly himself.[12]

The Kellys' version was that Fitzpatrick had arrived drunk, attempted to molest one of the Kelly girls, and generally insulted and bullied those present. Whatever actually took place that day in Greta, the outcome was the arrest of Skillion, Williamson, and Mrs Kelly, and a £100 reward for the capture of Ned Kelly. At her trial, Mrs Kelly was given the unusually severe sentence of three years in Pentridge, solely on Fitzpatrick's questionable evidence. Williamson and Skillion received six years apiece. These sentences were one of the earliest components of the Kellys' image as the victims of official persecution and injustice. Popular opinion in the north-eastern district at the time held Fitzpatrick in contempt as a liar, while the Kellys were seen as the victims of police harassment[13]—sentiments that find an outlet in a number of the Kelly ballads.

From the time of their mother's arrest, Ned and Dan stuck to the bush, rocking a gold cradle and nursing their anger at the ultimate proof of police tyranny. In October 1878, Sergeant Kennedy and Constables Scanlon, Lonigan and McIntyre were sent from Mansfield into the rugged Wombat Ranges to search for Ned and Dan Kelly. About 5 p.m. on 26 October, together with Steve Hart, Joe Byrne, and Tom Lloyd jun.,[14] the Kellys came upon the policemen's camp on the banks of Stringybark Creek. There was a gunfight that ended with three dead policemen. Only Constable McIntyre escaped to bring the shocking news to Mansfield.

When details of the murders reached Melbourne, the public reacted with revulsion, encouraging the Berry government to rush an adaptation of the New South Wales Felons Apprehension Act through the Victorian parliament. This legislation, a throwback to the bushranging heyday of the 1860s, the earlier penal years, and even further back to the medieval institution of outlawry, was essentially a means of imposing what amounted to martial law on any given area. Under the Act, those proclaimed as outlaws could be shot on sight by anyone at all. Anyone suspected of harbouring or aiding outlaws could be arrested and presumed guilty on the unsupported allegation of another person. The maximum sentence for this offence was fifteen years' hard labour. Any Justice of the Peace or police officer was empowered to enter and search premises without a warrant if he suspected outlaws were being harboured there. As in New South Wales, the police were able to requisition horses, arms, or supplies when in pursuit of outlaws, the amount of compensation for such requisitions being decided by the government.[15]

Locally, though, the reaction to the killings was rather different, as the following ballad indicates. The police are presented as objects of ridicule and the entire bloody sequence of events is treated in a humorously offhand

and callous manner, even Kelly's well-known and apparently genuine regret for killing Sergeant Kennedy.

STRINGYBARK CREEK[16]

A sergeant and three constables set out from Mansfield town,
Near the end of last October for to hunt the Kellys down.
So they travelled to the Wombat and they thought it quite a lark
And they camped upon the borders of a creek called Stringy-bark.

They had grog and ammunition there to last them many a week,
And next morning two of them rode out all to explore the creek,
Leaving McIntyre behind them at the camp to cook the grub,
And Lonigan to sweep the floor, and boss the washing tub.

It was shortly after breakfast Mac thought he heard a noise,
So gun in hand he sallied out to try and find the cause;
But he never saw the Kellys planted safe behind a log,
So he slithered back to smoke and yarn, and wire into prog [i.e. food].

But bold Kelly and his comrades thought they'd like a nearer look,
For being short of grub, they wished to interview the cook;
And of firearms and of cartridges they found they had too few,
So they longed to grab the pistols, guns and ammunition too.

Both the bobbies, at the stump alone, they then were pleased to see,
A-watching of the billy boiling for the troopers' tea.
There they smoked and chatted gaily, never thinking of alarms,
Till they heard the fearful cry behind, 'Bail up! Throw up your arms.'

The traps they started wildly, and Mac then firmly stood,
And threw up his arms, while Lonigan made tracks to gain the wood;
Reaching for his revolver, but before he touched the stock,
Ned drew his trigger, and dropped him like a cock.

Then after searching McIntyre, all through the camp they went
And cleared the guns and cartridges and pistols from the tent;
But brave Kelly muttered sadly as he loaded up his gun
'Oh, what a —— pity the —— tried to run!

The Victorian Felons Apprehension Act became effective on 12 November 1878. From that day, north-eastern Victoria became an occupied province. Individuals and homes were under continuous surveillance and were frequently made the objects of misguided police raids and searches. Parties of armed police constantly patrolled the district, often descending upon groups of innocent men thought to be the Kellys. Police spies and informants abounded, and in December, seventy of the Garrison Artillery were posted in the district to guard the banks. The earliest ballad, 'Stringybark Creek', dates from this time. But support and sympathy for the Kellys were far more extensive than the singing of songs. The success and survival of the bushrangers for nearly two years was largely a result of their bush telegraph system. As with Frank Gardiner, Ben Hall and other bushrangers, this system revolved around the nucleus of immediate family and relatives and was extremely effective in protecting the outlaws from the forces of the law.

The Victorian government of 1878, when faced with the same predicament, was no more able to resolve it within the normal legal framework than the New South Wales government. The Victorian Felons Apprehension Act became law and two months later, as in New South Wales, its provisions were used to subvert the liberty of selected individuals. Beginning on 2 January 1879, the police arrested thirty suspected Kelly sympathisers and lodged them in Beechworth gaol. Twenty-three were charged, and over the next four months many of these unfortunates were continually remanded in custody while the court awaited the presentation of police evidence against them. By 22 April eleven men were still inside the gaol without having had any police case laid against them. Finally, an embarrassed presiding magistrate could no longer ignore the blatant illegality of the situation, and released the prisoners.

The period during which these men were imprisoned coincided with harvest time, and many families consequently experienced great difficulty and hardship getting their crops in. Not surprisingly, this whole episode further alienated both sympathisers and non-sympathisers from the police and their whole campaign. Along with this policy of intimidation, the police could, and did, ensure that suspected sympathisers were prevented from selecting land needed to extend their farms. But sympathisers still provided horses, food, shelter, ammunition, and intelligence of police movements to the gang.[17] They also carried out the undoubtedly pleasurable task of providing the police with false information concerning the activities of the outlaws.[18] Of the 127 reported sightings of the Kellys between November 1878 and April 1879, not one of those followed up by the police yielded even a glimpse of the gang.[19] This was the result of false information, police bungling, and the pre-arranged system of warning signals that the telegraphs used to inform the bushrangers of police presence.[20]

At the other end of Victorian society, the law-abiding classes expressed their disgust not only at the murders but also at the disturbing extent of sympathy for the Kellys. The existence of a group of hereditary criminals, setting the law at defiance and aided by a vast network of sympathisers, was seen as a positive danger to the character and social stability of Victoria, echoing fears expressed in New South Wales a dozen or so years earlier. So great were the apparent dangers of such a situation that the suspension of the legal rights of individuals was not merely necessary but absolutely justifiable. This withdrawal of the forms of liberty from 'degraded' men was seen to be the means of maintaining the substance of liberty for the 'respectable portion of society'.[21] No consideration was given to the possibility that such strong and extensive manifestations of sympathy for a gang of bushrangers might indicate the existence of more fundamental discontents than those which produced mere criminality.

These fears proved to be unfounded. No subsequent bushranging outbreaks occurred, and the authorities were free to concentrate their efforts upon rooting out the 'tribe of hardened criminals who had taken possession of the land and for years defied the law'.[22] And although the *Argus* doubted that 'the Dick Turpin and Jack Sheppard sentiment had any serious prevalence in the land', two days later the same writer was complaining that Kelly sympathisers were everywhere, and aiding the bushrangers so effectively that they should all be arrested.[23]

Of course, this extensive network of sympathisers needed financing in order to continue for more than a few months. Robbing banks was the most immediate means of securing money. To the Kellys and their sympathisers this had the additional advantage of striking at the enemy's resources. The bushrangers would then be able to maintain both themselves and their Robin Hood image, ensuring continued local support and sympathy. Their first bank hold-up was in the small sleepy town of Euroa near the southern extremity of the Kelly country, barely six weeks after Stringybark Creek.

Firstly, the Kellys took over Younghusband's Faithfull Creek station on the morning of 9 December 1878. The subsequent proceedings were quite civilised, though firmly carried through by the Kellys. All the station-hands were taken into custody, while the bushrangers made themselves at home for the remainder of that day and the following night. The women present were treated with great respect and civility by the gang in the best highwayman style. As would become usual on these occasions, Ned spoke grimly of the police persecution of his family, particularly his mother, and also discussed his duffing prowess and the fight at Stringybark Creek.

The next morning, Ned, Dan, and Steve Hart, leaving Joe Byrne at the station to guard the prisoners, set off for the town in two carts. After spying out the town, the bushrangers parked their carts at the back and front of the bank. The manager, Mr Scott, his wife and family, together with the accountant and two clerks, were politely bailed up and the bank's strongroom relieved of over £2000 in cash and gold. Ned also took a number of mortgages from the bank, leaving most of the securities and the like behind. As the bank was officially closed, the robbery proceeded without a hitch. Over the next few weeks a lot of the Kellys' poor friends in north-eastern Victoria were able to pay some of their debts, and to run up more in the public houses. As Mrs Scott later recalled: 'They took a great deal of silver from Euroa and a fairly large account was paid next day by one of their friends, in sixpences and shillings.'[24]

The police were helpless, unable to get even a smell of the gang except for false leads that started them on wild-goose chases, including one across the Murray River into New South Wales. The press, adopting a tone that would become the norm during the outbreak, raged against the ineptitude of the police and the daring of the Kellys: 'the whole country is in the hands of an extensive criminal community, who do not hesitate to impudently manifest their power', thundered an *Age* editorial. The following ballad appeared in a pamphlet:

STICKING UP OF THE EUROA BANK[25]

So Kelly marched into the Bank,
   A cheque all in his hand,
For to have it changed for money
   Of Scott he did demand.

And when that he refused him,
   He, looking at him straight,

Said 'See here, my name's Ned Kelly
    And this here man's my mate.'

With pistols pointed at his nut,
    Poor Scott did stand amazed,
His stick he would have liked to cut [i.e. he would have liked to
    leave],
    But was with funk half crazed.

The poor cashier with real fear,
    Stood trembling at the knees,
But at last they both seen 'twas no use
    And handed out the keys.

The safe was quickly gutted then,
    They drawers turned out as well,
The Kellys being quite polite,
    Like any noble swell.

With flimsies, gold and silver coin,
    The threepennies, and all,
Amounting to two thousand pounds
    They made a glorious haul.

Less than two months later, the Kellys were 'to impudently manifest their power' yet again by robbing the town of Jerilderie across the New South Wales border on 8 and 9 February.[26] The local branch of the Bank of New South Wales was part of the same building as the Royal Hotel. The bushrangers went into the hotel for a drink, but it was not long before Ned and Joe excused themselves from the bar, entered the bank and invited the manager, two clerks and an astonished customer to join the party at the hotel—though not before they had 'withdrawn' over £2000. Ned also burned the mortgages and some ledgers, to the lusty cheers of the crowd in the hotel, who were enthused by sympathy, fear, alcohol, or a combination of all three. According to one eye-witness, the bushranger commented that the banks were crushing the life's-blood out of the poor struggling man and this was a good reason for destroying all the mortgages.[27] Ned Kelly gave his standard speech for such occasions, stressing the injustice he and his peers had suffered and the general villainy of the police force. The three bushrangers mounted up and Steve Hart completed the show with a display of horsemanship. As with most of the Kelly raids, this had been a highly public affair.

One of the earliest Kelly songs to be published, 'The Bold Kelly Gang' emphasises the extent of local support for the Kellys and includes the significant lines: 'We thin their ranks, We rob their banks . . .'. The avenging, terrorising element of the tradition is also prominent here, as is the gang's cunning in eluding capture. The extremely partisan nature of this text is largely due to its publication by a newspaper within the 'Kelly country' itself.

THE BOLD KELLY GANG[28]

Oh there's not a dodge worth knowing
or showing, that's going
but you'll learn (this isn't blowing [i.e. boasting]),
from the BOLD KELLY GANG.

We've mates where-e'er we go
that somehow let us know
the approach of every foe
to the BOLD KELLY GANG.

There's not a peeler riding
Wombat Ranges hill or siding
but would rather be for hiding,
though he'd like to see us hang.

We thin their ranks, we rob their banks
and say no thanks for what we do,
Oh the terror of the camp
is the BOLD KELLY GANG.

Then if you want a spree
come with me, and you'll see,
how grand it is to be
in the BOLD KELLY GANG.

The New South Wales government, under pressure from the Bank of New South Wales, reversed its earlier refusal to offer a reward for the Kellys and matched the £4000 offered by the Victorian government. The gang was now worth a total of £8000, dead or alive, an amount generally considered to be the largest ever offered for bandits. But in spite of this, and frantic police activity on both sides of the border, the Kellys could not be found anywhere, though the Kelly country received another sudden economic stimulus.

The last act of the Kelly saga was played out at the Glenrowan railway station where, in June 1880, the bushrangers hoped to derail a police train. What the Kellys planned to do next is still a matter of dispute.[29] It has been said that they merely intended to rob as many banks as possible; others have argued that they hoped to establish a republic of north-eastern Victoria. Whatever their aims, Glenrowan was definitely to be the final confrontation between the outlaws and the forces of the state. The plans of the outlaws went wrong, however. The four bushrangers spent a night in the Widow Jones' Glenrowan Inn with sixty or so hostages, awaiting the arrival of the police train. Everyone seems to have enjoyed this; the landlady's son even sang two outlaw ballads, 'The Wild Colonial Boy' and one of the current Kelly songs.[30] As a prisoner later testified, 'He did not treat us badly—not at all.'

By ten o'clock the train had still not arrived and Ned, perhaps more relaxed than he should have been, allowed some of the prisoners to go home. One of them was a schoolteacher, Thomas Curnow, who told Ned he was worried about his wife and family being alone at night. Curnow went home, got a lantern and began walking back along the railway line to warn the police of their danger. Just before three o'clock on Monday morning, the bushrangers heard the pilot engine's whistle warning the following police train of danger ahead and knew their plan had failed. Buckling on the suits of armour, weighing nearly 100 pounds each, which they had fashioned from stolen and donated ploughshares in readiness for a possible final pitched battle, the four members of the Kelly gang took up their positions by the hotel as the police train drew into the Glenrowan station.

Ned Kelly stood in front of his companions shouting that he was made of iron and firing at the police. Ned soon received four or five wounds. The police took cover behind trees and in a shallow ditch near the inn. Dan Kelly, Joe Byrne, and Steve Hart retreated inside the hotel and Ned strolled through the police lines, firing at the police and apparently impervious to their bullets. He then faded into the dark surrounding bush.

A number of the hostages were killed or wounded by police bullets. Joe Byrne was killed as he stood at the bar toasting the bold Kelly gang. About this time, Ned Kelly walked effortlessly back through the scattered police lines and into the hotel. He found Joe Byrne's body, but he could not locate Dan or Steve, who were in one of the rear rooms. Assuming that they had escaped, he went out the back door of the hotel to make his own getaway, only to discover that his horse had bolted. Ned Kelly then pierced the police lines yet again, finally fainting in the bush from loss of blood and exhaustion.

Just before dawn, a newly revived Ned Kelly lumbered out of the bush blazing away at the police with a revolver. His wounds and the clumsiness of the armour ensured that Kelly did little more than frighten the police, some of whom thought the tall, macintosh-coated figure was the Bunyip, or even Old Nick. Ned was eventually brought down with a shotgun blast to the legs. The badly wounded outlaw was taken into custody at the Glenrowan railway station, where he was made as comfortable as possible. He was not expected to live, and the last rites were given by Father Gibney, a passing Catholic priest.

The police continued to fire on the inn, which still contained hostages, until 10 a.m. when the large crowd of spectators who had congregated on the railway station compelled Superintendent Sadleir to call a cease-fire and the hostages were allowed to leave. Dan Kelly and Steve Hart attempted to escape after the release of the hostages, but were driven back to the hotel by the police. The police decided to burn the hotel down at three that afternoon, even while a wounded hostage still lay inside. He was rescued by the priest, only to die a few hours later.

Being in excellent health, Ned Kelly once again refused to do what was expected of him and remained alive. He was taken to Melbourne the day after the siege and soon nursed back to health to stand trial. The same judge who had sentenced Mrs Kelly to a three-year sentence over the Fitzpatrick affair, and thereby precipitated the outbreak, presided at her son's trial on 28 and 29 October 1880. Judge Redmond Barry directed the jury to consider a verdict of murder rather than manslaughter. The jury took half an hour to find Kelly guilty. In the process of sentencing the bushranger to death, Barry and Kelly exchanged bitter words that well illustrate the extent of support the Kellys had and the fears the authorities entertained about such support. The judge said:

> 'An offence of the kind which you stand accused of is not of an
> ordinary character . . . A party of men took up arms against
> society, organised as it was for mutual protection and regard for
> the law.'

'Yes, that is the way the evidence brought it out,' interrupted Kelly.

'Unfortunately,' the judge continued, 'in a new community, where society was not bound together so closely as it should be, there was a class which looked upon the perpetrators of those crimes as heroes ... It is remarkable that although New South Wales had joined Victoria in offering a large reward for the detection of the gang, no person was found to discover it. There seemed to be a spell cast over the people of this particular district, which I can only attribute either to sympathy with crime or dread of the consequences of doing their duty.'[31]

Ned Kelly was held in the condemned cell of Melbourne gaol until 10 a.m. on 11 November when he was to be hanged. Despite considerable public support for his reprieve, the sentence was carried out. That morning, Ned woke early and, according to tradition, was heard singing one of the Kelly songs, 'Farewell to My Home in Greta'. He received the last rites and walked steadily to the gallows, telling the hangman that there was no need to tie his arms. On the scaffold he sighed, 'Ah well, I suppose it had to come to this.' (He did not say 'Such is life', as tradition more romantically has it.) Then the trap was sprung. Ned Kelly died game in the best traditions of the outlaw hero.

THE BALLAD OF THE KELLY GANG[32]

Oh, Paddy dear, and did you hear the news that's going round,
On the head of bold Ned Kelly they've placed two thousand
    pounds
For Dan, Steve Hart, and Byrne, two thousand each they'll give,
But if the sum were double, sure the Kelly boys will live.

'Tis sad to think such plucky hearts in crime should be
    employed,
But with great persecution they've all been much annoyed,
Revenge is sweet, but in the bush they can defy the law,
Such stickings up and plunderings Colonials never saw.

'Twas in November '78 the Kelly gang came down
Just after shooting Kennedy to famed Euroa Town;
Blood horses rode they all upon, revolvers in their hand,
They took the township by surprise, and gold was their demand.

161

Into the Bank, Ned Kelly walked and bail up he did say,
Unlock your safes, hand out your cash, be quick, do not delay;
Without a murmur they obeyed the robbers' bald [sic] command
Two thousand pounds in notes and gold they gave into his hand.

Now hand out all your arms you have, the audacious robbers said,
And all your ammunition, or a bullet through your head.
Your wife and children, too, must come, and make them look
    alive,
Get into these conveyances, we'll take you for a drive.

They drove them to a station about five miles away,
Where twenty men already had been bailed up all the day.
A hawker also shared the fate, which everybody knows
And came in handy to the gang, supplying them with clothes.

They next destroyed the telegraph by cutting down the wire
And of their left-off wearing clothes they made a small bonfire,
Throughout the whole affair, my boys, they never fired a shot,
The way they worked was splendid and will never be forgot.

Oh, Paddy dear, do shed a tear, I can't but sympathise,
Those Kellys are the devils, and they've made another rise.
This time across the Billybong Creek, on Morgan's ancient beat,
Where they robbed the Bank of thousands, and safely did retreat.

The matter may be serious, Pat, but sure I can't but laugh,
To think the tales the Bobbys [sic] told should all amount to
    chaff;
They said they had them all hemmed in—they could not get
    away,
But they did turn up in New South Wales, and made their
    journey pay.

They rode into Jerilderie town at 12 o'clock at night,
They roused the troopers from their beds who were in dreadful
    fright;
And took them in their nightshirts, ashamed I am to tell,
They covered them with revolvers, locked them in a cell.

They next acquaint the women folks that they intend to stay
And take possession of the camp until the following day.

They fed their horses in the stalls, without the slightest fear,
And go and rest their weary limbs till daylight does appear.

Next morning being Sunday, of course, they must be good,
They dressed themselves in troopers' clothes and Ned he
    chopped some wood,
No one there suspected them, for troopers, and all, they pass,
And Dan, the most religious, took the trooper's wife to mass.

They spent the day most pleasantly, had plenty of good cheer,
Beefsteaks and chops, tomato sauce and several pints of beer.
The ladies in attendance indulged in pleasant talk,
And just to ease the troopers' mind, they took them for a walk.

On Monday morning early, the masters of the ground,
They took their horses to the forge, and had them shod all
    round.
Then back were brought and mounted, their plans all laid so
    well.
In company with the troopers they stick up Cox's Hotel.

They bailed up all the servants and placed them in a room,
Saying, 'Do as we command you, or death will be your doom',
The Chinaman cook, 'no savvy' cried, not knowing what to fear,
But they brought him to his senses with a lift under the ear.

All who had approached the house just shared a similar fate,
In a very short time the number was nearly twenty-eight.
They shouted freely for all hands and paid for what they drank,
And two of them remained in charge and two went to the bank.

The force [sic] was here repeated, that I've already told,
They bailed up all the banker's clerks and robbed them of their
    gold.
The manager could not be found, and Kelly in great wrath
Searched high and low, and luckily found him in his bath.

They destroyed communication, by telegraph at least,
Of threatening and of robbery they had a perfect feast,
Where they've gone's a mystery, and coppers cannot tell
Until we hear from them again I bid you all farewell.

163

THE CONTINUING IMAGE OF NED KELLY

Popular interest in the executed bushranger began to express itself in both oral and media forms, much as occurred in the cases of the British and American equivalents of the Kellys. Orally, the creation of Kelly folklore within the framework of the outlaw hero tradition continued, and songs, poems, legends, and sayings proliferated.

Many of Ned Kelly's actions seemed tailor-made for the genesis of an Australian Robin Hood. Like many of his Australian predecessors he was well aware of the ethics required of a bushranger. To retain vital sympathy and support, he and his companions had to act in the same manner as the outlaw heroes of traditional song and story. That meant not killing and plundering indiscriminately or without just cause, showing courtesy and generosity to women and the poor, and generally behaving in a manner appropriate to a ballad hero.

From the very first raid, Ned had been at pains to ensure that things were done in proper highwayman style. Mrs Scott, wife of the Euroa bank manager, was greatly impressed by the outlaw's courtesy and manly bearing. 'Ned Kelly was a gentleman,' she stated on several occasions, inspiring the title of a later Kelly ballad. No-one seems to have been unduly interfered with by the gang, except the murdered accomplice, Aaron Sherritt, another young man of the region who had played a dangerous game of double agent and go-between for the police and the bushrangers. Sherritt was the Judas who, in terms of the outlaw hero tradition, suffered a just and proper fate.[33] Ned made Steve Hart return watches he ungraciously tried to pocket at Jerilderie, and also returned a horse he intended to 'borrow' for himself upon being told that it was the favourite mount of the publican's daughter. The gang always socialised with their captives, drank with them (at the bushrangers' own expense, it seems), danced, sang, and played party games with them, and generally gave everyone a roaring good time! That at least is the impression given by most of the eye-witness accounts of the Kelly raids. And, of course, Ned made public performances of burning the mortgages at Euroa and Jerilderie.

These apparently trivial acts were the stuff of Ned Kelly's popularity and continuing support. This was given a final and enduring boost by the public and violent nature of the events at Glenrowan, followed by Ned's trial and execution. A more suitable candidate for the image of the traditional outlaw hero would be difficult to come by. His early attainment of this mantle is evident from the publication of a number of Kelly songs while the outlaws were still active, as quoted above. After Kelly's death, though, songs were still made and sung about his exploits.

'Kelly Was Their Captain' contains many central motifs of the outlaw hero tradition. Ned is a fine, manly specimen; he is oppressed by the forces of authority in the form of the 'Governor of Victoria', a representative of the Crown; he defends his mother's honour and is righteously violent and angry; he is betrayed and, at the last, goes out in a defiant bang of blood and fire at the Glenrowan Station, terrifying the craven police. As the song puts it, the bushranger 'put their blood to shame'.

KELLY WAS THEIR CAPTAIN[34]

Come all you wild colonial boys and attention to me pay,
For in my song I will unfold the truth without delay.
'Twas of a famous outlawed band that roamed this country round,
Ned Kelly was their captain and no better could be found.

But the Governor of Victoria was an enemy of this man,
And a warrant he likewise put out to take his brother Dan.
But, alas, one day some troopers came young Dan to apprehend,
And he like a tiger stood at bay, his mother to defend.

Five hundred pounds reward was made for Ned, where'er was
    found,
And from place to place was hunted as if he was a hound.
Now driven to desperation to the bush brave Ned did take,
Young Dan, Steve Hart and brave Joe Byrne, all for his mother's
    sake.

And although they deemed them outlaws, brave men they proved
    to be,
And vengeance ranked [sic] in every breast for Kelly's misery.
They burnt his mother's vine-clad hut, which caused his heart to
    yearn,
And angered his companions, Dan, Steve Hart, and brave Joe
    Byrne.

One day as Ned and his comrades in ambush were concealed,
They spied three mounted troopers and their presence did reveal.

165

They called to them 'Surrender', these words to them he said,
'Resist a man among you and I'll surely shoot you dead.'

Now Kennedy, Scanlon and Lonnergan in death were lying low,
When Ned amongst them recognised his old and vitrous [*sic*]
    foe;
Then thoughts came of his mother with a baby at her breast,
And it filled Ned's heart with anger and the country knows the
    rest.

It was at the Wombat Ranges where Ned Kelly made his haunt,
And all those Victorian troopers at that name would truly daunt.
For months they lay in ambush until finally were betrayed
By traitor Aaron Sherritt, and his life the treachery paid.

It was at the Glenrowan station where the conflict raged severe,
When more than fifty policemen at the scene then did appear.
No credit to their bravery, no credit to their name,
Ned Kelly terrified them all and put their blood to shame.

While songs and poems like these were defending the Kellys or
mourning their deaths, another oral tradition associated with popular
heroes was trying to bring at least one, often two, of the gang back to
life. There was a persistent rumour that Dan Kelly and Steve Hart
somehow survived the fire at Glenrowan. The two bushrangers were
variously supposed to have made their getaway to America, South Africa,
or, rather less exotically, to Goondiwindi in Queensland. There was a
strong popular belief that the two outlaws fought in the Boer War, sometimes with the Boers, sometimes against them, as in these letters, the
first from a Melbourne *Herald* of 1930: 'It was reported when I was in
South Africa during the Boer War that two of the gang were there, but
I knew that couldn't be true. How the rumour originated I do not know,
but I was asked about it more than once.'[35] This particular belief was
still about in 1967 when Ian Jones, Kelly scholar and film-maker,
received a letter containing this statement: 'My uncle a mining engineer
was in South Africa during the Boer War. He met Dan Kelly and Steve
Hart—they were fighting with the Boers.' In 1933 the *Bulletin* commented upon the great number of men roaming around the country
during the 1920s and early 1930s, claiming to be Dan Kelly. Somebody

was even inspired to put pen to paper about the apparently universal survivor.[36]

The legend of Dan Kelly's survival after the Glenrowan fire also spawned its share of media exploitation. As early as 1911 a prolific sensationalist, Ambrose Pratt, foisted a cleverly conceived book upon the Australian public. It was comprehensively titled, *Dan Kelly, Being the Memoirs of Daniel Kelly (Brother of Edward Kelly, Leader of the Kelly Gang of Bushrangers), Supposed to have been Slain in the Famous Fight at Glenrowan*. In fact, the book was one of Pratt's concoctions, though this did not prevent it from running into numerous reprints over the next few years. The extent and persistence of this particular tradition is an expression of popular reluctance to accept the death of certain heroes. As mentioned in chapter 1, this is a widespread phenomenon of folklore and includes figures as diverse as Arthur, 'the once and future king', Alexander I of Russia, and even Jesus of Nazareth, to name only some.[37] Ned Kelly was undoubtedly the central hero of the Kelly saga, but he was just as surely executed in 1880. The popular need to believe in the survival of the hero was accordingly transferred to Dan and Steve, whose bodies were charred beyond recognition in the final conflagration at Glenrowan. Perhaps this legend began in the whispering of the onlookers at Glenrowan station, many of whom later said they heard the sound of horses coming and going to the scene throughout the siege. However it began, the survival legend has been a continuous strand woven through the fabric of Kelly oral tradition and has been one of many points of interchange between it and the media tradition that evolved from the bushrangers' notoriety.[38]

From the very beginning, the Kellys' outlawry had been a media event. After Stringybark Creek the urban and provincial newspapers had been almost continually agog with breathless reports and rumours about the gang. Within months of the murders, postcards of the bushrangers were being sold throughout Victoria, a substantial pamphlet had been published in Mansfield, and a broadsheet of Kelly songs had appeared in Hobart, Tasmania. While the gang was still at large, a dramatic production that apparently portrayed the gang as heroes and the police as blundering oafs was, not surprisingly, suppressed by the authorities in Melbourne. By 1880 an anonymous pamphlet called *History of the Outlaws* did not even need to specify its subject in the title. The same year saw the first issue of the *Bulletin* providing extensive coverage of the outlaws, which it continued up to the time of Ned Kelly's execution.

Poster for 1906 feature film The Story of the Kelly Gang.
(Documentation Section, National Film and Sound Archive.)

Succeeding years were filled with a constant stream of Kellyana from a variety of sources, including the press, book publishers, magazines, poets, and playwrights.

In 1906 the new medium of cinematography made its first full-length Australian debut[39] with *The Story of the Kelly Gang*. So concerned were the authorities with the potential of this film, produced a quarter of a century after the events it portrayed, to lead the youth of Australia into criminal rampages through the bush, that it was banned. Initially the Victorian authorities banned the film in the Kelly country itself, though this was soon followed by a broader prohibition. The success of the film with audiences prompted later cinematic entrepreneurs to film the exploits of other bushranger heroes. These productions also alarmed the authorities, especially in New South Wales where such films were banned until the 1940s. While this ban was long-lasting, it seems to have been relatively ineffective. At least six Australian feature films on the Kellys have been released, including the 1969 version starring rock singer Mick Jagger. A mini-series, *The Last Outlaw*, filled Australian TV screens from 1980, along with a number of documentaries. Despite the failure of the official proscription on producing bushranger films, the existence of the bans provides further evidence of the long-lasting official unease with the subject of outlawry.

During the 1930s an infant local broadcasting and recording industry finally found its Australian voice in the form of country music, originally copies from American recordings. Country music in the United States had its own tradition of 'badman' heroes and, after the initial wave of imitation had subsided a little, Australian singers began looking for local heroes to balladise. In a country still reeling from the effects of the Great Depression they did not have to look far to find an Australian champion of the poor and dispossessed. In 1939 Tex Morton and 'Smiling' Billy Blinkhorn (an immigrant from Canada) both recorded approving songs about Ned Kelly,[40] with acerbic comments on the depression economy. Blinkhorn sang, 'Poor Ned Kelly, it's easier to do today / Poor Ned Kelly, you don't even have to run away.' Tex Morton commented on 'the prices of things that we buy' and concluded 'I think to myself, perhaps after all—old Ned wasn't such a bad guy.' These were to be followed by numerous Australian country songs celebrating the Kellys and sung by such popular and big-selling artists as Slim Dusty, Smoky Dawson, and Buddy Williams.[41]

The basic ingredients of these media treatments of the Kelly story were derived from existing oral traditions. Probably the most widely used aspect was the concept of the outlaws, particularly Ned, as brave, resourceful men who died game. Even the earliest pot-boilers, while deploring the violence of Stringybark Creek, generally admire the gang's daring, bushmanship, and sheer style. Twelve years after the outbreak, even *The Banker's Magazine* felt able to admit that Ned Kelly was 'a thorough bushman and a born general . . . He was a powerful, handsome man and an all-round athlete; he never interfered with women', and that he went to his death 'very quietly and coolly'.[42]

Thirty-odd years later, the same mixed feelings were still evident. A romance titled *The Girl Who Helped Ned Kelly*[43] created a greater sensation than any other Australian romance when it appeared serially in *Table Talk* during 1928. The foreword to the 1929 publication in book form of this work had this to say about Ned: 'Superb qualities of leadership, almost unexampled endurance and uncanny bushcraft, would have taken him far if Fate had willed for him a more honest career.'[44]

Media productions also used the highwayman concept of the outlaw as the victim of circumstances largely beyond his control. In the oral tradition, this takes the form of unjust police persecution. The media were often concerned to whitewash the activities of the police as much as possible, so the same basic idea was expressed in a number of ways. Number 44 of the Boy's Friend 3d. Library, for instance, was titled *Ned Kelly: A Tale of Trooper and Bushranger* and written as an Australian western complete with faithful steeds, ranches, and an Aboriginal who talked like a Hollywood Red Indian—'Me see um track,' and so on. In this undated paperback Ned is said to have 'gone wrong' because of a woman and does not seem able to make up his mind whether he should be wearing the black hat or the white.[45] There have been many similar Deadwood Dick fabrications over the last hundred and fifteen years.[46]

A wildly inaccurate film made in 1951, *The Glenrowan Affair*, shows the police as bullying heavies and says that Mrs Kelly is in Melbourne gaol merely for 'being Ned Kelly's mother'. The film *Ned Kelly* also takes the view that economic circumstances and persecution were the main causes of Ned's outlawry. And if Ned was not exactly robbing the rich to give to the poor in a very early popularisation, *Ned Kelly, the Ironclad Australian Bushranger*, published in thirty-eight weekly instalments during 1911 by a quick-witted English publisher, at least his heart was in the right place. Between fictional travels around the world to undertake a stunning variety of criminal activities, Ned finds time to tell

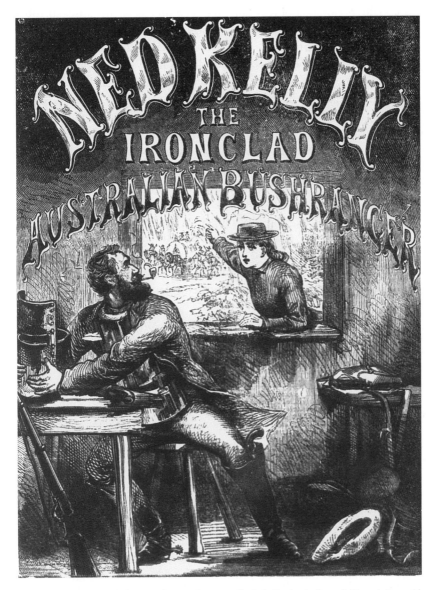

Ned Kelly, The Ironclad Australian Bushranger *(by J. S. Borlase). One of thirty-eight weekly instalments published in England.*

his equally fictional adopted daughter: 'It's no sin, in my case, to rob a rascally government who robbed my father and mother of life.'[47]

Douglas Stewart's play, *Ned Kelly*, gathers into itself many of the Kelly traditions. Broadcast as a radio drama in 1942 and published the following year, the play treats Ned as a direct successor to Ben Hall and the notion of the gallant highwayman: 'Bow to the ladies! Kiss the blooming babies', a disgruntled Steve Hart says to Ned in Act 2, Scene 2, when the outlaw leader makes him return the watch stolen from Reverend Gribble. Stewart sees Kelly as an ambivalent Australian archetype and, significantly, ends the play with the capture of the defiant armoured outlaw rather than with his execution.

'Ned Kelly Was a Gentleman' is a 1940s evocation of the Kelly legend, again casting the bushranger as the hero of the poor and oppressed against the rich. In accordance with the gradual elevation of Kelly from the status of folk hero to national hero, this poem puts forward the suggestion that Ned and his like would be the ideal warriors to save the nation from the then-advancing Japanese army.

NED KELLY WAS A GENTLEMAN[48]

Ned Kelly was a gentleman: many hardships did he endure.
He battled to deprive the rich then gave it to the poor.
But his mode of distribution was not acceptable to all,
Though backed by certain gunmen known as Gilbert and Ben Hall.

I think it was a pity they hanged him from a rope;
They made Australian history but they shattered Kelly's hope.
If they'd sent him into Parliament his prospects would be bright,
He'd function for the masses if not for the elite.

And perhaps now in Australia we'd have millions trained with him,
All laughing with vengeance at the little yellow men.
If Ned and such guerillas were here with us today
The Japs would not be prowling round New Guinea and Milne Bay.

Since Ned went over the Border there has been many a change,
Yet we may adopt his tactics around the Owen Stanley Range.
Poor Ned, he was a gentleman but never understood.
We want men of such mettle now to stem the yellow flood.

These elements—Ned Kelly's bravery, his forced or, at least unintentional, outlawry, his championing of the poor, and the survival legends—were digested and regurgitated by the media in one form or another to cater for a voracious appetite for Kellyana. But the media also contributed some new ingredients to the mix. One of these was a fascination with the armour worn by the outlaws at Glenrowan. This occurs without fail in books, films, poems, plays, even Nolan's paintings, but is not found in oral tradition—with the minor exception of a line in Billy Blinkhorn's 'Poor Ned Kelly' which mentions the armour in passing.

Another prominent feature of the media rarely found in oral tradition is the tendency to moralise about the Kellys. This was seen at its most blatant in the film *The True Story of Ned Kelly* (1923) and it may be found in the last verse of 'Ye Sons of Australia', a long and dreary poem by J. K. Moir, first published in the *Bulletin*. But in a version of this poem, collected as a song from oral tradition during the 1950s, the moralistic conclusion and the details of the armour have been dropped. The lyrics have been considerably pruned and amended to create a totally different meaning from the original.

The considerable number of popular stage presentations of the Kelly saga also wavered between romanticising the bushrangers, usually by sending up the police, and, as official disapproval loomed, sanitising the drama through moralisation. Bushranging, as it would be for the silent cinema, was a favourite subject of melodrama. Playwrights were not slow to recognise the wide appeal of Ned and his exploits, however fancifully embroidered. The first known production, *Catching the Kellys*, appeared in Melbourne while the bushrangers were still at large in March 1879. It was followed in July the next year by an advertised Sydney production of *The Capture and Destruction of the Kelly Gang*. This never opened, being banned by the government. In Melbourne a Kelly play by E. C. Martin made it to the stage in August 1881, and later toured the country. These productions and near-productions established the Kellys as staple figures of the Australian popular stage. An anonymous play titled *The Kelly Gang* was first staged in March 1898. The following year Arnold Denham's comprehensively titled *The Kelly Gang; or, the Career of Ned Kelly, the Ironclad Bushranger of Australia* opened in Sydney, beginning a run of almost continual revivals in one version or another that lasted until 1929. The opening night publicity described the play as 'being a grand moral lesson, showing the rising generation of Australia that in the words of Ned Kelly himself, "After all HONESTY IS THE BEST POLICY."[49] In the first decades of the twentieth century, tent shows, a combination of theatre and imitation wild west shows under circus tents, staged such extravaganzas as *Hands Up! Or Ned Kelly and His Gang, The Iron-Clad Bushranger*, as well as productions about Thunderbolt and Ben Hall. These were aimed at family audiences and combined rootin' tootin' gunfights with a note of warning.

The desire to draw a moral from the Kelly tale is absent from, and antagonistic to, the folk tradition. But as 'Ye Sons of Australia' illustrates, one media innovation that did find a degree of acceptance in oral tradition is the (inaccurate) notion of Kate Kelly as heroine.[50] This is a commonplace of all the Kelly media material, and is also found in those traditional songs that are recognisably derived from literary, nineteenth-century sources, such as 'Farewell to Greta' and 'The Kelly Gang'. It is, of course, also a common feature of the outlaw hero wherever and whenever he is romanticised.

The media continue to offer an overwhelming variety of material to the apparently insatiable public fascination with Ned Kelly. Barely a year has passed since 1879 without the publication of one—or, more often, several—works aimed at this seemingly eternal audience. To a greater or lesser extent they all display the same ambiguities and bewilderment about Ned Kelly. Was he a hero or a villain? A good illustration of this continuing ambivalence towards Ned Kelly is contained in a work published by its author, Henry H. Neary, in Sydney, probably sometime during the 1930s. In this book, barely more than a pamphlet, Neary succinctly and accurately delineates the essence of Ned Kelly's popular image:

> The Kellys became a sort of tradition in Australia, much as Dick Turpin did in England and the James brothers in U.S.A. Until 1915 their memory was regarded in a somewhat heroic light, but after the advent of the Anzacs and their deeds on Gallipoli and the deeds of the Light Horse in Egypt and Palestine, this country found itself with a new and much worthier tradition— the tradition of Anzac, with its spirit of mateship, sacrifice and courage. All the same, it was the same daring blood that inspired the bushmen of the first A.I.F. that had enabled the Kelly gang to defy the police for so long and gave them the courage to fight to the death when cornered. Wrong as they were, and black as was their criminal record, they had two great

attributes in their bushmanship and bravery, and it was probably that which led so many people to see only their courage rather than their criminality in the years that followed their violent end.[51]

Uncertainty about Ned's proper position on the spectrum between righteousness and damnation is also found in Australian folk speech. Because they are largely subconscious, formalised expressions are an interesting indication of the conflicts and tensions generated by the coexistence of the oral and media Kelly traditions. Sayings like 'game as Ned Kelly' or 'game as the Kelly Gang' reflect admiration for the pluck and daring of the bushrangers. On the other hand, to accuse someone of using 'Kelly methods', or to hint at unfair tactics with the statement 'They hanged Ned Kelly', is to recognise the criminal aspects of the bushranger. Interestingly, the same phrase can also be used as a response suggesting unfairness, as in 'I don't think that's fair', with the reply 'Well, they hanged Ned Kelly.'[52] The presence of these contrasting expressions in the Australian vernacular is a further illustration of the ambiguous attitudes towards Ned Kelly that persist in the minds of many Australians. That uneasy ambivalence is a result of the interaction of both the folk and the media Kelly traditions, which themselves draw upon the much older tradition of the outlaw hero.

As well as the songs,[53] books and films discussed above, Ned Kelly's persistent appeal is exploited in a number of other modes and arenas, including tourism. In the Kelly country proper, the tourist industry celebrates the outlaw for all he is worth, much as Britain's Dick Turpin and America's Billy the Kid, Jesse James and other outlaws have become consumer items. The duality of Ned's image—hero and villain—continues unabated.

Further evidence of Ned Kelly's uncertain status appeared during the centenary year of 1980. A not entirely tongue-in-cheek campaign was mounted to gain a pardon for Ned Kelly. The centenary year also saw the Australian government issue a commemorative stamp to mark the date, much to the expressed disgust of the Victorian state government. That government's official attitude to the Kelly centenary was to ignore it. Not urprisingly, the Victoria Police Force was reluctant to have one of its less than glorious episodes dragged through the historical mire. Indeed, the Mansfield monument to the three troopers who died at Stringybark Creek, erected in 1880, bears the unequivocal inscription 'in memory of the three brave men who lost their lives while endeavouring to capture a band of armed criminals in the Wombat Ranges ... ' It is no surprise, then, to find that there is no touristic celebration of the Kellys around Mansfield. Nor is there much around Euroa or the 'Kelly Tree', site of the murders at Stringybark Creek.

Since 1980 a number of books have been published on the Kelly story, including one in which a leading legal authority has examined the trial of Ned Kelly under the then-Chief Justice of Victoria, Sir Redmond Barry. In his book *The Trial of Ned Kelly*, John H. Phillips, Supreme Court Judge, concludes that Barry's summing up to the jury in Kelly's trial

> would have effectively removed from the jury's consideration the
> issue central to Kelly's defence. Sir Redmond should have told the
> jury that it was for them to decide whether the police [at
> Stringybark Creek] were acting as ministers of justice or summary
> executioners and then reviewed for the jurors the evidence
> relevant to this issue. Instead the matter was put to the jury in
> terms that were conclusive in favour of the Prosecution.

Phillips goes on to write:

> Accordingly, the conclusion is inescapable that Edward Kelly was
> not afforded a trial according to law. Whether the result would
> have been any different had the jury been correctly directed is, of
> course, entirely another matter.[54]

Phillips shows the extent to which the Victorian establishment of the time was prepared to go in order to dispose of Kelly and the very real threat they believed he and his sympathisers might pose to social order.[55] The magnitude of the rewards offered for Kelly's capture during 1878–80 and the extent of the armoury the Victoria Police brought to bear at Glenrowan also indicate the fear that the Kelly outbreak engendered among 'the respectable classes' of Victorian society.

Historian Bob Reece has conducted extensive research into the Irish background of Ned's father, John 'Red' Kelly. Reece discovered that, far from having been transported for a 'social' crime of an honourable kind—stealing from an English landlord as legend had it—Ned Kelly's father was known to the police as 'a notorious character' and probably involved in the organised theft of animals from his neighbours. Not only that, but Ned Kelly's father was a police informer and, quite possibly, an *agent provocateur*.[56] Other historians and writers, such as Dagmar Balcarek, have tracked down further threads of history and legend in the

Kelly story, including the nature of that remarkable woman Ellen Kelly, mother of Ned and the rest of the brood.[57] John Molony has given us an interestingly imaginative biography of Ned, originally titled *I Am Ned Kelly*, though now in print simply as *Ned Kelly*.[58] Melbourne University Press has reissued in paperback John McQuilton's classic account of the Kellys, *The Kelly Outbreak*, originally published in 1979.[59]

Australian creative artists have also continued to be fascinated by various aspects of the Kelly story. Jean Bedford published *Sister Kate* in 1982, using Ned's youngest sister Kate as the central character.[60] A decade later Robert Drew published *Our Sunshine*, an imaginative reworking of the history and mythology surrounding the Kellys.[61] At least two children's books based on the Kelly story have been published. Kelly scholar and film-maker Ian Jones produced the TV mini-series *The Last Outlaw* in 1980 and also made an important contribution to knowledge and understanding of the internal relationships of the Kellys and their supporters in his 1992 book, *The Friendship that Destroyed Ned Kelly: Joe Byrne and Aaron Sherritt*. Apart from its scholarship, this book is remarkable for reproducing some facsimile pages of Ned Kelly's Jerilderie Letter, long believed lost to the world and previously known only in copies of varying accuracy.[62]

Publication of a book-length study of an aspect of the Kelly myth is in itself an indication of the return of the Kelly mythology to the centre of historical interest. Far more telling in terms of popular culture has been the recent Yahoo Serious film, *Reckless Kelly*, a zany treatment of the Kelly story that revolves around the bushranger's Robin Hood characteristics, updated, satirised and sanitised. Serious (writer, director, co-producer, star, stuntman, etc.) presents a powerfully nationalistic re-telling of the Kelly story, a kind of 1990s *Crocodile Dundee* aimed as much at the American as at the local market. American and Australian film producers obviously believe that the subject of Ned, suitably retooled, is worth twenty millions of their dollars. Despite this offshore funding (something of a contradiction given the film's attitude towards foreign investment in Australia), *Reckless Kelly* is only occasionally crass and sometimes clever, and it makes some reasonably serious points about Australian culture and economics. The film ends with the bushranger/bank-robber and his 'Australian' values triumphant, and with a dedication to Ned Kelly, the 'larrikin' fighter against oppression and injustice.

Even though Ned's mortal remains have been laid to rest, there is no sign of the Kelly legend dying. Lawyers, historians, film-makers,

Ned Kelly *(Mick Jagger)*
(© 1970 Woodfall Limited. All Rights Reserved.)

novelists and journalists continue to approach Ned Kelly, his story and his folklore, in a variety of ways. Ned, like the saint that Keith Dunstan called him in his 1980 book of the same title,[63] has his hagiographers, his mythologists, his forgers, his fakers, his salespeople and, apparently, even his would-be saviours. Need a national hero, an Australian myth, provide any further evidence of his sanctification and commodification? They have all ensured that the bushranger persists at the centre of Australian myth-making. National hero or national villain, Ned Kelly's legend will not lie down and die.

How relevant is Ned to the new Australia? Can Aboriginal people, for instance, identify with an Anglo-Celtic bushranger? It seems so. As a sobering example of how the past may return to haunt the present, descendants of the Aboriginal trackers who worked with the police during the Kelly hunt are now claiming their share of the reward—plus interest. In the Northern Territory, Aborigines have adopted Kelly into their cultures, in some cases conflated with Jesus, other biblical figures and Captain Cook.[64] Ned's defiance of duly constituted authority and his insistence on the repressive nature of the Victorian government and its police has caused some Western Australian Aborigines to see Kelly as an appropriate representative of their own grievances and struggle. It is this Robin Hood element of the bushranger that may also resonate with Australians from backgrounds other than Anglo-Celtic. Kelly is the epitome of the Australian branch of an international 'noble robber' tradition. But the noble robber or Robin Hood figure, who redresses the political and economic wrongs done to the poor by the rich and powerful, is a cultural constant throughout the world, appearing in many guises in many nationalities. Ned Kelly's struggle and his mythology present no barriers to Australians whose cultural precedents are not those of the British Isles. It may be that Ned proves to be as adaptable and flexible in the new Australia as he was in the old.

In April 1994, the Western Australian-based Challenge Bank began an expensive print and television advertising campaign featuring Ned Kelly. Although Ned's legend has only limited appeal in Western Australia, the bank's advertising agency still managed to sell this rather odd sales pitch. Perhaps the myth has come full circle. Australia's most famous bank-robber has become an appropriate icon for promoting respectable banking. From folk hero to national hero, from outlaw to advertising gimmick, from bank-robber to bank seller: there seems to be no end to the convenience of Ned Kelly in Australian culture.

CHAPTER SEVEN

Interpreting the Legend

FACT AND FOLKLORE

The problematic relationship of history and folklore has been a long and fiery one.[1] While the relationship is important, it is not important in the sense in which it has mainly been pursued—that is, whether or not folklore is 'truthful' or 'reliable'. It is not the purpose of folklore to provide 'historical truth', though its bearers often believe it does. Rather, folklore is a complex cultural process in which history, belief, tradition and popular discourse are intertwined in a complex web of past and present meaning.

Meaning is a notoriously slippery concept and its study is difficult. The relationship of folklore and history is particularly difficult for a number of reasons. One of these is the force of tradition. The existence of a tradition is itself a powerful validating influence, providing the subject(s) of the tradition with an aura of sanctity simply by virtue of its having persisted for a reasonable length of time. Reinforcing this 'sacred cow' factor is the ability of a tradition to provide an internally logical framework of belief for the bearer of the tradition. The veracity of the view of history presented in the tradition is rarely questioned, no matter how unlikely or how challenged by other sources of information. In folk tradition, Turpin *did* ride from London to York in one day, Jesse James *was* the victim of post-Civil War injustice and Ned Kelly's last words *were* 'Such is life.' Together, these factors impart a considerable sustaining power to any tradition, a power that is easily able to override the claims of history, should these be presented.

The persistence of a tradition over time and space also means that a variety of meanings becomes accreted around the central concept, depending upon the period, place and circumstances in which the tradition has been found to be convenient. A tradition will have different meanings to different social groups. One relevant example of this is in the often deep meanings that an outlaw hero tradition may have for residents of the area, almost always rural or semi-rural, where a historical outlaw operated. With local associations of persons, places, topography and events, the tales and ballads of the outlaw have an especially powerful resonance. Yet essentially the same tradition may be equally relevant to groups with no local associations at all. Such groups may be urban factory workers in a depression, soldiers on active duty, or even the members of an oppressed ethnic minority. Examples of these wider uses of particular outlaw hero traditions may be found in relation to many of the outlaws studied here. In these cases, a particular facet or even motif of the outlaw hero tradition may become the focus of the outlaw's popularity, such as his Robin Hood aura, or his bravery and manliness. Because a tradition is essentially a device for linking the past to the present, such fragmentations and re-emphases, as well as accretions of detail, mean that interpretation is a complex undertaking, particularly when attempted from a diachronic perspective. Despite these difficulties, some effort must be made to account for such factors in studying a tradition.

The outlaw hero tradition identified, delineated, described and traced in this book is a case study of the interaction of many, often disparate, elements over time and space. Among other things, this study shows that history, folk tradition and popular culture are intermixed at all levels and that the nature of that mixture, the effects it has on historical groups and individuals and the effects that their activities have on the folklore or legends of their lives (and other outlaw heroes) should be the focus of scholarly concern, rather than the arid debate about whether folklore is 'true' or 'historically accurate'. It does not matter whether folklore presents an accurate picture of the past, if indeed such a thing is even possible. What matters is the manner in which the past is reworked and re-presented through folklore and the way in which that representation can affect the attitudes and the actions of men and women in the present. In the case of the cultural tradition of the outlaw, the perceived past has continually made possible communally sanctioned acts of law-breaking and violence. The same tradition that made this possible also provided a moral code that guided the actions of outlaw heroes and their supporters.

The issues and actions proceeding from these acts involve life-and-death situations which are likely to be the most crucial social experiences in the lives of the participating groups and individuals. 'The everyday', a term being increasingly applied to folkloric manifestations, is therefore an inadequate concept for understanding these events. The generation, support and celebration of outlaw heroes is a matter far removed from the everyday and is one important reason for the continued coherence of the tradition and the codes of conduct and attitude that it provides. Like the 'carnivalesque' operating in festival, the outlaw hero tradition provides a set of boundaries and signposts for actors in cultural scripts to negotiate a situation which is outside the everyday and which violently flouts everyday norms. While the world is turned upside down briefly and largely symbolically in festival, in outbreaks of outlawry the period of disruption is extended and actual. People are killed, wounded, oppressed, humiliated, imprisoned and otherwise permanently affected through the operation of forces largely outside their control. While festival is a controlled *excess*, communally validated and sanctioned within a particular time and space, outlawry is an uncontrolled and dangerous *distress* in which any number of serious consequences may occur. The cultural need for a set of rules and boundaries to contain and control the deep discontents, frustrations and aggressions unleashed by the outlaw is therefore imperative. This need is provided by the outlaw hero tradition.

The incessant relationship of folklore and the popular is also relevant here, as forms of cultural production and representation in post-industrial societies are powerful and interrelated. The nature and occurrence of these interactions are significant and have been discussed at various points in this book. They indicate that it is not sufficient to look at folklore as a unique, separate and individual aspect of culture. It clearly interacts with all other aspects of culture and society at all levels and in all ways. At the same time, the folkloric processes underpinning this interaction are a discrete, if not autonomous, strand of culture. Those processes have characteristics, imperatives and meanings of their own. Folklore, or 'the hidden culture', as I have called it elsewhere,[2] can be understood in relation to all these intersecting areas but, finally, needs to be understood on its own terms and for what it can contribute to our understanding of the world — a world we are forever making and unmaking, not only through our actions but also through the fictions that we weave to explain, justify and extend those actions.

CONVENIENT FICTIONS

While the process of delineating the persistence and diffusion of the outlaw hero tradition is necessary and valuable in itself, it does not tell us why the tradition persists in such a stable and coherent form over numerous centuries and continents. The reasons for the extraordinary tenacity of this cultural complex are to be found in the convenience or appropriateness of the tradition and in the meanings and functions of its narrative features. Outlaw heroes are created and perpetuated through the construction of 'convenient fictions'.

A fiction is a story, a sequence of events and variously motivated characters arranged in a usually causal relationship. Such arrangements of characters and events are imaginary. That is, while based on actual or perceived events in the real world, they are conventionally held to be artful untruths about which we temporarily suspend our disbelief, drawn into the story by our identification with, or against, the characters and empathy with the events that constitute the fiction. While such artifices are imaginary, they nevertheless convey deep truths, or lasting values of one kind or another. This is often held to be an important reason for the longevity of folkloric fictions.

Recent approaches to communication forms have tended to show how such supposedly 'factual' genres as news and documentary are equally artificial constructs or fictions, merely presented or 'inflected' as fact. Generally, such analyses of factual texts indicate how the processes of fiction—narrative construction—can be seen operating to produce heroes/heroines, villains/villainesses, various stereotypes of gender, race, class and power, in a manner related to the complex social, economic, political and cultural formations of the industrial capitalist world. The fiction/factual texts and narratives thus produced are seen as both reflections of the ideology of capitalism and, in the more sophisticated formulations, also tend to reinforce that ideology as they circulate through the social formations within a culture. In brief, the point of such analyses is to reveal the means and methods through which cultural texts of all kinds perpetuate ideology and so ensure the continued hegemony of the powerful class(es).

Some analysts, particularly those who have paid attention to popular culture, have argued that, while the purpose of these discourses may be hegemonic, the consumers or 'audiences' of such texts and narratives do not simply 'read' or interpret them in the ideologically appropriate

184

manner. Rather, they read and respond to these texts in a variety of ways, depending on their backgrounds, their beliefs, the context(s) in which they receive the message, and their socio-cultural position.[3] In the most extreme formulations of this view, any text may mean anything to anybody, and no objective interpretation of 'meaning' is possible. There is only a multitude of meanings circulating among millions, even billions, of individuals.

As a mode of analysis, this reduction of cultural and historical experience to 'meaningless meaningfulness' is enervating rather than enlightening. Ethnographic, social psychological and historical studies show that there are commonly agreed meanings operating within culture, and that these meanings are generally articulated, even applied, often symbolically, in the expressions and practices of particular, homogeneous social groups and communities. Even more importantly, at least from a folkloristic perspective, is the fact that groups of human beings articulate and otherwise express agreed meanings in many of the verbal and behavioural activities of everyday life—and in the reversals of the everyday that constitute much festival and ritual activity.[4] Such practices and expressions are not all simply 'ideological' or 'hegemonising', but can also be intentionally oppositional, subversive and/or otherwise antagonistic to the maintenance of the status quo. The complicated truth is that many folkloric activities and expressions are simultaneously hegemonic and oppositional.

Despite these differences of orientation and emphasis, it does seem that there are illuminating insights to be derived from these areas of textual analysis and in the problematic but important relationships between text and context, between fiction and fact, and between the artifice and the actual. The study of the intersections and interrelationships between the folklore of the outlaw hero and the historical actualities of his life is especially useful in relation to questions of this type. The notion of a fiction is therefore a useful concept to apply to the verbal articulations of the outlaw hero tradition, for a number of reasons.

Most obviously, and as this book has demonstrated, such traditions are clearly expressed in story form, whether as ballads or oral prose narratives. These narratives are fictions that are at once 'artful untruths' insofar as they tell a tale that may bear little relevance to 'truth'—yet they are also believed to be the truth, or at least to hold some degree of verisimilitude by those who make and continue these expressions. Finally, the individual elements that go to make up the tradition are themselves stylised fragments of fiction, or motifs. Like any other narrative elements, these can be combined, added, subtracted, altered in details if not essentials, and so used by singers and storytellers to construct an appropriate account of any particular outlaw hero, real or imagined. In this sense, we can apply the term 'morphology', in which the various elements of the outlaw hero tradition form a relatively stable group of connected motifs from which a singer or storyteller is able to select the most appropriate in order to construct a satisfactory narrative. This narrative must be 'appropriate', 'meaningful' or otherwise necessary to the social, political and economic circumstances in which it is created and circulated. It must be convenient.

The notion of 'convenience' must go together with that of fictions in this instance, because stories are made and told and retold for a variety of complex individual and communal reasons. These reasons may not be unique to particular individuals or groups within a society, but may be equally convenient for other, even antagonistic groups. Examples of this process are the persistence of Billy the Kid folklore among Mexican-Americans and the adoption of Ned Kelly as a culture hero by Australian Aborigines. Variants of the same essential fiction about a particular event or personality will circulate within a society, often constructed from the same pool of motifs, though perhaps investing the motifs with a negative rather than a positive value, a type of narrative flexibility recognised and allowed for by Propp in his structural analysis of the folktale.[5] As well, certain motifs may be left out, while others are given a privileged status in order to reflect the prejudices and intentions of the producer of the text and to cater to what he or she believes to be the requirements of the text's intended audience.

So, for example, the essential narrative structure of the Robin Hood legend is that of an unjustly treated man taking to the woods and robbing the rich to give to the poor in a heroic trickster manner, only succumbing to the inevitable at the hands of a treacherous nun or friar, depending on which version of the legend we prefer. Later embellishments, such as Maid Marian, do not significantly alter this basic narrative structure, which may be utilised or interpreted in various ways. The story can be understood as a true tale of historical events and characters, which indeed was how it was presented for many centuries. Or it can be seen as a metaphor for social and economic distress and as a fanciful wish-fulfilment mechanism for the poor. It could be read as a text for political rebellion of a rather more serious kind than whispered resentments. It

The Adventures of Robin Hood. *(© 1938 Turner Entertainment Co. All rights reserved.)*

can also be read as a form of chivalrous romance, in which Robin Hood functions as an ideologically appropriate figure for righting a few wrongs and keeping the peasants in their place while the nobles get on with exploiting them. This indeed, it has been suggested, was how the Robin Hood stories later came to be viewed by the rising British merchant class of the seventeenth century.[6] Later still, but only a short step away, we get the thorough romanticisation of Robin Hood by Sir Walter Scott and a host of other literary workers. This media romanticisation contin- ues throughout the nineteenth century in various kinds of popular lit- erature, including 'penny dreadfuls', and is picked up in the twentieth century by Hollywood and the television industry, for which the story of the outlawed archer has long been especially convenient for generating income.

The Robin Hood narrative, variously inflected, has clearly been appropriate and convenient for some dramatically different social configurations, all of which have interpreted the character and his story (or stories) in quite disparate ways. A similar progress can be charted for the most outstanding of the outlaw hero figures discussed in this book. Just as Robin Hood became a stock character of children's literature, so did Dick Turpin. Glamourised at first for adults in broadsides and chapbooks, then in *Rookwood*, 'The short, dumpy, balding butcher's assistant, horse-thief and robber, renowned for his brutal methods of torture, became a gay blade with magnificent moustachios, a bold and daring highwayman, a gentleman of the road, a protector of the weak and oppressed'[7] in the Victorian 'penny dreadfuls' and the boys' comics that succeeded them until quite recent times. The imperatives that keep particular narratives, such as those of Robin Hood and Dick Turpin, in continual oral and formal circulation for centuries are related to the utility, or convenience of the outlaw hero tradition for various social groups and historical actors. These groups certainly include children, especially males, who have long consumed the sanitised doings of the likes of Turpin, and even Ned Kelly,[8] through reading matter produced explicitly for them. By such means was established a *Boys' Own* environment of knowing in the mainstream popular culture. Through this environment an expectation was created in which the particular modes of criminality associated with highway, bank and train robbery could be invested with some positive, heroic features.

But the most important of the social groups for whom these fictions were convenient were those who generated, sympathised with and supported outlaw heroes. Such groups have, usually with some justification, seen themselves as 'the poor', or the oppressed of some particular political-economic configuration. The conflicts and tensions inherent in such situations eventually throw up an individual or number of individuals who, deliberately or accidentally, rebel violently against their circumstances, infringing the laws controlled by the powerful groups in their society. Once this occurs, a significant sequence of events and tradition is initiated in which the individual is obliged to avoid the clutches of the controlling authorities, leave his usual haunts and companions (other than those who may follow him) and seek a place of safety, such as the hills or the woods, away from the usual byways and highways. Often the individual's infringement of power is taken as serious enough for a formal proscription against him, classically a declaration of outlawry, a legal separation of an individual from the body of the community. In any case, the individual in such circumstances is ideally situated for sympathy and support in accordance with the pre-existent tradition of the outlaw hero. The individual has stepped beyond the bounds of the everyday and, however clumsily, struck a blow against the hated system of oppression, the blow that every other oppressed man and woman would wish to strike. From this point onwards, the actual and the artificial tend to merge, as the case studies of Turpin, James and Kelly indicate.

A second major interested party for whom the tradition is convenient is the outlaw himself and, usually to a lesser extent, the members of his gang. In order to remain at large and survive, the outlawed individual must have a number of things: the sympathy and support of his peers, and money, arms, transport and food. While supporters are generally able and willing to give shelter, information and silence, they are usually not economically able to provide the considerable material means of existence required for a life on the run. The outlaw is therefore forced to rob those who do have these things—the rich or, at least, the richer. Once this begins the outlaw becomes even more of a nuisance to the ruling powers, and resources are committed to capturing him, inevitably bringing the interest of the communication channels of the period and consequent popular notoriety. The status of celebrity villain is inevitably foisted upon the outlaw.

Whether he retains this celebrity and, far more importantly, the approbation of his social group and other groups who identify with his rebellion depends largely upon the outlaw's actions. It is now that the intelligent outlaw must make some crucial decisions about his mode of operation. Not only should he refrain from robbing his own kind—who are probably not worth robbing anyway: he must be seen to be robbing the rich, preferably those members of the rich who can be identified with the oppressors of the outlaw's own group. The Sheriff of Nottingham enforcing King John's unjust taxes and the corrupt clergy (never the church itself) are ideal targets for the medieval outlaw. Rich lawyers, lords and ladies are fair game for the highwayman. The impersonal railroad companies are ideal targets for Jesse James, while that master of public relations, Ned Kelly, goes out of his way to rob the banks that hold the mortgages of his supporters, publicly burning the documents and making grand-sounding speeches about social injustice to his captives. While little, if any, of the proceeds of such robberies may actually find their way to the poor, the spirit, if not the letter, of the outlaw hero creed is more than satisfied. And so the stories and the ballads begin to weave the legend of yet another doomed bandit snatching a few brief months of freedom before the overwhelming resources of the law and the power of those who operate it inevitably capture or kill him.

Before that happens, the outlaw is expected to conform to the traditional code, at least as far as possible in such a situation. The details, the facts, are relatively unimportant, for the stereotype has been established and brought into operation and will obligingly fill in the finer details, if only the outlaw refrains from excessive violence, acts courteously to women, orphans, children and unfortunates, robs the odd bank or railroad and manages to go out stoically or flamboyantly, but in any case, bravely. If any of these matters can be managed with even a modicum of *éclat*, so much the better. When these requirements are met, or seen to be met, reasonably well, the outlaw can be assured of becoming and remaining a hero.

Here the tradition itself has a dynamic of its own that is certainly related to actual events, yet is greater than the combined energy of those events. The cultural stereotype takes over from the historical and provides a framework of narrative, a basis for belief and an impelling power that thrusts the resultant legend of the outlaw through the present and into the future. This motivating intersection of fact and fiction can be seen at its simplest in the statement of one Henry Bliss to the judge at his trial for highway robbery in 1696: 'the poor I fed, the rich likewise I empty sent away',[9] almost a verbatim quotation from one of the Turpin ballads that were published forty-five and more years later. Similar examples of outlaws anxious to assert their status as friends of the poor and upholders of the outlaw hero's moral code are not difficult to find. The bushranger Frank Gardiner wrote to a local newspaper to defend himself against the charge that he had stolen a poor man's boots, as well as his money. Gardiner's letter reveals his familiarity with the tradition of the outlaw hero and of his British historical precedents. In America, the James gang wrote to a newspaper claiming that they acted only within the confines of what has been described here as the outlaw hero tradition. Many other examples have been discussed in the previous pages.

Another important group or segment of society for whom the

fiction of the outlaw hero is especially convenient is the producers of popular or commercial literature, music, film and television. The production of materials for the consumption of 'the masses' has been a constant facet of the outlaw hero tradition. Popular interest in the activities, trials and executions of great criminals has always been immense in Anglophone cultures, and from the earliest days of printing it has provided the publishing industry with a large slice of its bread and butter. Later the closely related entertainment industries of the popular theatre, the magic lantern show, the cinema and television have likewise found the outlaw a particularly valuable stock item. The badman and the bushranger have been the subjects of the country and western ballad industries of both America and Australia. Popular artists like Bob Dylan and the Eagles, among others, have recorded songs and even entire albums dedicated to the myths of John Wesley Hardin (mis-spelled 'Harding' in Dylan's album of the same name) and the Dalton gang. Closely related to these urban transmutations of rural tradition is the rock and roll mythology of the road, in which the performers (and their attendant 'roadies') take on certain inflections of outlawry, usually expressed in various forms of anti- or non-social behaviour such as smashing up (expensive) hotel rooms, drug abuse and alleged acts of colossal, sometimes aberrant, sex. Contemporary fragments of outlawry have also been attached to terrorists, Hell's Angels and similar 'bikie' groups, and even serial killers.

The continuing trade between the tradition and the media—micro as well as mass—can also be seen in other fragmentary continuations of the outlaw hero that persist in modern society. This takes two main forms: the attempts of the press to typecast certain criminals as outlaw hero types; and the relationship of modern mythic figures to the outlaw hero. These can be usefully seen as opposite faces of the same coin.

In Australia there has been a degree of celebration (and self-promotion) in the public profiles of a number of criminal figures. These include the late Darcy Dugan and Ray Denning, both of whom were noted for their defiance of the police and the legal/penal systems. In the United States there has been popular affection for depression criminals such as Bonny and Clyde (Bonny Parker and Clyde Barrow) and Alphonse 'Al' Capone, considerably enhanced by later Hollywood treatments of such figures. These individuals were certainly aware of their popular and media status and, to varying degrees, attempted to project a positive Robin Hood image in their activities and their communications with the press, which was only too pleased to promote the gangsters as celebrities. But Capone, unlike Dillinger and Floyd, perhaps the last of the frontier outlaw heroes, belonged to the developing milieu of the professional urban gangster. Mired in urban and suburban politics, manipulation and violence, such characters were generally unsuitable heirs to the tradition of Robin Hood, Dick Turpin and Jesse James. Missing from their profiles were the essentials of social, economic and political injustice and oppression.

Most recently, this celebration of criminality has reached new heights in the Oliver Stone film *Natural-Born Killers*. In the bizarre events of the O. J. Simpson case, the process perhaps reached its logical conclusion. Instead of criminality conferring celebrity, as had previously been the case, Simpson's celebrity status was fused almost indistinguishably with his alleged criminality. There were serious doubts that the man would be able to obtain a fair trial. In these circumstances, Simpson's criminal heroism might have effectively subverted the very judicial processes he is accused of offending.

While these criminal personalities have attracted or manufactured some elements of the outlaw hero, they are unlikely to join the pantheon of the outlaw hero tradition. The popular images of these individuals also lack a number of the essential attributes of the outlaw hero. They do not represent the interests and the perceived injustices of a supporting socio-economic group, as did Ned Kelly, Jesse James and others. They are not widely perceived as Robin Hood figures, robbing the rich to help the poor. And, most importantly, they do not eschew violence. Indeed, violence is at the heart of their real and alleged activities. For the outlaw hero of tradition, violence is incidental, justifiable, and always regrettable. For the criminals mentioned above, violence is either their way of life or the cause of their celebrity. The outlaw hero of tradition is almost invariably an ordinary man driven to violence by the injustice he and his supporters have suffered.

The other side of the coin from those criminals who are celebrated are those celebrities whose actions are—necessarily, if fantastically— outside the law. Appearing originally in the genre of the comic book, the superheroes have survived, multiplied and spun off into a variety of marketing media. The Phantom, Superman, Green Lantern, Spiderman, Batman, Captain America, to name only a few, share some traits with the heroes of myth and of folklore. Many of these characters have the ability to disguise and shape-shift, to perform superhuman feats and to avoid danger or, trickster-like, to escape from their (evil) captors. But while these heroes operate outside the law, their actions are always ultimately in harmony with the law and the currently dominant values of civil society and morality. The 'outlawry' of the superheroes is therefore a type of nonconformism rather than a radical challenge to the status quo which, finally, these comic-book characters support.

It is not only the supporters and exploiters of outlaws who find the traditional fictions convenient. The antagonists of the outlaw hero, the forces of authority and oppression, may also utilise the outlaw for their own ends. It may be politically appropriate for these forces to manipulate elements of the tradition to portray the outlaw in a convenient light, either to the outlaw's supporters or to the wider public. The most commonly utilised element of the tradition by such forces is the power and violence of the outlaw hero. The police or other representatives of the establishment, in their haste to establish the criminality of the outlaw and so defuse any potentially serious political and destabilising effect, represent him as a particularly violent, unprincipled type. This was a popular ploy in Australia, where bushranging was viewed as a potentially serious threat to a fragile civil society. The bushranger Daniel 'Mad Dog' Morgan was so represented in the 1860s by the police and the popular media, even though Morgan himself was considered by those of his own community to be 'the traveller's friend' and an appropriate type for outlaw balladry. The effectiveness of such propaganda was well displayed after Morgan was shot at Peechelba station in 1865, when police removed his beard, facial skin and, according to some accounts, his scrotum, to make tobacco pouches. Here a human had effectively been reduced to the status of the hunted wolf in the minds of his pursuers, and so treated.

Similar processes have been at work in the representation of Billy the Kid, apparently the least deserving of individuals to be selected for heroisation, yet one who is persistently made an outlaw hero. The political and economic rivalries in which Billy the Kid was enmeshed produced continuingly contradictory images of him as murdering scum and outlaw hero. The tensions of this ambivalent image have never been resolved. Rather, they have been happily exploited by film-makers and other media producers who, down to *Young Guns 2*, continue to be fascinated by the Kid's duality.[10] While the time and trouble involved in putting down bandit outbreaks is a nuisance to the authorities, their end does allow a theatrical display of the power of the state, either through the final overpowering of the outlaws by police and sometimes the armed forces, or in the trial and execution of the outlaw. The case of Ned Kelly provided an ideal excuse for the public parade of such official power in 1880.

The overwhelmingly male nature of the Anglophone outlaw tradition[11] is also explicable as a specific manifestation of one of the largest convenient fictions of all. The cultural space which the outlaw inhabits is clearly designated 'men only', whether that space be in fiction or in fact. While there have been one or two real 'female highwaymen',[12] a few fictional concoctions in broadside ballads, and women such as Annie Oakley and Belle Starr in the traditions of the American west, these women and their legendry are not part of the outlaw hero tradition outlined here. Like the female cabin boy and the female soldier, these figures belong to a tradition other than that of the outlaw hero. They are women in drag. The intrigue of their stories is that they dress as men and adopt male roles, transgressing gender boundaries rather than any very serious boundaries of law and order. They are out of gender rather than out of law.

It seems that the patriarchal structure of Anglophone culture is as effective outside the law as within the law. When women do appear in outlaw traditions, they are definitely cast in supporting roles: Maid Marian provides assistance and succour to Robin Hood; Billy the Kid has a Mexican sweetheart; Ned Kelly's younger sister, Kate, assists him and his gang by bringing food, ammunition and information and by throwing the police off the gang's tracks. These are all subsidiary roles, revolving around and supportive of the outlaw hero. The powerful cultural spaces allowed for women criminals in western folk and popular discourses are apparently restricted to those of the feared abomination (axe-murderer Lizzie Borden), the witch (Lindy Chamberlain) and the temptress (any number of female figures, beginning with Eve).

VIRTUAL OUTLAWS ON THE POSTMODERN FRONTIER

Is the outlaw hero tradition a thing of the past, simply a means of better understanding certain historical events and processes? It seems not. Even on the frontier of postmodernism, the Internet, the ancient imperatives of resistance and power can be seen in action. While these struggles occur in the as-yet sparsely peopled world of cyberspace, they are rapidly becoming 'real' as different interest groups compete for access, control or simply use of this new frontier. Given these circumstances, we are perhaps unsurprised to see the outlaw hero tradition assert itself yet again, the old problems in another new world.

Motifs of the outlaw hero tradition have accreted around computer hackers like Phiber Optik (Mark Abene), a young American hacker hero, referred to as 'the Robin Hood of cyberspace' and 'a digital Robin Hood'.[13] The rapidly proliferating magazines and other media that cover the Internet use language like 'Internet bandits' and 'hardcore hacker heroes'. There is a compelling intertextuality between the notion of 'highway robbery', the standard operation of the outlaw, and the possibilities for individual freedom and defiance of authority along the 'information superhighway'. Well-defined groups of mostly young males, it seems, who do travel this virtual highway in cyberspace also espouse codes not unlike those followed by outlaw heroes. In hacker culture, it is claimed, the computer systems of banks, corporations, NASA, the Pentagon and other defence and scientific systems around the globe are penetrated and 'robbed'. Hacker groups claim they are not doing this for themselves. Apart from the thrill of simply being able to crack security provisions, hackers have typically simply thrown the information obtained to anyone else who cruises the Internet. In this sense, their activities may be seen as noble cyber-robbery, taking from the information-rich and redistributing the proceeds among the information-poor. Importantly, the very 'virtuality' of their crimes removes any necessity for violence. No 'person' gets hurt, only the impersonal, abstract equivalents of the frontier railroad and the colonial bank, the multinational corporation, the global communications network, NASA, the Pentagon . . .

Such romanticism has, not surprisingly, claimed the attention of the global mass media, just as the activities of Turpin, Kelly, James and their peers claimed the attention of the media of their times. With an ease born of long practice and superficial inquiry, the press has deployed the rhetoric of outlawry in its treatment of Kevin Mitnick, apparently the world's most wanted computer hacker, who began his illegal deeds along the information superhighway at a tender age when he broke into the United States air defence system. Since then Mitnick's obsessively illegal cyberspace activities have made him 'a legendary outlaw on the computer frontier'.[14] After a gaol term and breaking parole, this post-modern cyberpunk was recaptured in February 1995. His picture, looking remarkably like that of a terrorist, was published in the papers with the caption 'Mitnick . . . legendary outlaw'. An article in *Time* continued to cast Mitnick in the role of modern outlaw—single-parent upbringing, youthful crimes, his sense of humour and trickster-like pranks such as overriding the microphones at fast-food driveways so that Mitnick could berate startled customers for eating junk food. Like the outlaw hero of tradition, Mitnick was elusive and disdainful of the forces of authority and was only caught by the FBI in 1988 when betrayed by a trusted friend. The *Time* article even made the specific American outlaw connection, describing Mitnick's eventual capture through the superior computer skills of Tsutomu Shimomura as 'Shimomura, playing Pat Garrett to Mitnick's Billy the Kid'.[15]

In the cases of Abene and Mitnick, the media have manipulated selected motifs of the outlaw hero tradition to suit their own ends and what they imagine, possibly accurately, to be the ends of those who consume their products. But with Mitnick and other Internet outlaws we may be witnessing more than a convenient media fiction. Instead we are watching the emergence of the latest redaction of the outlaw hero, this time in cyberspace. The Internet belongs to no-one. It also belongs to everyone. It is a global electronic commons, a virtual common land on which those with access have 'squatted' wherever and whenever their various interests and needs have dictated. Like the commons, the Internet is free, or at least relatively cheap to use. Like the wild spaces that have always sheltered outlaw heroes, the Internet has been beyond the clutches of authority. In the anarchy of cyberspace, the Internet community has evolved its own rules and regulations, its own moral and ethical code, just as all social groups have done. These rules have been 'policed' by the members of the group themselves rather than by any outside authority. The Internet is the first postmodern frontier.

As with the frontiers of the New World, conflicting interests have ridden largely unchecked across the unfenced expanses of the virtual plains and bush. But in 1993–94, the phenomenal growth of the Internet sparked by the home computer revolution had two important consequences. Firstly, it attracted the interest of commercial parties wishing to exploit its potential for advertising, shopping and a host of other fee-for services. Exactly the same process occurred in Britain during the seventeenth to the nineteenth centuries with the enclosure and related expropriations of common land and rights by agrarian capitalists, canal, tollway and railway companies. As with the commons of Britain, the global electronic commons has become an opportunity to be grasped and is currently being commercialised with great speed.

The second consequence of the Internet explosion has been the concern of governments and their agencies about the potential of the network for all sorts of potentially subversive activities, ranging from the relatively minor bizarre sex and other weird newsgroups up to and including the hacking of banks, corporations, and ultimately national security and defence systems. Concerns for economic and political destabilisation and a related fear of social disorder on a global scale (if only in virtual reality) have modern governments reacting in ways similar to their predecessors in seventeenth-century Britain and in nineteenth-century America and Australia. The Internet has become a threat, a problem, a site of political, social and economic struggle. As with the earlier sites of struggle outlined in this book, these circumstances too have begun to throw up individuals whose actions and attitudes seem appropriate for the processes of folklore and popular culture to represent as outlaw heroes. Unlike the space through which they ride, people such as Mitnick are real, not 'virtual'. Their actions, justifiably or not, have the old Robin Hood aura of stealing and redistributing wealth, in this case knowledge-wealth to other users of the net, who are likewise real, not virtual, people. The postmodern outlaw hero's weapons may be microprocessors rather than guns, knowledge rather than violence. His booty may be information rather than gold. But he—and it continues to be 'he'—still arises from the age-old struggle between those who have and those who have not. Nothing much has really changed.

OUTSIDE THE LAW–INSIDE THE LORE

Turpin, James, Brennan, Kelly and others were not celebrated because they were criminals and robbers. There were and are any number of those about. These outlaws were celebrated because they were seen, rightly or wrongly, to embody a spirit of defiance and protest, a symbolic striking back of the poor and dispossessed against those perceived as their oppressors. The criminality of the outlaw hero has a definite political dimension, even if this is crudely formed and poorly, if at all, articulated—except in their folklore. Even if the outlaw heroes did not themselves espouse political views or ends, their activities were viewed in that light by their own and other communities, who saw the outlaw's individual rebellion as symbolic of their own desires and as a vicarious blow against their oppressors. And, given the nature of the balance between the law and the lore, between the official and the unofficial, any activities that presumed to set the informal imperatives of lore over those of the law inevitably had a political significance, striking as they did against the equilibrium of the social order.

Those who used the law as a weapon of oppression also perceived the outlaw hero's activities in a political light. The outlaw was a threat not simply to life and property but to the official structures of power, wealth and the mechanisms for ensuring that these stayed in the hands of those who already possessed them. This explains the extraordinary efforts and expenses often made to capture or kill certain outlaw figures, including Turpin, James and Ned Kelly, involving large rewards, the passage of special legislation and the mobilisation of large numbers of coercive state apparatuses—the police, and, in Ned Kelly's case, even the army, together with all the resources required to sustain such forces.

In tracing the tradition of the outlaw hero in Britain, America and Australia, we see the intersection of the universal and the local, the general and the specific, the law and justice, of divergent perceptions of actuality, of 'the rich' and 'the poor', of the powerful and the powerless. These are the fundamental issues at the base of every society and inevitably are the focus for tension and conflict. Mostly such tensions are kept beneath the surface, expressed in mutters, whispers, jokes and gossip, and kept more or less in check by the machinery of law and order and coercion or cajoling by those groups who control that machinery. But in some circumstances discontent may become so great, oppression so unbearable, or ineptitude and corruption within the legal system so blatant, that the outlaw hero arises and his tradition is invoked. As we have seen, rarely is such a hero a deliberate figure of political rebellion. More usually, local circumstances throw up a reasonably appropriate male lawbreaker and the wider web of economic and political problems lead to his acceptance and presentation as a figure of revenge, rebellion and protest. It is these aspects of the outlaw that are most consistently expressed in the tradition of the outlaw hero, while the criminality and assumed romance of his activities form the basis of his popular image as projected in and through the mass media. Of course, the folkloric and the popular are symbiotic, autonomous yet interacting, constituting a social and cultural process that effectively acts as a social regulator, a force for mediating conflict within society, a cultural milieu of last resort upon which social groups fall back when the formal regulatory modes fail, in their perception, to deliver a just share of resources, wealth and power. The outlaw hero tradition, and by extension other folkloric

198

traditions, can be understood as an alternative set of values and beliefs which groups in crisis and in conflict with the legitimate order and its power are able to fall back upon as a framework for moral resistance.

This unofficial order is related to ancient notions of common law and of customary rights and privileges. Most, if not all, of these have long since been eroded by the official apparatus of statute law, legislation and the machinations of the powerful, but they persist in folklore as cherished rights and beliefs about the ultimate communality of nature, especially of wild food sources, domesticated food resources and the land that, beneath everything, supports all these necessities of life.[16] We continually encounter outlaw heroes in the company of poachers, smugglers and others who inhabit the grey zone of resistance between the official and the unofficial, between law and lore. There is a persistent thread twining the archetypal commons of Robin Hood's 'greenwood' to the frontier outlaw heroes and those anonymous figures whose nominally criminal activities also embodied social and political protest. One day in early August 1242, English poachers slew a buck and mounted its head on a stake, with its dead mouth snarling at the sun, 'in great contempt of the King and his foresters'.[17] Wat Tyler's doomed grievance in 1381 was that the poor and hungry were forbidden to hunt the food the rich could take at will. Tyler and his peasant insurrectionaries also wanted the sentence of outlawry struck from the statutes.[18] In the eighteenth century, the poachers of Windsor and Waltham Forests were directly and intimately connected with the highwaymen of the period, including Dick Turpin, whose varied criminal career also involved smuggling. Australia's Ned Kelly began stealing cattle and horses ('duffing') from a very early age, in an area where livestock roaming free was considered common property. Billy the Kid's noted shootouts blazed in the context of a 'range war', essentially a dispute over which power faction would control access to and use of the American commons, the open range.[19] The same struggle is now taking place on the electronic commons of the Internet.

One of the numerous consistencies between highwaymen, badmen and bushrangers is the extent to which notions of common law, natural justice and customary rights recur as justifications and explanation for their outlawry. This is not only a matter of stereotype or cliché, either on the part of the outlaws themselves or their defenders. It is a matter of belief, of assumption that when the legally ordained system of control, order and distribution of resources breaks down or is subverted in some way, that recourse to a more fundamental law or lore is not only sensible but justified and valid. The changes to the means and modes of production that exacerbated highway robbery in eighteenth-century Britain were a direct result of capitalist enclosure of commons and encroachments on previously existing rights, such as the right of way, brazenly commercialised by private turnpikes and tollgates.[20] In such circumstances of expropriation, the individual who 'goes outside the law', or 'takes the law into his own hands', is likely to be viewed in heroic light by those who feel similarly deprived or threatened. It then becomes crucial that the outlaw maintain his heroic status in the eyes of his supporters by attempting to adhere to a set of moral guidelines.

This comparative study of the outlaw legend has highlighted instances and practices in which alternative forms of law have been instituted. These include the rule of the mob in eighteenth-century England, the role of vigilantism in America, and the outbreaks of outlawry across all three national groupings. These are all species of 'rough justice' that have parallels in the folkloric institution known in English as 'rough music' or, more generically, by the French term 'charivari'.[21] A charivari is a relatively spontaneous public demonstration of communal dissatisfaction. It takes many forms, but its aims are generally to identify wrongdoers and, often, to see that 'justice is done' in situations where it is thought that the formal judicial institutions of the police or the courts have ignored justice, failed it, or have simply got it wrong. Charivari may result in the expulsion of individuals from a community and/or their marking in some way, as in the American frontier custom of 'tar and feathering'. Whatever the means applied, the motivation for a charivari and its ends remain essentially similar in Anglophone tradition. Charivari is intimately associated with folkloric notions of what is 'right', regardless of statute law. It belongs to the same unspoken constellation of 'commonsense' that motivated attitudes towards customary rights, such as occupational perquisites, the taking of the flora and fauna of the commons, and access to common land itself. In many ways, outlaw heroes are ongoing forms of charivari. They are the vicarious representatives of their communities, avenging wrongs and putting the customary world, however briefly and bloodily, back in order by reasserting 'the rightness' of the lore rather than the 'justice' of the law.

This is the ultimate function and meaning of the outlaw hero tradition—the maintenance outside the law of another, alternative law that is considered, for the moment at least, to be a more likely means of attaining 'true justice' than the formally sanctioned legal system that supposedly is in operation for the good of all. It is not surprising that outlaw heroes arise in circumstances where formal law and order is weak, or is blatantly subverted or perverted by one group at the expense of others. The history of Anglophone social bandits supports this view, while the folklore of the outlaw hero provides the knowledge, the framework of appropriate action and the moral justification for certain kinds of robbery and justified violence.

In 1908, more than two centuries after William Nevison 'suffered' at Tyburn, Joseph Taylor sang this highwayman's obscure life and death into Percy Grainger's primitive cylinder phonograph.[22] The final terse lines of Nevison's ballad, addressed to the judges of the court, can stand for all the outlaw heroes of history and legend:

> I have never robbed no man of tuppence,
>   And I've never done murder nor killed,
> Though guilty I've been all my lifetime,
>   So, gentlemen, do as you please.

Notes

Preface

1 Manifold to Parker, c. 1955? in A. L. Lloyd Collection, Goldsmith's College Library, London, in binder titled 'Aust. Song Notes, Correspondence, etc.'.

Chapter 1   The Outlaw Legend

1 Some well-known hero studies include O. Rank, *The Myth of the Birth of the Hero*, New York, 1914; Lord Raglan, *The Hero: A Study in Tradition, Myth and Drama*, London, 1936; J. Campbell, *The Hero With A Thousand Faces*, Princeton, 1968; S. Hook, *The Hero in History*, London, 1945; B. Poli, 'The Hero in France and America', *Journal of American Studies* 2: 2, 1968; O. Klapp, 'The Folk Hero', *Journal of American Folklore* 62, 1949. Some studies related particularly to outlaw heroes include R. Pike, 'The Reality and Legend of the Spanish Bandit Diego Corrientes', *Folklore* 99: ii, 1988; A. Paredes, *With His Pistol in His Hand: A Border Ballad and its Hero*, Austin, TX, (1958) 1990; E. Stenbock-Fermor, 'The Story of Van'ka Kain', in A. Lord (ed.), *Slavic Folklore: A Symposium*, Philadelphia, 1956; Kent L. Steckmesser, 'Robin Hood and the American Outlaw', *Journal of American Folklore* 79, 1966; W. E. Simeone, 'Robin Hood and Some Other American Outlaws', *Journal of American Folklore* 71, 1958; P. Butterss, 'Bold Jack Donahue and the Irish Outlaw Tradition', *Australian Folklore* 3, 1989; G. Seal, *The Highwayman Tradition in Australia*, Folklore Occasional Paper 9, Sydney, 1977; G. Seal, *Ned Kelly in Popular Tradition*, Melbourne, 1980; J. W. Roberts, '"Railroad Bill" and the American Outlaw Tradition', *Western Folklore* 40, 1981; R. Meyer, 'The Outlaw: A Distinctive American Folktype', *Journal of the Folklore Institute* 17, 1980; and P. Kooistra, *Criminals as Heroes: Structure, Power and Identity*, Bowling Green, 1989. See also R. Cavendish (ed.), *Legends of the World*, London, 1982, for a sample of folk outlaw hero figures from many cultures.

2 E. Hobsbawm, *Bandits*, London, 1969. See also his *Primitive Rebels*, Manchester, 1963.

3 A. Blok, 'The Peasant and the Brigand: Social Banditry Reconsidered', *Comparative Studies in Society and History* 1: 4, September 1972, and Hobsbawm's response in the same issue; P. O'Malley, 'Social Bandits, Modern Capitalism and the Traditional Peasantry', *Journal of Peasant Studies* 6: 4 1979; P. O'Malley, 'Class Conflict, Land and Social Banditry: Bushranging in Nineteenth Century Australia', *Social Problems* 26: 3, 1979.

4 See Roberts, '"Railroad Bill"'; Simeone, 'Robin Hood'; Steckmesser, 'Robin Hood'; Paredes, *With His Pistol in His Hand*; and R. Meyer, 'The Outlaw'.

5 R. B. Dobson and J. Taylor, *Rymes of Robin Hood: An Introduction to the English Outlaw* (1976), 2nd rev. edn. Gloucester, 1989; R. H. Hilton, 'The Origins of Robin Hood', *Past and Present* 14, 1958; J. Holt, 'The Origins and the Audience of the Ballads of Robin Hood', *Past and Present* 18, 1960; M. Keen, 'Robin Hood: A Peasant Hero', *History Today*, October 1958; M. Keen, *The Outlaws of Medieval Legend*, London, 1961; J. R. Maddicott, 'The Birth and Setting of the Ballads of Robin Hood', *English Historical Review* 93, 1978; J. Ritson, *Robin Hood*, 1795; and A. Stapleton, *Robin Hood: The Question of His Existence*, 1899. On the continued importance of Robin Hood in popular literature, see B. Capp, 'Popular Literature', in B. Reay (ed.), *Popular Culture in Seventeenth Century England* (1985), London, 1988.

6 The *Gest of Robyn Hode*, also 'A True Tale of Robin Hood'. See Dean Alan Hoffman, 'The Minstrelsy of the Greenwood: The Medieval English Outlaw Ballad in Literary and Social History', unpublished PhD dissertation, University of California, Riverside, 1987; and Dobson and Taylor, *Rymes of Robin Hood*.

7 Variously known as 'Jesse James' or 'The Ballad of Jesse James', some representative texts being in M. Larkin, *The Singing Cowboy*, New York, 1931, and reprinted in B. Botkin (ed.), *A Treasury of American Folklore*, New York, 1944, p. 108. Other versions of this extremely widespread song are noted in H. Belden and A. Hudson (eds), *Folk Ballads from North Carolina* (vol. 2 of *The Frank C. Brown Collection of North Carolina Folklore*, 7 vols), Durham, NC, 1952, pp. 557–62. They give ten versions plus references to additional variants. There are at least two other distinctive songs about James that also treat the badman in outlaw hero terms, in H. Belden (ed.), *Ballads and Songs Collected by the Missouri Folklore Society*, Columbia, MO, 1940, pp. 403–4. See also H. H. Kruse, 'Myth in the Making: The James Brothers at Northfield, Minnesota, and the Dime Novel', *Journal of Popular Culture* 10: 2, 1976.

8 R. White, 'Outlaw Gangs of the Middle Border', *Western Historical Quarterly* 12: 4, 1981.

9 D. J. Shiel, *Ben Hall: Bushranger*, St Lucia, Qld, 1983; J. McQuilton, *The Kelly Outbreak: The Geographical Dimension of Social Banditry*, Melbourne, 1979.

10 'Bold Ben Hall', in J. Bradshaw, *The Only True Account of Ned Kelly, Frank Gardiner, Ben Hall and Morgan*, Sydney, 1911.

11 Quoted, together with a local variant, in S. Williams, *A Ghost called Thunderbolt*, Woden, ACT, 1987, p. 162.

12 The outlaw hero as a friend of the poor is the most frequent and consistent motif in song and narrative texts, occurring in almost all of the fifty or so texts upon which this study is based.

13 'My Name is Edward Kelly', collected from Cyril Duncan by W. Fahey and in G. Seal, *Ned Kelly in Popular Tradition*, Melbourne, 1980.

14 'Song of Billy the Kid' in J. Lomax and A. Lomax, *American Ballads and Folk Songs*, New York, 1934, pp. 137–8, for notes on the legendry of Bonney, including the fact that he was driven to crime, was a friend to the poor, and lived on after his death until at least 1926. See also Kent L. Steckmesser, *The Western Hero in History and Legend*, Norman, OK, 1965; L. Hollon, *Frontier Violence: Another Look*, New York, 1974; and J. C. Dykes, *Billy the Kid: The Bibliography of a Legend*, Norman, OK, 1952.

15 White, 'Outlaw Gangs'; and W. A. Settle jnr, *Jesse James Was His Name, or, fact and fiction concerning the careers of the notorious James brothers of Missouri*, Columbia, MO, 1966. James had been a member of the irregular Confederate guerilla force under the command of William Clarke Quantrill (1837–65) formally outlawed by the Union in 1862 and himself treated as an outlaw hero; see the song 'Quantrell' [*sic*] in R. Lingenfelter *et al.* (eds), *Songs of the American West*, Los Angeles, 1968, pp. 314–15, taken from C. Finger, *Frontier Ballads*, 1927, and noting further variants. See also Belden, *Ballads and Songs*, pp. 353–4, for further Quantrill folklore.

16 Representative texts of 'The Highwayman Outwitted' in *Journal of the Folk Song Society* 1, 1899–1904, p. 236, collected by Kidson from Mrs Thompson of Knaresborough; 'The Yorkshire Farmer' in F. Kidson, *A Garland of English Folk Songs*, London, 1926, pp. 141–2; 'The Yorkshire Bite' and 'Two Jolly Butchers', in A. Williams, *Folk Songs of the Upper Thames*, London, 1923, pp. 253–4, 275–6. See also ch. 2.

17 See the narrative concerning the Fermanagh outlaw, 'Black Francis', told by Hugh Nolan, in H. Glassie (ed.), *Irish Folk History: Texts from the North*, Philadelphia, 1982, p. 48.

18 The story is told of Brennan (see J. Healy, *Ballads from the Pubs of Ireland*, Dublin (1965), 1976, p. 120; H. Glassie, *Irish Folk Tales*, New York, 1985, for a narrative collected from Thomas O'Riordan, Cork, by Sean O'Sullivan in 1934), Turpin, Sam Bass, Jesse James and other outlaw heroes.

19 'Bold Nevison', collected from Mr J. Taylor, Brigg, Lincs by Percy Grainger,

1908. Transcribed from LP disk *Unto Brigg Fair*, Leader LEA4050-B, 1972.

20 Turpin's violence is discussed in C. Hibbert, *The Roots of Evil: A Social History of Crime and Punishment* (1963), Westport, CT, 1978; and C. Hibbert, *Highwaymen*, London, 1967. See also C. Winslow, 'Sussex Smugglers', in D. Hay *et al.* (eds), *Albion's Fatal Tree: Crime and Society in Eighteenth Century England*, London, 1975, for references to Turpin's pre-highwayman activities as smuggler and housebreaker and for the links between such activities as smuggling, poaching and social protest. Also relevant are many of the other articles in the same book. For a different view of the 'social' nature of crimes of this type, see F. McLynn, *Crime and Punishment in Eighteenth Century England*, Oxford, 1991, particularly ch. 10. A comprehensive study of Turpin's activities, together with some discussion of Turpin balladry, is D. Barlow, *Dick Turpin and the Gregory Gang*, London, 1973.

21 'Stringybark Creek', a version collected by Rev. Dr P. Jones and given in C. Cave *et al.* (eds), *Ned Kelly: Man and Myth*, Sydney, 1968.

22 Most versions of 'The Wild Colonial Boy' contain these lines or variants.

23 'My Name is Edward Kelly'; see ch. 6.

24 Quoted in P. Linebaugh, *The London Hanged: Crime and Civil Society in the Eighteenth Century*, New York, 1992, p. 187.

25 Healy, *Ballads from the Pubs of Ireland*. Also the songs 'Willie Brennan' and 'Captain Grant'.

26 P. Radin, *The Trickster: A Study in American Indian Mythology*, New York, 1956; A. Harrison, *The Irish Trickster*, Sheffield, 1988.

27 On James gang disguise and on Jesse James folklore in general, see R. Dorson, *American Folklore*, Chicago, 1960, pp. 236–43; Settle, *Jesse James*; and Steckmesser, *The Western Hero*.

28 See McQuilton, *The Kelly Outbreak*, and Seal, *Ned Kelly*.

29 'Jesse James' and common to most versions.

30 'The Death of Ben Hall', apparently appearing first in *Smith's Weekly*, 24 September 1924, credited to Will Ogilvie. See H. Anderson, 'On the Track with "Bill Bowyang"', *Australian Folklore* 6, 1991. Also a version collected from Sally Sloane in J. Meredith and H. Anderson (eds), *Folksongs of Australia*, Sydney, 1967.

31 'Frank Gardiner'. See ch. 5.

32 See Steckmesser, *The Western Hero*.

33 See Seal, *Ned Kelly*.

34 Meredith and Anderson (eds), *Folksongs of Australia*, vol. 1, p. 165.

35 'Black Francis', in Glassie (ed.), *Irish Folk History*, p. 51.

36 On Sam Bass and his treasure see F. J. Dobie, *Tales of Old-Time Texas* (1928), London, 1959, p. 89ff. Also C. L. Martin, *A Sketch of Sam Bass, the Bandit*, 1880; J. B. Gillett, *Six Years With the Texas Rangers*, 1925.

R. Lingenfelter *et al.* (eds), *Songs of the American West*, print a Sam Bass ballad on pp. 316–17, noting numerous variants. See also Belden, *Ballads and Songs*, pp. 399–400; and C. Sandburg, *The American Songbag*, New York, 1927, pp. 422–3.

37 See B. Beatty, *A Treasury of Australian Folk Tales and Traditions*, Sydney, 1960, p. 62ff. for hidden loot traditions of Gardiner, Hall and Thunderbolt. Also K. Byron, *Lost Treasures in Australia and New Zealand*, Sydney, 1964, pp. 99–112, 119–124.

38 Seal, *Ned Kelly*.

39 Shiel, *Ben Hall*; Seal, *The Highwayman Tradition*.

40 On medieval outlaws, see the above references to Robin Hood and outlaws, and J. Bellamy, *Crime and Public Order in England in the Later Middle Ages*, London, 1973.

41 On law and order on American and Australian frontiers, see Steckmesser, *The Western Hero*, ch. 4 and elsewhere; Hollon, *Frontier Violence*; R. M. Brown, *Strain of Violence: Historical Studies of American Violence*, Oxford, 1975; H. Graham, and T. Gurr (eds), *Violence in America: Historical and Comparative Perspectives* (rev. edn), Beverly Hills and London, 1979. Also relevant is J. Greenway, *The Last Frontier: A Study of the Development of the Last Frontiers of America and Australia*, London, 1972.

42 See ch. 5 for a full discussion of this point.

43 It is worth noting that individuals with strong repertoires of outlaw hero traditions in America and Australia often claim to be related in some way to the outlaw. This is true of one of Dorson's informants (*op. cit.*, p. 243) and Sally Sloane in Australia (Meredith and Anderson (eds), *Folksongs of Australia*), for instance.

44 Meyer, 'The Outlaw', p. 113.

45 P. O'Farrell, *The Irish in Australia*, Sydney, 1987; W. Wannan, *The Wearing of the Green: The Lore, Literature, Legends and Balladry of the Irish in Australia*, London, 1968; R. Reece, 'Ned Kelly and the Irish Connection', in C. Bridge (ed.), *New Directions in Australian History*, London, 1990.

46 White, 'Outlaw Gangs'; Steckmesser, *The Western Hero*.

47 See Steckmesser, *The Western Hero*, on Billy the Kid. See also ch. 5 for the adoption of Ned Kelly by some Australian indigenous peoples, a similar process.

48 Steckmesser, *The Western Hero*; Settle, *Jesse James*.

49 Seal, *Ned Kelly*; see also ch. 5.

50 G. Seal, 'Narrative Structure and Cultural Function in the Highwayman Tradition', paper presented to the American Folklore Society Centennial meeting, October 1989. Also related to this argument is G. Seal, 'Tradition and Protest in Nineteenth Century England and Wales', *Folklore* 100: 2, 1988.

Chapter 2   Outlaws of Myth

1 On the development of the medieval outlaw tradition see J. de Lange, *The Relation and Development of English and Icelandic Outlaw-Traditions*, Haarlem, 1935.

2 There is some controversy about the date of 'The Geste's' composition. It could be as early as c. 1400 or as late as the 1460s; see S. Knight, *Robin Hood: A Complete Study of the English Outlaw*, London, 1994, pp. 46–8.

3 J. Bellamy, *Crime and Public Order in England in the Later Middle Ages*, London, 1973, p. 70. See also F. J. Child, *The English and Scottish Popular Ballads*, 5 vols, 1882–1908, New York, 1965.

4 Knight, *Robin Hood*, p. 108, citing documents of the King's Bench, 1441.

5 Knight, *Robin Hood*, pp. 108–9 and p. x.

6 Child, *Popular Ballads*, vol 3, p. 31. Walter Bower's extension of the *Scotichronon*, c. 1441, describes Robin Hood as a popular hero.

7 'A True Tale of Robin Hood', from Child, *Popular Ballads*, vol. 3. no. 154, pp. 227–33, verses 19–21, 51–2, 107. Also relevant here is the discussion of Robin Hood balladry in W. Chappell, *Popular Music of the Olden Time* (1859), 2 vols, New York, 1965, vol. 2, pp. 387–90.

8 Child, *Popular Ballads*, vol. 3, p. 213.

9 Child, *Popular Ballads*, vol. 3, pp. 42–3.

10 The essential recent works are M. Keen, *The Outlaws of Medieval Legend*, London, 1961; J. R. Maddicot, 'The Birth and Setting of the Ballads of Robin Hood', *English Historical Review* 93, 1978; R. B. Dobson and J. Taylor, *Rymes of Robin Hood: An Introduction to the English Outlaw*, (1976) 2nd rev. edn, Gloucester, 1989; and, most recently, Knight, *Robin Hood*. However, Robin Hood has attracted serious consideration for centuries, see J. Ritson, *Robin Hood*, 1795; A. Stapleton, *Robin Hood: The Question of His Existence*, 1899; and J. M. Gutch, *A Lytell Geste of Robin Hood*, 2 vols, London, 1847, for some examples. Comprehensive bibliographies appear in Dobson and Taylor and in Knight.

11 Dobson and Taylor, *Rymes of Robin Hood*.

12 'Bold Robin Hood', in A. Williams, *Folk Songs of the Upper Thames*, London, 1923, p. 237.

13 Knight, *Robin Hood*, p. 58 and elsewhere.

14 'Robin Hood and Little John', in Williams, *Folk Songs of the Upper Thames*, p. 296.

15 A. Lloyd, *Folksong in England*, London, 1967, p. 149.

16 For some representative oral examples of Robin Hood songs, see F. Purslow, (ed.), *The Wanton Seed: More English Folk Songs from the Hammond and Gardiner Mss*, London, 1968, p. 97 ('Robin Hood and the Tanner', a composite based on two versions collected in Hampshire by Gardiner in 1905 and 1908); R. Vaughan Williams and A. Lloyd (eds), *The Penguin Book of*

English Folk Songs, 1959, p. 88 ('Robin Hood and the Pedlar', collected by Vaughan Williams from Mr Verrall, Horsham, Sussex in 1906). Lucy Broadwood published a version of the same song collected by her in 1893 in her *English Traditional Songs and Carols*, London, 1908, pp. 4–5. Other versions were being sung in Essex and Yorkshire at the same period, and Sharp collected some Robin Hood songs in southern England. See also Chappell, *Popular Music of the Olden Time*, pp. 307ff.; and C. Simpson, *The British Broadside Ballad and its Music*, New Brunswick, 1966, pp. 606–11.

17 L. Shepard, *The History of Street Literature*, Newton Abbot, 1973, Appendix. Robin Hood ballads were a staple of the broadside catalogues well into the nineteenth century. See also V. Neuberg, *Popular Literature: A History and Guide*, Harmondsworth, 1977, pp. 51–2, for the outlaw's continued popularity in print.

18 Knight, *Robin Hood*.

19 The provenance of Robin Hood ballads in folklore is problematic. Despite an abundance of texts, there is little evidence that they were widely sung, either during the period of their composition or after. On this point see Lloyd, *Folksong in England*, p. 149; Knight, *Robin Hood*, p. 49; and B. Bronson, *The Traditional Tunes of the Child Ballads*, 1966, vol. 3, pp. 13–14. None of this absence of melody would preclude the ballads being popularly recited, of course, as they appear to be in the earliest literary reference by Langland, who writes of 'rymes of Robyn hood'. Nor is there any need to assume a single 'audience' for the ballads. In some contexts they may have been sung, in some recited, in yet others read.

20 There are a number of other songs from the tradition that deal with non-historical aspects, such as 'Johnny Troy' and 'My Bonny Black Bess', though these are discussed elsewhere.

21 A version of this song was collected in Holne, 1890, with no outlaw hero characteristics at all. G. Hitchcock (ed.), *Folksongs of the West Country*, London, 1974 (the Sabine Baring-Gould MS collection), pp. 56–7. This is sometimes the case with 'floating' verses that may be easily inserted, or not, into songs without substantially altering the general narrative flow. Songs like 'Newry Town' which belong to a genre other than that of the outlaw hero have only a fluctuating relationship with the tradition discussed here.

22 'The Highwayman' from F. Kidson, *A Garland of English Folk-Songs*, London, 1926, pp. 96–7. See also M. Karpeles (ed.), *Cecil Sharp's Collection of English Folk Songs*, London, 1974, vol. 2, pp. 160–3 for another three versions, No. C of which contains the same verse 5. *Journal of the Folk Song Society* 1, 1899–1904, pp. 114–15, has a 9-verse version with the song's more usual title of 'In Newry Town', collected from Mr Henry Hills by W. P. Merrick, c. 1899–1900. *Journal of the Folk Song Society* 2, 1905–07,

p. 291, has the first verse and tune only of a version collected in Liverpool by Kidson.

23 'The Jolly Highwayman', collected from Mr Henry Stansbridge and Mr George Blake, Lyndhurst, Hants., 1906, by J. F. Guyer, in *Journal of the Folk Song Society* 3, 1909, p. 284.

24 'The Maltman and the Highwayman' from Williams, *Folk Songs of the Upper Thames*, pp. 250–1. Williams notes: 'Perhaps of Wiltshire origin, though I discovered it at Bampton. As my informant was once employed near Malmesbury, Wilts, he may have learned it there in his young days. Obtained of Charles Tanner, Bampton, Oxon.'

25 'The Flying Highwayman' from J. Holloway and J. Black (eds), *Later English Broadside Ballads*, London, 1975, vol. 1, pp. 103–4. Undated but probably late seventeenth or early eighteenth century.

26 G. Seal, 'The Wild Colonial Boy Rides Again: An Australian Legend Abroad' in I. Craven (ed.), *Australian Popular Culture*, Cambridge, 1994.

27 The fact that 'The Wild Colonial Boy' was often sung to the tune of 'The Wearing of the Green', a melodic icon of Irish revolt, is a further indication of the importance of the 'Celtic connection'. However, the relationship of 'The Wild Colonial Boy' to the broader Anglophone tradition of the outlaw hero is suggested in a contribution to the British *Notes and Queries* 159: 6, 9 August 1930, p. 101, where W. H. Dixson states that 'The Wild Colonial Boy' was current in Australia during the 1870s and that it was sung to a similar tune to what he called a Somerset song, 'Brennan on the Moor' (see following chapter). Explicit connections between political dissent and outlawry are made in one version collected by Bill Scott from Mr H. Beatty, Brisbane, where the boy 'turned out as a Tory boy, as I'd often done before': J. Meredith, *The Wild Colonial Boy: The Life and Times of Jack Donahoe, 1808–1830*, Sydney, 1960, p. 52. On this see G. Seal, *Ned Kelly in Popular Tradition*, Melbourne, 1980, and G. Seal, 'Tradition and Protest in Nineteenth Century England and Wales', *Folklore* 100: 2, 1988.

28 Meredith, *The Wild Colonial Boy*, in a version from *Walton's 132 Best Irish Songs and Ballads* (n.d.).

29 See Cozens, *The Journal of Capt. Henry Thomas Fox*, 1852, quoted in Meredith, *The Wild Colonial Boy*, p. 95.

30 From A. B. Paterson's *The Old Bush Songs*, Sydney, 1905. See also notes on the American and British versions of this song, and Seal, 'The Wild Colonial Boy Rides Again'.

31 'The Yorkshire Farmer' in Kidson, *A Garden of English Folk-Songs*, pp. 48–9, where it is titled 'Saddle to Rags'. Originally published by Kidson in his *Traditional Tunes: A Collection of Ballad Airs*, London, 1891, pp. 141–2 (S.R. Publishers reprint 1970, with new foreword by A. E. Green). Another version is in H. Logan, *A Pedlar's Pack of Ballads and Songs*, Edinburgh,

1869, pp. 128–30. This is a broadside c. 1796, and Logan also cites an 1846 reference to the song being widely sung in Yorkshire.

32 'The Yorkshire Bite' from Williams, *Folk Songs of the Upper Thames*, pp. 253–4. Logan, *A Pedlar's Pack*, pp. 131–3, has a 16-verse broadside of the song, c. 1782, and the Broadside Collection of Elizabeth Davison contains a 15-verse Glasgow broadside by Robertson, 1801 (BL 11606 aa 24). The Library of Congress holds at least one Texas version of this song, at 2905 A4.

33 'The Highwayman Outwitted', collected from Mrs Thompson, Knaresborough, by Frank Kidson and published in *Journal of the Folk Song Society* 1, 1899–1904, p. 236. No date given, but according to R. Palmer, *Everyman's Book of British Ballads*, London, 1980, p. 246, it was November 1891. Kidson also printed a version in *A Garland of English Folk-Songs*, pp. 14–15, that appears to be a collation of this oral version and a broadside(s).

'The Highwayman Outwitted' in various forms is an extremely widespread song. See Karpeles (ed.), *Cecil Sharp's Collection*, vol, 2, p. 47; F. Purslow, *The Constant Lovers*, London, 1972, p. 40; K. Stubbes, *The Life of a Man*, London, 1970, p. 64; Logan, *A Pedlar's Pack*, pp. 134–6, for a longer version titled 'The Maid of Rygate'; E. McColl and P. Seeger, *Traveller's Songs from England and Scotland*, London, 1977, pp. 279–80, also mentioning three broadside versions in the British Museum; another undated broadside there by Johnston, Falkirk, of 20 verses at BL 11606 aa 22 (titled 'The Crafty Farmer'). A recorded version collected from Joseph Jones, Kent, by Mike Yates, appears on *Songs of the Open Road*, LP disk, Topic Records 12T253, 1975. A broadside version is in Holloway and Black (eds), *Later English Broadside Ballads*, pp. 109–10. American versions appear in G. Laws, *American Balladry from British Broadsides*, Philadelphia, 1957, pp. 165–6; and in J. H. Combs, (ed. D. K. Wilgus), *Folksongs of the Southern United States* (1925), American Folklore Society Reprint, 1967, pp. 130–2, titled 'Selling the Cow' and said to be 'a secondary form' of Child 283.

34 'Two Jolly Butchers' from Williams, *Folk Songs of the Upper Thames*, pp. 275–6, collected from Thomas King, Castle Eaton. Williams also prints the first verse of another version he had collected.

35 Such as 'The Bold Robber', a version of which was collected from a Mr Anderson in Essex, by Ralph Vaughan Williams, in 1905, and seems to be a species of the 'highwayman outwitted' type, as Kidson surmises in his comment on the published version in *Journal of the Folk Song Society* 2, December 1905, pp. 165–6. There are also echoes of the noble robber in traditions associated with figures such as 'Railroad Bill' and other American desperadoes. See J. W. Roberts, '"Railroad Bill" and the American Outlaw Tradition', *Western Folklore* 40, 1981.

Chapter 3   British Highwaymen

1 For outlaw traditions in other English-speaking countries see H. Evans and E. Evans, *Hero on a Stolen Horse: The Highwayman and His Brothers-in-Arms the Bandit and the Bushranger*, London, 1977; E. Hobsbawm, *Bandits*, London, 1969, and *Primitive Rebels*, Manchester, 1963; and G. Seal, *Ned Kelly in Popular Tradition*, Melbourne, 1980.

2 See B. Capp, 'Popular Literature', in B. Reay (ed.), *Popular Culture in Seventeenth Century England* (1985), London, 1988, p. 207: 'The other most popular heroes of seventeenth-century popular literature were the outlaws of legend, such as Robin Hood and Adam Bell.' Anthologies and studies of popular literature abound (see Sources and References). Vast collections of popular literature are to be found in the libraries and archives of Britain, mostly uncatalogued and rich in potential insights.

3 See A. L. Hayward, *Lives of the Most Remarkable Criminals*, London, 1735, pp. 57, 111–12, 425–7, 513.

4 'Bold Nevison' (broadside) from P. O'Shaughnessy (ed.), *Yellowbelly Ballads* (Part 1), Lincoln, 1975, pp. 9–10, taken from C. J. Ingledew, *The Ballads and Songs of Yorkshire*, London, 1860, pp. 125–8. See also C. Hindley, *Curiosities of Street Literature*, 1871, p. 169.

5 'Bold Nevison' from the singing of Mr Joseph Taylor, Brigg, Lincolnshire. Collected by Percy Grainger, 1908, and transcribed from *Unto Brigg Fair*, LP disk, Leader, LEA4050-B, 1972.

6 As related in *The Complete Newgate Calendar*, cited in Capp, 'Popular Literature', p. 230.

7 For some account of this see Evans and Evans, *Hero on a Stolen Horse*, itself an addition to the popular mythologising of the outlaw hero.

8 Capp, 'Popular Literature', p. 207.

9 Information on Turpin's life and activities may be found in the *Dictionary of National Biography*; Ash and Day's *Immortal Turpin*; Captain Alexander Smith, *A Complete History of the Lives and Robberies of the Most Notorious Highwaymen*, 1719; D. Barlow, *Dick Turpin and the Gregory Gang*, London, 1973; C. Hibbert, *Highwaymen*, London, 1967.

10 Quoted in C. Mackay, *Extraordinary Popular Delusions and the Madness of Crowds*, London, 1841, pp. 251–2.

11 P. Linebaugh, *The London Hanged: Crime and Civil Society in the Eighteenth Century*, New York, 1992, p. 204.

12 See A. L. Humphreys, 'The Highwayman and His Chap-Book', *Notes and Queries*, May–June 1940; V. Neuberg, *Popular Literature: A History and Guide*, Harmondsworth, 1977.

13 D. Barlow, *Dick Turpin and the Gregory Gang*.

14 Dick Turpin Ballad: Brit.Mus./C 136 bb 2 and also quoted in Barlow, *Dick Turpin and the Gregory Gang*, pp. 310–12.

15 A. Williams, *Folk Songs of the Upper Thames*, London, 1923.

16 'Turnpin's Valour' was published in 1803 by J. M. Robertson of Saltmarket, Glasgow. (BL 11606 aa 23). Compare with the version in W. H. Logan, *A Pedlar's Pack of Ballads and Songs*, Edinburgh, 1869, pp. 118–21, dated c. 1796. The song is also known in an Australian version collected by Ron Edwards and published in *Northern Folk* 42.

17 This cockfighting term means a 'craven' cock, one who does not behave 'gamely' (also a cockfighting term). Thus Turpin's heroism is further implicated in this ballad. See Linebaugh, *The London Hanged*, p. 210.

18 'Turpin Hero': in M. Karpeles (ed.), *Cecil Sharp's Collection of English Folk Songs*, London, 1974, vol. 2, p. 164, No. 244A. See also Sharp's version in his *A Book of British Song, for Home and School*, London, 1902, pp. 146–7. Other versions include one collected from Mrs May Bradley of Shropshire by Fred Hamer and published in the latter's *Garner's Gay*, London, 1967, p. 6; and one from George Messenger, Suffolk, in 1956, by Peter Kennedy and published in his *Folksong of Britain and Ireland*, London, 1975.

Kennedy also provides references to numerous other printed and oral versions of the song (including nine in the Cecil Sharp MS collection), in Britain and Canada. Two versions are in *Folk Songs of the Upper Thames*, Williams, pp. 99–100. As well, see versions in G. S. Maxwell, *Highwayman's Heath* (new edn, 1949), p. 196; Ash and Day, *Immortal Turpin*, p. 129, and BL 11621 h 12 and C 116 h 2 (44); *Journal of the English Folk Song Society* 2, 1905–6, pp. 279, 280, for an 8-verse version from Chappell, an oral 3-verse version, and one variant *against* Turpin. See also W. Chappell, *Popular Music of the Olden Time*, New York, 1965, vol. 2, pp. 661–2, for the statement that Chappell noted the tune from a singer in 1840 and also a reference to a similar song titled 'Captain Freney' (see below). Kidson has a 5-verse version, similar to that of Sharp reproduced here, in *A Garland of English Folksongs*, London, 1926, pp. 60–1. There is a Glasgow(?) broadside, n.d., in the Kidson collection, vol. 5, p. 39 in the Mitchell Library, Glasgow; reproduced in R. Edwards (ed.), *The Convict Maid*, Kuranda, Qld, 3rd edn, 1987, p. 35. The song has also been collected in Australia on several occasions; see R. Edwards, *200 Years of Australian Folksong Index, 1788–1988*, Kuranda, Qld, p. 107.

19 'Poor Black Bess' issued by Such around 1865. (See 'Old Broadside Ballads', in *The Chapbook*, no. 15, September 1920, p. 22.) An earlier version, pre-1850, is reproduced by L. James in *Print and the People, 1819–1851*, London, 1976, p. 265. V. de Sola Pinto, and A. Rodway print a ballad of the same name in their *The Common Muse: An Anthology of Popular British Broadside Ballad Poetry, XVth–XXth Century*, London, 1957, but this seems to have little or no relation to that discussed here. See also Ashton's *Modern Street Ballads*, London, 1888, pp. 366–7, and the American version printed

later in this book. Williams, *Folk Songs of the Upper Thames*, p. 101, has a version titled 'Dick Turpin's Ride', and there are two different versions from Fortey in T. Crampton, *Ballads Collected by . . .* , BL 11621 h 11, London, 1868–70.

20 'Dick Turpin and Black Bess' from Mrs May Bradley, Shropshire, in Hamer (comp.), *Garner's Gay*, p. 44.

21 There are also occasional references to songs that present a point of view antagonistic to a particular outlaw hero. There is a version of the well-known song 'Turpin-Hero' that portrays the highwayman in a negative light in *Journal of the English Folk Song Society* 2, 1905–06, p. 279, for instance. See also note 14 above. Such songs, though, are extremely rare and perhaps are the product of an individual rather than a traditional, communal point of view.

22 Linebaugh, *The London Hanged*, p. 205.

23 The popular theatre has been an important perpetuator of criminal and political heroes, including outlaws. London's Bartholomew Fair during the eighteenth century included plays about Wat Tyler, Jack Sheppard and Robin Hood.

24 Linebaugh, *The London Hanged*, ch. 6.

25 Quoted in Linebaugh, *The London Hanged*, p. 217. Interestingly, this was one of the few lines of the song that the octogenarian reformer could remember.

26 On enclosures as the major cause of agrarian discontent in the sixteenth to eighteenth centuries see M. Beloff, *Public Order and Popular Disturbances, 1660–1714*, London, 1938, pp. 76ff. On smugglers and their relationship to protest see C. Winslow, 'Sussex Smugglers', in D. Hay *et al.* (eds), *Albion's Fatal Tree: Crime and Society in Eighteenth Century England*, London, 1975, particularly pp. 120, 127, 132, 156, 158–60. For a rather different view on the 'social' nature of smuggling see F. McLynn, *Crime and Punishment in Eighteenth Century England* (1989), Oxford, 1991, ch. 10. McLynn is unwilling to accept that highway robbery, or even smuggling, poaching, arson and other symptoms of rural discontent, are 'social crimes', by which he means having the support of the general populace. While his argument makes sense from the historian's point of view and from the sources typically used by the historian, McLynn conveniently ignores folk and popular expressions of the type examined here, which clearly indicate significant support and sympathy for certain criminals. Rather curiously, the only crime that McLynn considers to be really social is that of 'rioting', where the rioters sought to enforce a fair, just or moral price or conditions for commodities, usually corn. Rioting was 'The one activity that satisfies the moral criterion of altruistic social resistance' (p. 241). This rather quaintly moralistic position adopted by McLynn seems blind to the realities of everyday life.

Individuals and groups rarely act without a mixture of motives. The argument that social dissatisfaction and political dissent, no matter how primitively articulated, could not figure in the motives of smugglers, highwaymen, poachers and others at the same time as they either ensured or extended their economic security seems simplistic, or optimistic, in the extreme. In McLynn's view, highwaymen are excluded from the category of social criminal because they often came from middle-class backgrounds; poachers were also from various classes and poaching was often carried out as a source of income, as were coining and smuggling. Wrecking, which he claims (without presenting any evidence) 'involved a clear-cut defiance of the law in the name of the sovereignty of local folkways' (p. 199), 'was beyond the moral pale by any standards' (p. 241), despite having the active support and connivance of entire communities. Of just what these local folkways might consist, we are not told. Indeed, we are not told what McLynn thinks 'folkways' are as he doesn't bother to define the term, despite asserting that 'In some ways wrecking was the century's most dramatic assertion of the supremacy of customary rights to statute law' (p. 199).

These conclusions demonstrate that the historian's concentration on the synchronic moment, while valuable and necessary, inevitably underrates, even ignores, the longer diachronic continuities, their persistence and their motivating power in social relationships and activities. An additional point might be made that the reliance on evidence from official primary sources that characterises McLynn's study not surprisingly leads to the conclusion that activities which threatened the status quo were irredeemably 'criminal' rather than 'social'.

27 Similar attitudes persisted in America. See, for instance, E. D. Ives, *George Magoon and the Down East Game War: History, Folklore and the Law*, Urbana and Chicago, 1988.

28 Some representative works dealing with this large topic are: E. P. Thompson, *Whigs and Hunters: The Origin of the Black Act*, London, 1975; Linebaugh, *The London Hanged*; M. Beloff, *Public Order and Popular Disturbances, 1660–1714*, London, 1938, on enclosures, corn riots and other forms of agrarian disturbance, including poaching, stock-maiming and rick burning; also on relationships between poaching and enclosures and on popular support for smugglers and other kinds of 'justified' or sanctioned infractions of the law, pp. 95–8, for connections of smugglers with Jacobites and foreign spies, pp. 96–7. See also G. Seal, 'Tradition and Protest in Nineteenth Century England and Wales', *Folklore*, 100: 2 1988.

29 McLynn, *Crime and Punishment*, p. 276. See also Linebaugh, *The London Hanged*, passim.

30 Linebaugh, *The London Hanged*, p. 213.

31 G. Zimmermann, *Songs of Irish Rebellion: Political Street Ballads and Rebel*

Songs, 1780–1900, Dublin, 1967, p. 24. See also J. J. Marshall, *Irish Tories, Rapparees and Robbers*, Dungannon, 1927.

32 H. Glassie, *Irish Folk Tales*, New York, 1985, collected from Cormic O'Holland by Rose Shaw, 1930. See also H. Glassie (ed.), *Irish Folk History: Texts from the North*, Philadelphia, 1982, pp. 47–51, for further oral traditions regarding the noble robber status of tories and the highwayman 'Black Francis'.

33 J. Healy, *Ballads from the Pubs of Ireland*, Dublin, 1965, pp. 121–3.

34 Zimmermann, *Songs of Irish Rebellion*, pp. 24–5.

35 Healy, *Ballads from the Pubs of Ireland*, pp. 127–8.

36 'Bold Captain Freney' from Healy, *Ballads from the Pubs of Ireland*, pp. 121–3, from Kilkenny Archaeological Society publications, new series, March 1856, no. 2, with indications that the song was of considerable age, probably eighteenth century. See also Chappell, *Popular Music of the Olden Time*, vol. 2, pp. 661–2, on this and the similarities between 'Turpin-Hero' and 'Captain Freney'.

Humphreys, 'The Highwayman and His Chap-Book', p. 404, mentions an undated Dublin chapbook, titled *The Life and Adventures of James Freney*, that includes the lives of several other highwaymen.

37 'Street Ballad' by W. Percy French and Houston Collin(s?)son from Healy, *Ballads from the Pubs of Ireland*, pp. 127–8.

38 Healy, *Ballads from the Pubs of Ireland*, p. 120.

39 'Brennan on the Moor' sung by Mr Tom Sprachlan, Hambridge, Somerset, collected by Cecil Sharp, 1903, in Karpeles (ed.), *Cecil Sharp's Collection*, vol. 2, pp. 166–7, No. 245. See also No. 224.

F. Kidson, *Traditional Tunes* (1891), S.R. Publishers reprint, 1970, pp. 124–6, includes a 12-verse version in which Brennan is 'basely betrayed'. Ralph Vaughan Williams' 'Book of Broadsides' in the English Folk Dance and Song Society's library, p. 3 (P6016) includes a 12-verse broadside by Such, undated, as does T. Crampton, *Ballads Collected by . . .* , vol. 2, p. 94 (by Disley, St Giles).

There are three American versions in the Library of Congress collected by Alan Lomax, who also published an 11-verse version collected in Oregon, 1938, in his *Our Singing Country*, New York, 1949, p. 317.

William Brennan is still a favoured figure of Irish folklore, particularly around Cork, Tipperary and Limerick. Cork broadsheets on Brennan date from at least 1850 and Joyce noted an oral version around 1860 in County Meath. Robert Ford's *Vagabond Songs and Ballads of Scotland*, 2nd series, London, 1910 (Norwood reprint, 1975), pp. 56-61, contains two versions of the song, together with the observation that it was as popular in Scotland as it was in Ireland during the 1840s. Broadside versions frequently carry a verse indicating that Brennan was betrayed by a trusted accomplice, as in this verse given in Kennedy, *Folksong of Britain and Ireland*, p. 725, which also shows the hero in appropriately defiant mood:

> Brennan being an outlaw upon the mountain high
> With cavalry and infantry to take him they did try
> He laughed at them with scorn, until at length, 'tis said
> By a false-hearted comerade [*sic*] he basely was betrayed.

In addition, Kennedy provides references to twenty-four recorded and printed versions of the ballad throughout Britain, in Canada and the United States. The song is also known in Australia, particularly in Irish versions. (See Edwards, *Australian Folk Song Index*.) According to Healy, *Ballads from the Pubs of Ireland*, p. 120, who also gives text and tune of a nineteenth-century Irish version similar to Mr Sprachlan's rendition included here, the ballad was for a long time more popular in America than in Ireland, at least until the 1960s. Clearly it is a widely known expression of the outlaw hero legend and is perhaps even more widely diffused than 'Jack Donohoe' and 'The Wild Colonial Boy', with which songs 'Brennan on the Moor' has some affinities, particularly in its opening verse.

40 'Willie Brennan' collected from Mr Thomas O'Riordan, Cork, by Sean O'Sullivan, 1934, and in H. Glassie (ed.), *Irish Folk Tales*, New York, 1985.

41 'Captain Grant' sung by Mr Charles Benfield, Bould, Gloucestershire, 1909, collected by Cecil Sharp and given in Karpeles (ed.), *Cecil Sharp's Collection*, pp. 169–70, No. 246. See *Journal of the Folk Song Society* 1, 1899–1904, p. 109, for a 5-verse version collected c. 1899 from Mr Hills of Lodsworth, Sussex by W. P. Merrick. E. McColl and P. Seeger, *Travellers' Songs from England and Scotland*, London, 1977, pp. 283–4, print a 3-verse, fragmentary version and on p. 282 note that Such printed a broadside of the song. Williams, *Folk Songs of the Upper Thames*, pp. 216–17, also has a version set in Scotland.

42 Zimmermann, *Songs of Irish Rebellion*, pp. 24ff.

Chapter 4   American Badmen

1 'My Bonny Black Bess' from H. Belden, and A. Hudson (eds), *The Frank C. Brown Collection of North Carolina Folklore*, 7 vols, Durham, NC, 1952, vol. 2, pp. 356–7, and derived from the Such broadside. Reported as traditional in Arkansas in V. Randolph, *Ozark Folk Songs*, Columbia, MO, 1946–50 (4 vols), vol. 1, pp. 11, 152–5. The *Library of Congress Archive of Folksong Checklist*, Washington, DC, 1942, lists two versions at 3287A2 and 4212AL. *Sing Out* 25: 4, 1977, p. 9, prints a version of unclear—probably British—provenance. See also notes to British version.

2 'Johnny Troy' in K. Porter, '"Johnny Troy": A "Lost" Australian Bushranger Ballad in the United States', *Meanjin Quarterly* 24, June 1965. See also *Journal of American Folklore* XLV, pp. 37–9, for a version from Michigan. 'Troy' is also mentioned in company with other convict bushranger heroes in Francis (Frank the Poet) MacNamara's 'The Convict's Tour of Hell'.

3 See discussion of 'The Wild Colonial Boy' in ch. 2.

4 O. Klapp, 'The Folk Hero', *Journal of American Folklore* 62, 1949.

5 W. E. Simeone, 'Robin Hood and Some Other American Outlaws', *Journal of American Folklore* 71, 1958.

6 Kent L. Steckmesser, 'Robin Hood and the American Outlaw', *Journal of American Folklore* 79, 1966; and Kent L. Steckmesser, *The Western Hero in History and Legend*, Norman, OK, 1965.

7 R. Meyer, 'The Outlaw: A Distinctive American Folktype', *Journal of the Folklore Institute* 17, 1980.

8 J. W. Roberts, '"Railroad Bill" and the American Outlaw Tradition', *Western Folklore* 40, 1981. Also relevant here is L. Inciardi, L. Block and L. Hallowell, *Historical Approaches to Crime*, Beverly Hills, 1977, pp. 55–6.

9 R. White, 'Outlaw Gangs of the Middle Border: American Social Bandits', *Western Historical Quarterly* 12: 4, 1981; G. Seal, *Ned Kelly in Popular Tradition*, Melbourne, 1980; W. A. Settle jnr, *Jesse James was his Name, or, fact and fiction concerning the careers of the notorious James brothers of Missouri*, Columbia, MO, 1966. See also N. Cohen, *Long Steel Rail: The Railroad in American Folksong*, Urbana, 1981, for folklore surrounding James and company.

10 'Quantrell' [*sic*] in R. Lingenfelter *et al.* (eds), *Songs of the American West*, Los Angeles, 1968, pp. 314–5, and taken from C. Finger, *Frontier Ballads*, 1927. Lingenfelter *et al.* also note three further variants. See also H. M. Belden (ed.), *Ballads and Songs Collected by the Missouri Folklore Society*, University of Missouri, Columbia, 1940, pp. 353–4, where there is a rather literary piece titled 'The Call of Quantrell' [*sic*], together with a report that the guerilla leader did survive his supposedly fatal shooting in 1865 and was alive in 1907. For further information on Quantrill, see W. E. Connelley, *Quantrill and the Border Wars*, 1910; J. N. Edwards, *Noted Guerillas*, 1877; W. Britton, *The Civil War on the Border*, 2 vols, 1890–99.

11 White, 'Outlaw Gangs', p. 394.

12 P. Kooistra, *Criminals as Heroes: Structure, Power and Identity*, Bowling Green, OH, 1989, pp. 51–2.

13 Quoted in Kooistra, *Criminals as Heroes*, p. 56.

14 Edwards, *Noted Guerillas*, p. 451.

15 Kooistra, *Criminals as Heroes*, p. 65.

16 'Jesse James' in Belden (ed.), *Ballads and Songs*, pp. 403–4. No title given.

Collected in 1916 by Miss Mary Alicia Owen from a man who dug post-holes: 'He said everybody used to sing it.' According to N. Thorp *et al.* (eds), *Songs of the Cowboys*, New York, 1966, p. 17 fn, 'There are a half-dozen Jesse James ballads with intricate interlinking of texts and tunes'.

17 Randolph, *Ozark Folk Songs*, p. 146.

18 White, 'Outlaw Gangs', p. 392.

19 Steckmesser, 'Robin Hood and the American Outlaw'; R. Dorson, *American Folklore*, Chicago, 1960, pp. 236–43.

20 Settle, *Jesse James*. Kooistra, *Criminals as Heroes*, p. 73, states: 'There is no doubt that Jesse James and his supporters consciously attempted to take advantage of the social context in which they lived by defining themselves as modern Robin Hoods. But John Newman Edwards, through his book *Noted Guerillas*, and by his incessant editorial support of the James gang (along with whatever other support he may have given them), stands out as the "father" of the James boys as creatures of legend.'

21 Kooistra, *Criminals as Heroes*, pp. 49–51.

22 Quoted in Kooistra, *Criminals as Heroes*, p. 48, who also refers to and quotes from a number of other letters apparently penned by Jesse or other gang members and in which their various grievances and defences are presented.

23 Kooistra, *Criminals as Heroes*, p. 51.

24 White, 'Outlaw Gangs', p. 393ff.

25 White, 'Outlaw Gangs', p. 392.

26 Kooistra, *Criminals as Heroes*, ch. 3.

27 Kooistra, *Criminals as Heroes*, p. 155, citing R. Love, *The Rise and Fall of Jesse James*, New York, 1940.

28 Settle, *Jesse James*, p. 201.

29 'The Ballad of Jesse James' from M. Larkin, *The Singing Cowboy*, New York, 1931, and reprinted in Botkin, *A Treasury of American Folklore*, New York, 1944, p. 108. Variants abound, including Belden and Hudson, *The Frank C. Brown Collection*, vol. 2, pp. 557–62; R. Abrahams (ed.), *A Singer and Her Songs: Almeda Riddle's Book of Ballads*, Baton Rouge, 1970, pp. 10–13; C. Sandburg, *The American Songbag*, New York, 1927, pp. 420–1; *Library of Congress Checklist* lists 12 versions to 1940; Randolph, *Ozark Folk Songs*, pp. 146–8.

30 Settle, *Jesse James*, p. 175.

31 Ibid., p. 196.

32 Settle, *Jesse James*, p. 190. Also H. H. Kruse, 'Myth in the Making: The James Brothers at Northfield, Minnesota, and the Dime Novel', *Journal of Popular Culture* 10: 2, 1976. R. Adams, *Six Guns and Saddle Leather*, Norman, OK, 1969, notes over 300 works on Jesse James, a number far outweighing those on any other single American badman.

33 Settle, *Jesse James*, p. 187.

34 The bandit as avenger of real or imagined injustices is an important element of Hobsbawm's social bandit and is also integral to the Anglophone outlaw hero, if in a usually less violent manifestation than in some other cultures. Billy the Kid may be a partial exception to this pattern.

35 B. Botkin (ed.), *A Treasury of American Folklore*, New York, 1944, pp. 69–72.

36 As noted by Meyer, 'The Outlaw', p. 114.

37 'Billy the Kid' from J. Lomax and A. Lomax, *American Ballads and Folk Songs*, New York, 1934, pp. 137–8. The Library of Congress holds a recording of the song by Woody Guthrie at 3412 B2. Bonney has been the focus of enormous scholarly and popular interest, reflected in J. C. Dykes, *Billy the Kid: The Bibliography of a Legend*, Norman, OK, 1952. Further forests have been felled on Bonney since then. Steckmesser, *The Western Hero*, provides the best overview of the media and folkloric representations of the outlaw and I have leaned heavily on his work here.

38 Kooistra, *Criminals as Heroes*, p. 98. Also G. Page, 'Was Billy the Kid a Superhero or a Superscoundrel?', *Smithsonian*, February 1991.

39 Kooistra, *Criminals as Heroes*, p. 97.

40 S. Tatum, *Inventing Billy the Kid: Visions of the Outlaw in America, 1881–1981*, Albuquerque, 1982, pp. 197–8.

41 Page, 'Was Billy the Kid . . . ?', pp. 137ff.

42 'Sam Bass' from Lingenfelter *et al.* (eds), *Songs of the American West*, pp. 316–17 and noting numerous variants. Another version is in Sandburg, *The American Songbag*, pp. 422–3. Numerous versions are in the Library of Congress, and see Belden (ed.), *Ballads and Songs*, pp. 399–400; Larkin, *The Singing Cowboy*, pp. 159–161. Thorp *et al.* (eds), *Songs of the Cowboys*, print three further texts and note another fifty significant printed versions and over twenty manuscript versions and field recordings of the same song. They also provide numerous references to discussions of the song and to the life of Bass, including: Charles L. Martin, *A Sketch of Sam Bass, the Bandit*, 1880; James B. Gillett, *Six Years With the Texas Rangers*, 1925; Frank J. Dobie, *Tales of Old Time Texas* (1928), London, 1959, pp. 78–90 (includes extracts from Bass ballad), among others. The compilers of *Songs of the Cowboys* are of the opinion that the ballad was originally composed very shortly after Bass's death in July 1878 (pp. 112–20).

43 'Jim Fisk', in H. Belden (ed.), *Ballads and Songs*, pp. 415–16. The version given here was untitled and found in materials written in the late 1870s by a William Dresia, of Kansas. A number of variants of the song are mentioned by Belden (Vermont and Minnesota), who also notes that it was sung to the tune 'Never Go Back on the Poor' and based on an earlier song known as 'Remember the Poor'.

44 E. Hollon, *Frontier Violence: Another Look*, New York, 1974.

45 R. M. Brown, *Strain of Violence: Historical Studies of American Violence*, Oxford, 1975; H. Graham and T. Gurr (eds), *Violence in America: Historical and Comparative Perspectives* (rev. edn), Beverly Hills and London, 1979, especially K. Lynn, 'Violence in American Literature and Folklore'. Also Steckmesser, *The Western Hero*.

46 Kooistra, *Criminals as Heroes*, pp. 128–32.

47 Meyer, 'The Outlaw', pp. 101, 110.

48 Meyer, 'The Outlaw', p. 97.

49 Kooistra, *Criminals as Heroes*, p. 137.

50 'Pretty Boy Floyd' by Woody Guthrie. See Lingenfelter *et al.* (eds), *Songs of the American West*, p. 235. The Library of Congress holds a number of recordings of Guthrie performing this song, which has also been released on numerous commercial recordings.

Chapter 5   Australian Bushrangers

1 Full details of First Fleet convicts have not survived: see R. Hughes, *The Fatal Shore*, London, 1987, ch. 3 and pp. 70ff and notes, p. 617.

2 J. Bonwick, *The Bushrangers: Illustrating the Early Days of Van Diemen's Land*, Melbourne, 1856, p. 89.

3 It is important to emphasise the selectivity of the outlaw hero process. As reported in *House of Commons Papers for 1837–8*, vol. xxii, paper no. 669, the amount of crime in New South Wales and Van Diemen's Land 'in proportion to the respective population of the two countries [Britain and Australia], the number of convictions for highway robbery (including bushranging) in New South Wales, exceeds the total number of convictions for all offences in England': quoted in M. Clark (ed.), *Sources of Australian History* (1957), London, 1971, p. 213. From this large pool of desperate criminality, only a tiny portion were celebrated as heroes.

4 For an overview of bushranging, see J. McQuilton, 'Australian Bushranging and Social Banditry with Special Reference to the Kelly Outbreak', *Royal Geographical Society of Australasia, South Australian Branch, Proceedings* 82, 1982. Also T. J. Barker, 'Bushranging: The History and the Legend', *Canberra Historical Journal*, March 1974; and R. B. Walker, 'Bushranging in Fact and Legend', *Historical Studies* 11: 42, April 1964. Other important documentation of bushranging includes C. White, *History of Australian Bushranging*, 2 vols, 1893, and G. Boxall, *History of the Australian Bushrangers*, Sydney, 1935. Historically fanciful, though full of folkloric information, is J. Bradshaw, *The True History of the Australian Bushrangers*, Sydney, n.d. (1930?). This is essentially a compilation of Bradshaw's equally colourful earlier works, including *Highway Robbery Under Arms*, Sydney, c. 1924, and *The Only True Account of Ned Kelly, Frank Gardiner, Ben Hall and Morgan*, Sydney, 1911.

5 J. Meredith, *The Wild Colonial Boy: The Life and Times of Jack Donahoe, 1808–1830*, Sydney, 1960. See also *Sydney Gazette*, 10 October 1829, 'Government Order No. 48' and White, *History of Australian Bushranging*, vol. 1, pp. 105, 107, 108, 109–13.

6 G. Zimmermann, *Songs of Irish Rebellion: Political Street Ballads and Rebel Songs, 1780–1900*, Dublin, 1967, pp. 25, 269–71.

7 C. Cozens, *The Adventures of A Guardsman*, London, 1847. See also Meredith, *The Wild Colonial Boy*, pp. 91–2.

8 'Bold Jack Donohoe' from A. B. Paterson, *The Old Bush Songs*, Sydney, 1905. Versions of this song have frequently been collected in the eastern states of Australia: see J. Meredith and H. Anderson (eds), *Folksongs of Australia*, Sydney, 1967. Essential relevant studies are J. Meredith, *The Wild Colonial Boy*, and, more tangentially, J. Meredith and R. Whalan, *Frank the Poet*, Melbourne, 1979.

   An English version of 'Jack Donohoe' was collected by Roy Palmer from Ned Costello, Birmingham, in 1971 and published in R. Palmer (ed.), *Everyman's Book of British Ballads*, London, 1981, p. 134. Versions of the song with Fenian sentiments are printed in Zimmermann, *Songs of Irish Rebellion*, pp. 269–71. The Library of Congress contains recordings of a number of American versions of the song.

   There are a number of other ballads about Donohoe extant, including 'Bold Jack Donohoe' collected from Mr Jack Goodwin, NSW, by John Meredith, in Meredith and Anderson (eds), *Folksongs of Australia*, and 'John Donahue [*sic*] and his Gang' in D. Stewart and N. Keesing (eds), *Old Bush Songs*, Sydney, 1957 (taken from a nineteenth-century source). See also Meredith, *The Wild Colonial Boy*, and Meredith and Whalan, *Frank the Poet*, and notes to 'The Wild Colonial Boy' therein.

9 Much of what follows is based on G. Seal, *The Highwayman Tradition in Australia*, Sydney, 1977, and G. Seal, *Ned Kelly in Popular Tradition*, Melbourne, 1980, ch. 2.

10 New South Wales Public Statutes, 11 Geo. IV, No. X.

11 A. Harris, *Convicts and Settlers* (1847), Melbourne, 1970, devotes a whole chapter to the iniquities of this system. See also A. Haydon, *The Trooper Police of Australia*, London, 1911, pp. 68–70. For Bourke's and Burton's qualms, see *Historical Records of Australia*, Series 1, vol. 17, pp. 520–36.

12 This account is based on T. O'Callaghan, 'Police Establishment in NSW', *Journal of the Royal Australian Historical Society* 9: 6, 1923; A. Potter, 'The Police Force of New South Wales', *Journal of the Royal Australian Historical Society* 6: 6, 1920; H. King, 'Some Aspects of Police Administration in NSW, 1825–51', *Journal of the Royal Australian Historical Society* 42: 5, 1956; Haydon, *The Trooper Police*. See also M. Brennan, 'A Police History of the Notorious Bushrangers of New South Wales and Victoria', Mitchell

Library, Sydney, MS A2030; M. Brennan, *Reminiscences of the Goldfields*, Sydney, 1907; and D. Chappell and P. Wilson, *The Police and the Public in Australia and New Zealand*, St Lucia, Qld, 1969.

13 See H. Haygarth, *Recollections of Bush Life in Australia*, London, 1861, pp. 91–3; and R. Therry, *Reminiscences of Thirty Years' Residence in New South Wales and Victoria*, London, 1863, p. 266.

14 Harris, *Convicts and Settlers*, p. 27.

15 S. H. Roberts, *History of Australian Land Settlement, 1788–1920* (1924), Melbourne, 1968, pp. 180–1.

16 Therry, *Reminiscences*, p. 213.

17 *The Lachlan Miner*, 1862, cited in Boxall, *History of the Australian Bushrangers*, pp. 200–1.

18 White, *History of Australian Bushranging*, vol. 2, pp. 220–1, 222, 229.

19 *Sydney Morning Herald*, 26 February 1863, p. 4.

20 *Sydney Morning Herald*, 9 July 1864.

21 Gilbert, probably the most famous locally of all the Forbes district bushrangers, is the subject of a very fine literary ballad by A. B. 'Banjo' Paterson, titled 'How Gilbert Died': 'the smallest child on the Watershed / Can tell you how Gilbert died.'

22 'Frank Gardiner' in Bradshaw, *The Only True Account of Ned Kelly, Frank Gardiner, Ben Hall and Morgan*, Sydney, 1911, p. 6. See also J. Bradshaw, *The Only True Account of Frank Gardiner, Ben Hall and Gang*, Orange, NSW, 189?, pp. 1–2. An additional verse from the singing of Mrs Popplewell in Meredith and Anderson (eds), *Folksongs of Australia*, p. 30, describes Gardiner as 'the poor man's friend'.

23 Quoted in White, *History of Australian Bushranging*, vol. 1, p. 297. Similar observations were made in *Sydney Morning Herald*, 2 February 1863 (editorial) and 4 July 1863, p. 8 (letter).

24 P. McPherson, 'H. M. Keightley, W. R. Rottan and the Bushrangers', *Journal of the Royal Australian Historical Society* 23: 1, 1937, p. 64; White, *History of Australian Bushranging*, vol. 2, pp. 88–9; *Sydney Morning Herald* 16 May 1865, p. 5 (from the *Western Examiner*).

25 *Sydney Morning Herald*, 2 August 1864.

26 *Sydney Morning Herald*, 9 July 1864.

27 Harris, *Convicts and Settlers*, p. 140. For a detailed treatment of Hall and the numerous other bushrangers associated with him, see D. J. Shiel, *Ben Hall: Bushranger*, St. Lucia, Qld, 1983.

28 See Mitchell Library, Sydney, Ah72/2 for a police warrant for burning Hall's property dated 14 October 1861. This appears genuine and indicates that the police suspected Hall of harbouring, if not of bushranging, at this early date. Presumably the police were saving this warrant for the right moment.

29 *Sydney Morning Herald*, 5, 7, 10, 11, 12, 17 October 1863; 24 May 1864;

18 January 1865. These views were also expressed in other sectors of the colonial press, including the *Lachlan Observer*, 17 March 1863; *The Yeoman*, 16 April 1863; *Burrangong Star*, 4 September 1863; *Yass Courier*, 7 June 1864; *Pastoral Times*, 18 October 1864.

30 *Sydney Morning Herald*, 10, 17 March, 3 April, 13 October 1863; 2 March, 10 June, 2, 18 August 1864; 1 March 1865; and *Lachlan Observer*, 21 October 1864.

31 *Sydney Morning Herald*, 10 March 1863; 10 August, 4 November 1864; 30 January 1865 (two letters).

32 *Sydney Morning Herald*, 17 May 1865 (editorial).

33 *Public Statutes of NSW*, 28 Vic. No. 2.

34 Collected as a recitation by John Manifold in the New England region of NSW, and published in J. Manifold (comp.), *The Penguin Australian Song Book*, Ringwood, Vic., 1964, p. 47.

35 'My Name is Ben Hall' in Paterson, *The Old Bush Songs*.

36 'The Death of Ben Hall', collected from Mrs Sally Sloane, Lithgow, by John Meredith, in Meredith and Anderson (eds), *Folksongs of Australia*.

37 'The Streets of Forbes', collected in Brisbane from Mrs Ewell, late of Bathurst, NSW, by John Manifold, and in *Penguin Australian Song Book*, pp. 60–1.

38 'How He Died' by John McGuire. This version is contained in a series of articles titled 'A Wild Colonial Boy' in *Truth*, 4 April – 4 June 1911. Another is in D. Stewart and N. Keesing, *Australian Bush Ballads*, Sydney, 1955, p. 4.

39 Meredith and Anderson (eds), *Folksongs of Australia*, pp. 165–6. In May 1976, Mrs Sloane was recorded by the author and Warren Fahey, at which time she again sang 'The Death of Ben Hall' and repeated sentiments similar to those quoted.

40 M. Carnegie, *Morgan the Bold Bushranger*, Melbourne, 1974, p. 117.

41 'The Death of Morgan', in Stewart and Keesing, *Australian Bush Ballads*, Sydney, 1955, p. 4. Other Morgan songs and ballads appear in Folklore Council of Australia, *A Collection of Australian Folk Songs and Traditional Ballads*, Melbourne, 1967.

42 See S. Williams, *A Ghost Called Thunderbolt*, Woden, ACT, 1987, for an excellent account of Thunderbolt and some examples of his folklore. Also relevant are A. Rixon, *The Truth About Captain Thunderbolt, Australia's Robin Hood*, Sydney, 1940 (and various subsequent editions); R. B. Walker, 'Captain Thunderbolt, Bushranger', *Journal of the Royal Australian Historical Society* 43, 1957; B. McDonald, 'Thunderbolt, Folksong and the Legend of the Noble Robber', *Australian Folklore* 8, 1993, and B. Tate, 'Thunderbolt and Morgan', *Australian Tradition*, October 1972.

43 'The Wild Colonial Boy' is presented and discussed in Chapter 2. For a

detailed discussion of this song, numerous variants and its relationship to the Donohoe ballads, see Meredith, *The Wild Colonial Boy*.

44 I. Elliot, *Moondyne Joe: The Man and the Myth*, Perth, 1978, pp. 96–7.

45 Elliot, *Moondyne Joe*, pp. 146–55.

46 'Moondyne Joe' quoted in Elliot, *Moondyne Joe*, p. 96. See also a set of verses on Moondyne Joe's later horse-stealing activities in *Early Days* (Journal of the West Australian Historical Society), December 1948, p. 37, and a story about Joe in the style of Robin Hood, *Early Days*, 1: v, 1929, p. 35.

47 Other bushranging ballads appear in various sources, including a song on Martin Cash known as 'the Robin Hood of Van Diemen's Land', in R. Ward (ed.), *The Penguin Book of Australian Ballads*, Ringwood, Vic., 1964; W. Wannan, *A Dictionary of Australian Folklore*, Sydney, 1981, p. 454; 'Bushranger Jack Power', in H. Anderson, *Colonial Ballads*, Melbourne (1955), 1962; see also *Australian Tradition* 2: 2, July 1965; R. Edwards, *The Overlander Songbook* (1956, 1969), St Lucia, Qld, 1990; and the Melbourne *Argus*, 19 August 1950. 'The Ballad of Jack Lefroy' is in Bill Scott (ed.), *The Second Penguin Australian Songbook*. 'Those Bold Bushrangers' was collected from 'Paddy the Poet' by P. Jeff Walker and published in the *Bulletin*, 17 August 1911. Thunderbolt items are in Williams, *A Ghost Called Thunderbolt*; and 'Fred Lowry' is in Meredith and Anderson (eds), *Folksongs of Australia*, and Meredith, Covell and Brown (eds), *Folksongs of Australia*. This list is by no means exhaustive. See also R. Edwards, *200 Years of Australian Folk Song Index, 1788–1988*, Kuranda, Qld, 1988.

48 K. Dunstan, *St Ned: The Near-Sanctification of an Australian Outlaw*, Melbourne, 1980.

Chapter 6   Outlaw to National Hero

1 R. Reece, 'Ned Kelly's Father', in R. Reece (ed.), *Exiles from Erin: Convict Lives in Ireland and Australia*, London, 1991.

2 W. Bate, 'Ned Kelly and His Times', in C. Cave *et al.* (eds), *Ned Kelly: Man and Myth*, Sydney, 1968, pp. 40ff.; J. Powell (ed.), *Yeomen and Bureaucrats: The Victorian Crown Lands Commission, 1878–9*, London, 1973. See also editorial in *Argus*, 4 March 1878, on exorbitance of land tax, especially in Benalla; J. McQuilton, *The Kelly Outbreak, 1878–1880: The Geographical Dimension of Social Banditry*, Melbourne, 1979, chs 2–5.

3 J. Sadleir, *Recollections of a Victorian Police Officer*, 1913, pp. 65–7; T. O'Callaghan, 'Police in Port Phillip and Victoria, 1836–1913', *Victorian Historical Magazine* 4, June 1928.

4 H. King, 'Some Aspects of Police Administration in New South Wales, 1825–51', *Journal of the Royal Australian Historical Society* 42: 5, 1956; T. O'Callaghan, 'Police Establishment in NSW', *Journal of the Royal*

Australian Historical Society 9: 6, 1923; M. Brennan, 'A Police History of the Notorious Bushrangers of New South Wales and Victoria', MS A2030, Mitchell Library, Sydney.

5 *Royal Commission on the Police Force of Victoria 1881* (hereafter *PC*) Minutes of Evidence, Questions 15488–93, 15797–800, 17566.

6 *PC*, pp. 719–20.

7 The inadequacies of the police were frequently noted by the Victorian press at this time. See *Age*, 2 November 1878, 7 February 1879; *Argus*, 8 November 1879, p. 7. See also G. Wathan, *The Golden Colony of Victoria in 1854*, London, 1855, pp. 142, 179–82; R. Henty, *Australiana, or My Early Life*, London, 1886; and D. Chappell and P. Wilson, *The Police and the People in Australia and New Zealand*, St Lucia, Qld, 1969, pp. 28ff.

8 This was certainly how Ned Kelly and his supporters saw the situation. See, for example, J. Kenneally, *The Complete Inner History of the Kelly Gang and Their Pursuers*, Moe, Vic., 1929, an insider's guide to local feelings.

9 The texts of these letters are given in full in G. Seal, *Ned Kelly in Popular Tradition*, Melbourne, 1980.

10 Powell, *Yeomen and Bureaucrats*; *PC*, Questions 8723–26; McQuilton, *The Kelly Outbreak*, pp. 48–56.

11 *PC*, Appendix 1, pp. 679–82 and Questions 29, 3237–559; and I. Jones, 'A New View of Ned Kelly', in Cave *et al.* (eds), *Ned Kelly*, pp. 154–89.

12 *PC*, Questions 12801–994. Mrs Kelly married George King in February 1874, but it is convenient and conventional to refer to her as Mrs Kelly.

13 *PC*, Question 13440, evidence of W. Foster, local police magistrate.

14 McQuilton, *The Kelly Outbreak*, p. 96.

15 Felons Apprehension Act, Victoria, 1878.

16 'Stringybark Creek' collected by the Rev. Percy Jones c. 1940? and published in Cave *et al.* (eds), *Ned Kelly*. Original print version in *Songs of the Kelly Gang*, Hobart, ?1879 784.4/12, Mitchell Library, Sydney.

17 *PC*, Questions 1365–8, 2382–90, 12688–95.

18 *PC*, Questions 269–71, 554–8, 9380–8.

19 *PC*, Appendix 5, pp. 690–5.

20 *PC*, Questions 1365–8, 1372.

21 *Argus*, editorial, 28 February 1879.

22 *Age*, 17 December 1878.

23 *Argus*, 16, 18 December 1978.

24 Mrs R. Scott, 'The Kelly Gang at Euroa' (typescript Mitchell Library A4143). Mrs Scott was the wife of the Euroa bank manager and the one who declared that 'Ned Kelly was a gentleman.'

25 'Sticking Up of the Euroa Bank' in G. Wilson Hall, *The Kelly Gang or The Outlaws of the Wombat Ranges*, Mansfield, Vic., 1879. Also in *Songs of the Kelly Gang*, Mitchell Library.

26 Rev. H. C. Lundy, *Jerilderie: 100 Years*, Jerilderie, NSW, 1958, especially the statement 'The Kelly Raid on Jerilderie by one who was there', pp. 64ff., written in 1913.

27 Lundy, *Jerilderie*, p. 78.

28 'The Bold Kelly Gang' from Hall, *The Kelly Gang*. See also J. Meredith, (ed.), *Six Authentic Songs from the Kelly Country*, Sydney Bush Music Club, Sydney, 1955.

29 See Cave *et al.* (eds), *Ned Kelly*.

30 *PC*, Questions 7719–29.

31 *Argus*, 1 November 1880.

32 'The Ballad of the Kelly Gang', collected from Mr J. Watson, Sydney, by Warren Fahey, in Fahey, *Joe Watson: Traditional Folksinger*, Sydney, 1975.

33 See I. Jones, *The Friendship that Destroyed Ned Kelly: Joe Byrne and Aaron Sherritt*, Port Melbourne, 1992.

34 'Kelly Was Their Captain', a recitation collected from Mr Bill Shawcross by John Meredith, in J. Meredith and H. Anderson (eds), *Folksongs of Australia*, Sydney, 1967.

35 *Herald* (Melbourne), 14 November 1930; *Sun News-Pictorial*, 11 November 1930; *Age*, 18 April 1931. Also Cave *et al.* (eds), *Ned Kelly*, pp. 202, 206, for more survival traditions; *Bulletin*, 4 October 1933; and H. Neary, *The Kellys, Australia's Famous Bushrangers*, Sydney, n.d., [1930?] p. 39.

36 See Seal, *Ned Kelly*, pp. 140–1, a poem titled 'The Mystery Man'.

37 See Ellis H. Davidson, 'Folklore and History', *Folklore* 85, 1974; and A. W. Smith, 'Some Folklore Elements in Movements of Social Protest', *Folklore* 77, 1966, and ch. 1.

38 Such is the power of this tradition that in early 1995 serious attempts were made to prove a certain James Ryan of Ipswich, Qld, who died in 1948, was, as he claimed, really Dan Kelly: *The Weekend Australian*, 26–29 January 1995, p. 12.

39 The earlier Salvation Army effort, *Soldiers of the Cross* (1905), is not generally thought to be a true 'movie', involving stills as well as moving images.

40 Regal-Zonophone 78 rpm releases G23895 and G23882. Both these songs, 'The Ned Kelly Song' and 'Poor Ned Kelly', persist in oral tradition.

41 See E. Watson, *Country Music in Australia*, vol. 1, Sydney, 1976.

42 'The Kelly Gang of Robbers' in *The Banker's Magazine* 5, January 1892, pp. 352, 354.

43 C. E. Taylor, *The Girl Who Helped Ned Kelly*, Melbourne, 1929.

44 Examples like these could be cited almost endlessly from the never-ending flood of Kelly literature. The same ambivalence was also a feature of the Kelly films. For example, a silent production of 1923, *The True Story of the Kelly Gang*, wobbled its confused way to a moralising conclusion through portrayals of Constable Fitzpatrick as a hard-line trooper, the police firing

first at Stringybark Creek, and the Kellys' 'countless sympathisers', whom, we are later informed, only did it for the money.

45 C. Hayter, *Ned Kelly: A Tale of Trooper and Bushranger*, n.d.

46 For a reasonably comprehensive listing of the considerable number of Kelly works up to the early 1940s, see C. Turnbull, *Kellyana*, Melbourne, 1943.

47 J. S. Borlase, *Ned Kelly, The Ironclad Australian Bushranger*, London, 1881.

48 'Ned Kelly Was a Gentleman' is a poem that first appears in J. Sweeney, *Original Australian Verse*, Sydney n.d. [1945?] referring to Malaya and claimed by Sweeney as his own composition. Russel Ward collected the version of it that appears here and published it in his *The Penguin Book of Australian Ballads*, Ringwood, Vic., 1964.

49 Quoted in M. Williams, *Australia on the Popular Stage, 1829–1929*, Melbourne, 1983.

50 Actually, it was another sister, 'Maggie' (married name Skillion) who carried out these supportive actions. The publicity-seeking and sadly tragic Kate Kelly, assisted by the alliterative appeal of her name, was 'heroinised' by the press of the time and by the popular media ever since.

51 Neary, *The Kellys*. Other examples in Seal, *Ned Kelly*, ch. 9. Neary was wrong about Ned's heroism being superseded by the Anzac tradition. As the verses titled 'Ned Kelly Was a Gentleman' show, Ned Kelly's qualities were felt to be just as appropriate for fighting the Japanese as for fighting the Hun two and a half decades earlier.

52 I am grateful to John McQuilton for pointing out this telling usage of the phrase.

53 A number of other Kelly songs should be mentioned here also. 'Ned Kelly Was An Irishman' was collected in Queensland from Mrs Andreau by Ron Edwards and published in his *The Big Book of Australian Folk Songs*, Sydney, 1976, p. 254. Kate Kelly features in a number of other Kelly songs, some of which appear here. See also 'The Kelly Gang', collected from Mr Tom Gibbons by John Meredith, and 'Ye Sons of Australia', collected from Mrs Scrivener by John Meredith, in Meredith and Anderson (eds), *Folksongs of Australia*, pp. 248–9, 99–100. The original poem by J. K. Moir first appeared in the *Bulletin*. 'My Name is Edward Kelly' was collected by Warren Fahey from Mr Cyril Duncan, Hawthorne, Qld, 1973. Another version is in Manifold, *The Penguin Australian Song Book*, pp. 64–5. 'Farewell to My Home in Greta' was collected from Mrs Barrie by Max Brown, and it appears in his *Australian Son*, Melbourne, 1948. See also Meredith, (ed.), *Six Authentic Songs*, and Manifold, *The Penguin Australian Song Book*, pp. 66–7, particularly 'Ned Kelly Was Born in a Ramshackle Hut' and 'Poor Ned Kelly' (see note 30). Also 'Farewell Dan and Edward Kelly', 'The Kelly Gang', 'The Bold Kelly Gang', 'The Kellys Are Having A Mighty Fine Time' are in Brown, *Australian Son*, and elsewhere. See Seal, *Ned Kelly*, for a full

discussion of these. The numerous recorded country and western treatments of the Kelly legend are covered in the discography in Watson, *Country Music in Australia*, vol 1. There are also verse treatments of various bushrangers, real and imaginary, in the 'Bill Bowyang' reciters and assorted songsters, such as *Small's Colonial Songster*. None of these appears to have attained significant oral or other informal circulation.

54 J. Phillips, *The Trial of Ned Kelly*, Sydney, 1987, p. 94.

55 More than 30 000 people signed a petition for Kelly's reprieve.

56 R. Reece, 'Ned Kelly's Father'.

57 D. Balcarek, *Ellen Kelly*, Glenrowan, Vic., 1984.

58 J. Molony, *I Am Ned Kelly*, Ringwood, Vic., 1981.

59 McQuilton, *The Kelly Outbreak*.

60 J. Bedford, *Sister Kate*, Ringwood, Vic., 1982.

61 R. Drew, *Our Sunshine*, Ringwood, Vic., 1992.

62 Jones, *The Friendship that Destroyed Ned Kelly*.

63 K. Dunstan, *St Ned: The Story of the Near Sanctification of an Australian Outlaw*, Sydney, 1980.

64 See D. Rose, *Dingo Makes Us Human: Life and Land in an Aboriginal Australian Culture*, Melbourne, 1992, pp. 198–202, 205, 208, 231.

Chapter 7　Interpreting the Legend

1 On this topic see, for instance, Lord Raglan, *The Hero: A Study in Tradition, Myth and Drama*, London, 1936; H. Halpert, 'Truth in Folk-Songs: Some Observations on the Folk-Singer's Attitude', in H. Halpert and G. Herzog, *Traditional Ballads from West Virginia*, New York, 1939; D. Buchan, 'History and Harlaw', in *Journal of the Folklore Institute* 5, 1968; A. Green, 'McCaffery: A Study in the Variation and Function of a Ballad', *Lore and Language* 3–5, 1970–71; R. Dorson, 'The Debate Over the Trustworthiness of Oral Traditional History', in Dorson, *Folklore*, Bloomington, 1972; J. Ashton, 'Truth in Folksong: Some Developments and Applications', *Canadian Folk Music Journal* 5, 1977; E. D. Ives, *George Magoon and the Down East Game War: History, Folklore and the Law*, Urbana and Chicago, 1988, 'Introduction' and 'The Summing Up'; M. Pickering, 'The Past as a Source of Aspiration: Popular Song and Social Change', in M. Pickering and A. Green, *Popular Song and the Vernacular Milieu*, Milton Keynes, 1987.

2 G. Seal, *The Hidden Culture: Folklore in Australian Society*, Melbourne, 1989; 1993.

3 See J. Fiske, *Understanding Popular Culture*, Boston, 1989, and his *Reading the Popular*, Boston, 1989, for a succinct exposition of such approaches. Also M. de Certeau, *The Practice of Everyday Life*, trans. S. Rendall, Berkeley, 1984.

4 A. Falassi (ed), *Time Out of Time: Essays on the Festival*, Albuquerque, 1987;

U. Eco, 'The Frames of Comic Freedom' in T. Sebeok and M. Erickson (eds), 'Carnival!', *Approaches to Semiotics* 64, Berlin, 1984.

5 V. Propp, *Morphology of the Folktale* (1929), trans. L. Scott, 2nd edn, Austin and London, 1968.

6 B. Capp, 'Popular Literature', in B. Reay (ed.), *Popular Culture in Seventeenth Century England* (1985), London, 1988, p. 210.

7 Quoted from K. Carpenter, *Penny Dreadfuls and Comics: English Periodicals for Children from Victorian Times to the Present Day*, London, 1983, p. 6.

8 See ch. 6.

9 From H. E. Rollins (ed.), *The Pepys Ballads*, Cambridge, Mass., 1929–31, vii, pp. 202–4, quoted in J. Sharpe, 'The People and the Law', in Reay (ed.), *Popular Culture*.

10 Although outside the scope of this book, A. Paredes, *With His Pistol in His Hand: A Border Ballad and Its Hero*, Austin, (1958) 1990, on Gregorio Cortez provides an excellent case study of the same process at work on the Mexican-American bandit.

11 Female noble robbers are relatively common in other cultural and linguistic traditions, such as those of Spain, Peru, the Balkans and China.

12 For instance, Marcy Clay, a.k.a. Jenny Fox, was one highway-woman who cheated Tyburn by poisoning herself in the condemned cell in 1665. Such acts of pathetic desperation were not, of course, the stuff of highwaymen legend. In 1690 the ballad hacks celebrated 'The Female Highway Hector'— not important enough to dignify by name. See also A. Hayward (ed.), *Lives of the Most Remarkable Criminals* (1735), London, 1927, pp. 373–5, for 'Frances', alias Mary Blackett.

13 *Time*, 23 January 1995, p. 51. See also K. Hafner and J. Markoff, *Cyberpunk: Outlaws and Hackers on the Computer Frontier*, New York, 1991, which includes the story of Mitnick's earlier career of 'superhighway robbery'; and E. Krol, 'Outlaws in Cyberspace', *The Sciences*, 5 January 1994.

14 So described by James Bone in *The Times* and reprinted in the *Weekend Australian*, 18–19 February 1995, p. 20, beneath an article on a latter-day bounty hunter and another on the O. J. Simpson trial.

15 *Time*, 27 February 1995, pp. 36–7.

16 E. P. Thompson, *Customs in Common*, London, 1991.

17 A. McCall, *The Medieval Underworld*, London, 1979, p. 103.

18 McCall, *The Medieval Underworld*, p. 109.

19 For a study of the local intricacies of perceived common rights in Maine in the nineteenth and early twentieth centuries, attitudes towards authority and at least embryonic outlawry see Ives, *George Magoon*.

20 For a detailed and incisive explication of this point, P. Linebaugh, *The London Hanged: Crime and Civil Society in the Eighteenth Century*, New York, 1992, ch. 6 and *passim*.

21 There is a considerable literature on charivari (itself a contested term) especially in English and French. The late E. P. Thompson was a leading scholar in this area; see his *Customs in Common*, London, 1991, ch. 8 'Rough Music', an update of his 1972 article 'Rough Music: Le Charivari anglais' in *Annales E.S.C.* For an account of the relationship between charivari, folk custom in general and political protest, see G. Seal, 'Tradition and Protest in Nineteenth Century England and Wales', *Folklore*, 100: 2 1988, and for the continuing potency of folk justice see G. Seal, 'Azaria Chamberlain and the Media Charivari', *Australian Folklore* 1, 1987.

22 B. Thomson, B. Leader, B. Bland, *Unto Brigg Fair: Joseph Taylor and other traditional Lincolnshire singers recorded in 1908 by Percy Grainger*, LP record, Leader LEA 4050, London, 1972.

Sources and References

Abrahams, R. (ed.), *A Singer and Her Songs: Almeda Riddle's Book of Ballads*, Baton Rouge, 1970.

Adams, R., *Six Guns and Saddle Leather*, Norman, OK, 1969.

Adamson, B., File on Ned Kelly (MS), Mitchell Library, Sydney.

Allen, H. C., *Bush and Backwoods: A Comparison of the Frontier of Australia and the United States*, East Lansing, 1959.

Alomes, S. and den Hartog, D. (eds), *Post Pop: Popular Culture, Nationalism and Postmodernism*, Footscray, Vic., 1991.

Anderson, H., 'On the Track with "Bill Bowyang"', *Australian Folklore* 6, 1991.

Anderson, H., *Colonial Ballads*, Melbourne (1955), 1962.

Ashton, J., *Modern Street Ballads*, London, 1888.

Ashton, J., 'Truth in Folksong: Some Developments and Applications', *Canadian Folk Music Journal* 5, 1977.

Australian Folklore Unit Tapes (W. Fahey), Macquarie University and National Library of Australia.

Balcarek, D., *Ellen Kelly*, Glenrowan, Vic., 1984.

Barker, T. J., 'Bushranging: The History and the Legend', *Canberra Historical Journal*, March 1974.

Barlow, D., *Dick Turpin and the Gregory Gang*, London, 1973.

Beattie, J. M., 'The Pattern of Crime in England 1660–1800', *Past and Present* 62, 1974.

Beatty, B., *A Treasury of Australian Folk Tales and Traditions*, Sydney, 1960.

Belden, H. M. (ed.), *Ballads and Songs Collected by the Missouri Folklore Society*, University of Missouri, Columbia, 1940.

Belden, H. and Hudson, A. (eds), *The Frank C. Brown Collection of North Carolina Folklore*, (7 vols), Durham, NC, 1952, especially vol. 2: *Folk Ballads from North Carolina*.

Bellamy, J., *Crime and Public Order in England in the Later Middle Ages*, London, 1973.

Beloff, M., *Public Order and Popular Disturbances 1660–1714*, London, 1938.

Bigsby, C. W. E. (ed.), *Approaches to Popular Culture*, London, 1976.

Blok, A., 'The Peasant and the Brigand: Social Banditry Reconsidered', *Comparative Studies in Society and History* 1: 4, September 1972.

Bonwick, J., *The Bushrangers: Illustrating the Early Days of Van Diemen's Land*, Melbourne, 1856

Borlase, J. S., *Ned Kelly, The Ironclad Australian Bushranger*, London, 1881.

Botkin, B., *A Treasury of Western Folklore*, New York, 1964.

Botkin, B. (ed.), *A Treasury of American Folklore*, New York, 1944.

Boxall, G., *History of the Australian Bushrangers*, Sydney, 1935.

Bradshaw, J., *The Only True Account of Ned Kelly, Frank Gardiner, Ben Hall and Morgan*, Sydney, 1911.

Brady, E. J., *Two Frontiers*, Sydney, 1944.

Brennan, M., 'A Police History of the Notorious Bushrangers of NSW and Victoria' (MS A2030), Mitchell Library, Sydney.

Brennan, M., *Reminiscences of the Goldfields*, Sydney, 1907.

Britton, W., *The Civil War on the Border*, 2 vols, 1890–9.

Brown, M., *Australian Son*, Melbourne, 1948.

Brown, R. M., *Strain of Violence: Historical Studies of American Violence*, Oxford, 1975.

Buchan, D., 'History and Harlaw', *Journal of the Folklore Institute* 5, 1968.

Butterss, P., 'Bold Jack Donahue and the Irish Outlaw Tradition', *Australian Folklore* 3, 1989.

Byron, K., *Lost Treasures in Australia and New Zealand*, Sydney, 1964.

Campbell, J., *The Hero With a Thousand Faces*, Princeton, NJ, 1968.

Capp, B., 'Popular Literature', in Reay, B. (ed.), *Popular Culture in Seventeenth Century England* (1985), London, 1988.

Cave, C. *et al.* (eds), *Ned Kelly: Man and Myth*, Sydney, 1968.

Cavendish, R. (ed.), *Legends of the World*, London, 1982.

Chappell, D. and Wilson, P., *The Police and the People in Australia and New Zealand*, St Lucia, Qld, 1969.

Chappell, W., *Popular Music of the Olden Time* (1859), 2 vols, New York, 1965.

Child, F. J., *The English and Scottish Popular Ballads*, 5 vols, 1882–98.

Clark, C. M. H. (ed.), (Harris, A.?) *Convicts and Settlers* (1847), Melbourne, 1953.

Clark, M. (ed.), *Sources of Australian History* (1957), London, 1971.

Clune, F., *The Kelly-Hunters*, Sydney, 1954.

Clune, F., *The Wild Colonial Boys: Ben Hall and His Gang*, Sydney, 1948.

Cockburn, J. S. (ed.), *Crime in England 1550–1800*, London, 1977.

Cohen, N., *Long Steel Rail: The Railroad in American Folksong*, Urbana, 1981.

Collison, R., *The Story of Street Literature*, London, 1973.

Combs, J. H. (ed. D. K. Wilgus), *Folksongs of the Southern United States* (1925), American Folklore Society Reprint, 1967.

Connelley, W. E., *Quantrill and the Border Wars*, 1910.

Cozens, C., *The Adventures of a Guardsman*, London, 1847.

Crampton, T., *Ballads Collected by . . .* (9 vols), London, 1868–70 (B.L. 11621 h 11).

Davidson, Ellis H., 'Folklore and History', *Folklore* 85, 1974.

Dobie, F. J., *Tales of Old-Time Texas* (1928), London, 1959.

Dobson, R. B. and Taylor, J., *Rymes of Robin Hood: An Introduction to the English Outlaw* (1976), 2nd rev. edn, Gloucester, 1989.

Dorson, R., 'The Debate Over the Trustworthiness of Oral Traditional History', in Dorson, R., *Folklore*, Bloomington, 1972.

Dorson, R., *American Folklore*, Chicago, 1960.

Dunstan, K., *St Ned: The Near-Sanctification of an Australian Outlaw*, Melbourne, 1980.

Dykes, J. C., *Billy the Kid: The Bibliography of a Legend*, Norman, OK, 1952.

Eco, U., 'The Frames of Comic Freedom', in Sebeok, T. and Erickson, M. (eds), *Carnival!*, Approaches to Semiotics 64, Berlin, 1984.

Edwards, J. N., *Noted Guerillas*, 1877.

Edwards, R., *The Overlander Songbook*, St Lucia, Qld, 1991.

Edwards, R., *200 Years of Australian Folk Song Index, 1788–1988*, Kuranda, Qld, 1988.

Edwards, R. (ed.), *The Convict Maid*, Kuranda, Qld, 3rd edn, 1987.

Edwards, R., *The Big Book of Australian Folk Songs*, Sydney, 1976.

Elliot, I., *Moondyne Joe: The Man and the Myth*, Perth, 1978.

Evans, H. and Evans, E., *Hero on a Stolen Horse: The Highwayman and His Brothers-in-Arms the Bandit and the Bushranger*, London, 1977.

Fahey, W., *Joe Watson:Traditional Folksinger*, Sydney, 1975.

Falassi, A. (ed.), *Time Out of Time: Essays on the Festival*, Albuquerque, 1987.

Finger, C., *Frontier Ballads*, New York, 1927.

Finger, C., *Bushrangers*, New York, 1924.

Folklore Council of Australia, *A Collection of Australian Folk Songs and Traditional Ballads*, Melbourne, 1967.

Ford, R., *Vagabond Songs and Ballads of Scotland*, 2nd series, London, 1910 (Norwood reprint, 1975).

Gillett, James B., *Six Years With the Texas Rangers*, 1925.

Glassie, H., *Irish Folk Tales*, New York, 1985.

Glassie, H. (ed.), *Irish Folk History: Texts from the North*, Philadelphia, 1982.

Gonner, E. C. K., *Common Land and Inclosure* (1912), London, 1966.

Gow, N., 'Frank Gardiner: "Prince of Tobymen"', *Canberra Historical Journal*, March 1974.

Graham, H. and Gurr, T. (eds), *Violence in America: Historical and Comparative Perspectives* (rev. edn), Beverly Hills and London, 1979.

Green, A., 'McCaffery: A Study in the Variation and Function of a Ballad', *Lore and Language* 3–5, 1970–71.

Greenway, J., *The Last Frontier: A Study of the Development of the Last Frontiers of America and Australia*, London, 1972.

Greenway, J. (ed.), *Folklore of the Great West*, Palo Alto, 1969.

Gurko, L., *Heroes, Highbrows and the Popular Mind*, New York, 1953.

Gutch, J. M., *A Lytell Geste of Robin Hood*, 2 vols, London, 1847.

Hafner, K. and Markoff, J., *Cyberpunk: Outlaws and Hackers on the Computer Frontier*, New York, 1991.

Hall, G. Wilson, *The Kelly Gang or The Outlaws of the Wombat Ranges*, Mansfield, Vic., 1879.

Halpert, H., 'Truth in Folk-Songs: Some Observations on the Folk-Singer's Attitude', in Halpert, H. and Herzog, G., *Traditional Ballads from West Virginia*, New York, 1939.

Hamer, F. (comp.), *Garner's Gay*, London, 1967.

Harper, C. G., *Half-Hours with the Highwaymen* (2 vols), London, 1908.

Harris, A., *Convicts and Settlers* (1847), Melbourne, 1970.

Harrison, A., *The Irish Trickster*, Sheffield, 1988.

Hay, D. *et al.* (eds), *Albion's Fatal Tree: Crime and Society in Eighteenth Century England*, London, 1975.

Haydon, A. L., *The Trooper Police of Australia*, London, 1911.

Haygarth, H., *Recollections of Bush Life in Australia*, London, 1861.

Hayter, C., *Ned Kelly: A Tale of Trooper and Bushranger*, n.d.

Hayward, A., *Lives of the Most Remarkable Criminals*, London, 1735.

Healy, J., *Ballads from the Pubs of Ireland*, Dublin (1965), 1976.

Hendricks, G., *The Bad Man of the West*, San Antonio, 1941.

Henty, R., *Australiana, or My Early Life*, London, 1886.

Hibbert, C., *Highwaymen*, London, 1967.

Hibbert, C., *The Roots of Evil: A Social History of Crime and Punishment* (1963), Westport, CT, 1978.

Hilton, R. H., 'The Origins of Robin Hood', *Past and Present* 14, 1958.

Hindley, C., *Curiosities of Street Literature*, 1871.

Hitchcock, G. (ed.), *Folksongs of the West Country*, London, 1977 (the Sabine Baring-Gould MS collection).

Hobsbawm, E., *Bandits*, London, 1969.

Hobsbawm, E., *Primitive Rebels*, Manchester, 1963.

Hoffman, Dean Alan, 'The Minstrelsy of the Greenwood: The Medieval English Outlaw Ballad in Literary and Social History', unpublished PhD dissertation, University of California, Riverside, 1987.

Hollon, L., *Frontier Violence: Another Look*, New York, 1974.

Holloway, J. and Black, J. (eds), *Later English Broadside Ballads*, London, 1975, vol. 1.

Holt, J., 'The Origins and the Audience of the Ballads of Robin Hood', *Past and Present* 18, 1960.

Hook, S., *The Hero in History*, London, 1945.

Howitt, R., *Impressions of Australia Felix &c*, London, 1845.

Hughes, R., *The Fatal Shore: A History of the Transportation of Convicts to Australia, 1787–1868*, London, 1987.

Hults, D. S., 'A Bibliographic Survey of Folklore in Australia 1790–1990', unpublished MA thesis, Deakin University, 1995.

Humphreys, A. L., 'The Highwayman and His Chap-Book', *Notes & Queries*, May–June 1940.

Inciardi, L., Block, L. and Hallowell, L., *Historical Approaches to Crime*, Beverly Hills, 1977.

Ingledew, C. J., *The Ballads and Songs of Yorkshire*, London, 1860.

Ives, E. D., *George Magoon and the Down East Game War: History, Folklore and the Law*, Urbana and Chicago, 1988.

James, L., *Print and the People, 1819–1851*, London, 1976.

Jones, D. E., 'Clenched Teeth and Curses: Revenge and the Dime Novel Outlaws', *Journal of Popular Culture* 7: 3, 1973.

Jones, I., *The Friendship that Destroyed Ned Kelly: Joe Byrne and Aaron Sherritt*, Port Melbourne, 1992.

Karpeles, M. (ed.), *Cecil Sharp's Collection of English Folk Songs*, London, 1974, vol. 2.

Keen, M., *The Outlaws of Medieval Legend*, London, 1961.

Keen, M., 'Robin Hood: A Peasant Hero', *History Today*, October 1958.

Kenneally, J., *The Complete Inner History of the Kelly Gang and Their Pursuers*, Moe, Vic., 1929.

Kennedy, P., *Folksong of Britain and Ireland*, London, 1975.

Kent, D., 'Customary Behaviour Transported: The Parramatta Riot', *Australian Folklore* 7, September 1992.

Kidson, F., *A Garland of English Folk-Songs*, London, 1926.

Kidson, F., *Traditional Tunes* (1891), S.R. Publishers, 1970.

King, H., 'Some Aspects of Police Administration in NSW, 1825–51', *Journal of the Royal Australian Historical Society* 42: 5, 1956.

Kirby, C., 'The English Game-law System', *American Historical Review* 38, 1932–33.

Klapp, O., 'The Folk Hero', *Journal of American Folklore* 62, 1949.

Knight, S., *Robin Hood: A Complete Study of the English Outlaw*, London, 1994.

Kooistra, P., *Criminals as Heroes: Structure, Power and Identity*, Bowling Green, 1989.

Kruse, H. H., 'Myth in the Making: The James Brothers at Northfield,

Minnesota, and the Dime Novel', *Journal of Popular Culture* 10: 2, 1976.

Lange, J. de, *The Relation and Development of English and Icelandic Outlaw-Traditions*, Haarlem, 1935.

Larkin, M., *The Singing Cowboy*, New York, 1931.

Laws, G., *American Balladry from British Broadsides*, Philadelphia, 1957.

Library of Congress Archive of Folksong Checklist, Washington, DC, 1942.

Linebaugh, P., *The London Hanged: Crime and Civil Society in the Eighteenth Century*, New York, 1992.

Lingenfelter, R. *et al.* (eds), *Songs of the American West*, Los Angeles, 1968.

Lloyd, A., *Folksong in England*, London, 1967.

Logan, H., *A Pedlar's Pack of Ballads and Songs*, Edinburgh, 1869.

Lomax, A., *Our Singing Country*, New York, 1949.

Lomax, J. and A., *American Ballads and Folk Songs*, New York, 1934.

Lundy, Rev. H. C., *Jerilderie: 100 years*, Jerilderie, NSW, 1958.

Lynn, K., 'Violence in American Literature and Folklore', in Graham, H. and Gurr, T. (eds), *Violence in America: Historical and Comparative Perspectives* (rev. edn), Beverly Hills and London, 1979.

Mackay, C., *Extraordinary Popular Delusions and the Madness of Crowds*, London, 1841. Also published in 2 vols as *Memoirs of Extraordinary Popular Delusions*, London, 1852.

Maddicott, J. R., 'The Birth and Setting of the Ballads of Robin Hood', *English Historical Review* 93, 1978.

Manifold, J. S., *Who Wrote the Ballads?: Notes on Australian Folksong*, Sydney, 1964.

Marshall, J. J., *Irish Tories, Rapparees and Robbers*, Dungannon, 1927.

Martin, Charles L., *A Sketch of Sam Bass, the Bandit*, 1880.

Maxwell, G. S., *Highwayman's Heath*, new edn, London, 1949.

McColl, E. and Seeger, P., *Travellers' Songs from England and Scotland*, London, 1977.

McDonald, B., 'Thunderbolt, Folksong and the Legend of the Noble Robber', *Australian Folklore* 8, 1993.

McLynn, F., *Crime and Punishment in Eighteenth Century England*, Oxford, 1991.

McPherson, P., 'H. M. Keightley, W. R. Rottan and the Bushrangers', *Journal of the Royal Australian Historical Society* 23: 1, 1937.

McQueen, H., 'Convicts and Rebels', *Labour History*, 15, November 1968.

McQuilton, J., 'Australian Bushranging and Social Banditry with Special Reference to the Kelly Outbreak', *Royal Geographical Society of Australasia, South Australian Branch, Proceedings* 82, 1982.

McQuilton, J., *The Kelly Outbreak: The Geographical Dimension of Social Banditry*, Melbourne, 1979.

Meredith, John, Tape Collection, National Library of Australia.

Meredith, J., *The Wild Colonial Boy: The Life and Times of Jack Donohoe, 1808–1830*, Sydney, 1960; reprinted Ascot Vale, Vic., 1982.

Meredith, J. (ed.), *Six Authentic Songs from the Kelly Country*, Sydney Bush Music Club, Sydney, 1955.

Meredith, J. and Anderson, H. (eds), *Folksongs of Australia*, Sydney, 1967.

Meredith, J., Covell, R. and Brown, P., *Folksongs of Australia*, vol. 2, Sydney, 1987.

Meredith, J. and Whalan, R., *Frank the Poet*, Melbourne, 1979.

Meyer, R., 'The Outlaw: A Distinctive American Folktype', *Journal of the Folklore Institute* 17, 1980.

Milner, A., 'Postmodernism and Popular Culture', in Alomes, S. and den Hartog, D. (eds), *Post Pop: Popular Culture, Nationalism and Postmodernism*, Footscray, Vic., 1991.

Molony, J., *I Am Ned Kelly*, Ringwood, 1981.

Neary, H., *The Kellys, Australia's Famous Bushrangers*, Sydney, n.d., [1930?].

Neuberg, V., *Popular Literature: A History and Guide*, Harmondsworth, 1977.

O'Callaghan, T., 'Police Establishment in NSW', *Journal of the Royal Australian Historical Society* 9: 6, 1923.

O'Callaghan, T., 'Police in Port Phillip and Victoria, 1836–1913', *Victorian Historical Magazine* No. 4, June 1928.

O'Farrell, P., *The Irish in Australia*, Sydney, 1987.

O'Malley, P., 'Class Conflict, Land and Social Banditry: Bushranging in Nineteenth Century Australia, *Social Problems* 26: 3, 1979.

O'Malley, P., 'Social Bandits, Modern Capitalism and the Traditional Peasantry', *Journal of Peasant Studies* 6: 4, 1979.

O'Shaughnessy, P. (ed.), *Yellowbelly Ballads* (Part 1), Lincoln, 1975.

Overland 84, July 1981.

Page, G., 'Was Billy the Kid a Superhero or a Superscoundrel?', *Smithsonian*, February 1991.

Palmer, R. (ed.), *Everyman's Book of British Ballads*, London, 1981.

Paredes, A., *With His Pistol in His Hand: A Border Ballad and its Hero*, Austin, TX, (1958) 1990.

Paterson, A. B. (ed.), *The Old Bush Songs*, Sydney, 1905 (various revised editions to 1931).

Phillips, J., *The Trial of Ned Kelly*, Sydney, 1987.

Pickering, M., 'The Past as a Source of Aspiration: Popular Song and Social Change', in Pickering and Green (eds), *Popular Song and the Vernacular Milieu*.

Pickering M. and Green, A. (eds), *Popular Song and the Vernacular Milieu*, Milton Keynes, 1987.

Pike, R., 'The Reality and Legend of the Spanish Bandit Diego Corrientes', *Folklore* 99: ii, 1988.

SOURCES AND REFERENCES

Pinto, V. de Sola and Rodway, A. (eds), *The Common Muse: An Anthology of Popular British Ballad Poetry, XVth–XXth Century*, London, 1957.

Poli, B., 'The Hero in France and America', *Journal of American Studies* 2: 2, 1968.

Police Commission: Minutes of Evidence Taken Before Royal Commission on the Police Force of Victoria, 1881, (facsimile) Adelaide, 1968.

Porter, K., '"Johnny Troy": A "Lost" Australian Bushranger Ballad in the United States', *Meanjin Quarterly*, 24, June 1965.

Potter, A., 'The Police Force of New South Wales', *Journal of the Royal Australian Historical Society* 6: 6, 1920.

Powell, J. M. (ed.), *Yeomen and Bureaucrats: The Victorian Crown Lands Commission, 1878–1879*, London, 1973.

Purslow, F., *The Constant Lovers*, London, 1972.

Purslow, F. (ed), *Marrow Bones: English Folk Songs from the Hammond and Gardiner Mss*, London, 1965.

Purslow, F. (ed), *The Wanton Seed: More English Folk Songs from the Hammond and Gardiner Mss*, London, 1968.

Quinault, R. and Stevenson, J. (eds), *Popular Protest and Public Order: Six Studies in British History, 1790–1920*, London, 1974.

Radin, P., *The Trickster: A Study in American Indian Mythology*, New York, 1956.

Raglan, Lord, *The Hero: A Study in Tradition, Myth and Drama*, London, 1936.

Randolph, V., *Ozark Folk Songs*, Columbia, MO, 1946–50 (4 vols).

Rank, O., *The Myth of the Birth of the Hero*, New York, 1914.

Reay, B. (ed.), *Popular Culture in Seventeenth Century England* (1985), London, 1988.

Reece, R., 'Ned Kelly's Father' in Reece, R. (ed), *Exiles from Erin: Convict Lives in Ireland and Australia*, London, 1991.

Reece, R., 'Ned Kelly and the Irish Connection', in Bridge, C. (ed.), *New Directions in Australian History*, London, 1990.

Ritson, J., *Robin Hood*, 1795.

Rixon, A., *The Truth About Captain Thunderbolt, Australia's Robin Hood*, Sydney, 1940 (and various subsequent editions).

Roberts, J. W., '"Railroad Bill" and the American Outlaw Tradition', *Western Folklore* 40, 1981.

Roberts, S. H., *History of Australian Land Settlement, 1788–1920* (1924), Melbourne, 1968.

Rollins, H.E. (ed.), *The Pepys Ballads*, Cambridge, MA, 1929–31.

Rose, D., *Dingo Makes Us Human: Life and Land in an Aboriginal Australian Culture*, Melbourne, 1992.

Royal Commission on the Police Force of Victoria 1881, Minutes of Evidence.

Rudé, G., *Protest and Punishment: The Story of the Social and Political Protesters Transported to Australia, 1788–1868*, London, 1978.

Rudé, G., 'Early Rebels in Australia', *Historical Studies* 16: 62, 1969.

Sadleir, J., *Recollections of a Victorian Police Officer*, 1913.

Sadleir, J., 'The Early Days of the Victorian Police Force', *Victorian Historical Magazine* 1: 3, September 1911.

Sandburg, C., *The American Songbag*, New York, 1927.

Schechter, H., *The Bosom Serpent: Folklore and Popular Art*, Iowa City, 1988.

Scott, Bill (ed.), *The Second Penguin Australian Songbook*, Ringwood, Vic., 1980.

Seal, G., 'Ned Kelly: His Past, Present and Future', *Australian Folklore* 10, 1995.

Seal, G., 'The Wild Colonial Boy Rides Again: An Australian Legend Abroad', in Craven, I. (ed.), *Australian Popular Culture*, Cambridge, 1994.

Seal, G., 'Deep Continuities and Discontinuities in the Outlaw Hero Traditions of Britain, Australia and America', *Lore and Language* 10: 1, 1993.

Seal, G., 'Narrative Structure and Cultural Function in the Highwayman Tradition', unpublished paper presented to the American Folklore Society Centennial meeting, Philadelphia, October 1989.

Seal, G., 'Tradition and Protest in Nineteenth Century England and Wales', *Folklore* 100: 2, 1988.

Seal, G., 'Azaria Chamberlain and the Media Charivari', *Australian Folklore* 1, 1987.

Seal, G., *Ned Kelly in Popular Tradition*, Melbourne, 1980.

Seal, G., *The Highwayman Tradition in Australia*, Folklore Occasional Paper 9, Sydney, 1977.

Settle, W. A. jnr, *Jesse James Was His Name, or, fact and fiction concerning the careers of the notorious James brothers of Missouri*, Columbia, MO, 1966.

Sharp, C., *A Book of British Song, for Home and School*, London, 1902.

Sharpe, J., 'The People and the Law', in Reay, B. (ed.), *Popular Culture in Seventeenth Century England* (1985), London, 1988.

Shaw, A. G. L., 'Violent Protest in Australian History', *Historical Studies* 15: 60, April 1973.

Shepard, L., *The History of Street Literature*, Newton Abbot, 1973.

Shiel, D. J., *Ben Hall: Bushranger*, St. Lucia, Qld, 1983.

Simeone, W. E., 'Robin Hood and Some Other American Outlaws', *Journal of American Folklore* 71, 1958.

Simpson, C., *The British Broadside Ballad and its Music*, New Brunswick, 1966.

Smith, A. W., 'Some Folklore Elements in Movements of Social Protest', *Folklore* 77, 1966.

Smith, Captain Alexander, *A Complete History of the Lives and Robberies of the Most Notorious Highwaymen*, 1719.

Songs of the Kelly Gang, Hobart, ?1879.

Songs of the Open Road, LP disk, Topic Records 12T253, 1975.

Spargo, J. W., *Juridical Folklore in England*, Durham, NC, 1944.

Spufford, M., *Small Books and Pleasant Histories: Popular Fiction and its Readership in Seventeenth Century England*, Athens, GA, 1982.

Stapleton, A., *Robin Hood: The Question of His Existence*, 1899.

Steckmesser, Kent L., 'Robin Hood and the American Outlaw', *Journal of American Folklore* 79, 1966.

Steckmesser, Kent L., *The Western Hero in History and Legend*, Norman, OK, 1965.

Stenbock-Fermor, E., 'The Story of Van'ka Kain', in Lord, A. (ed.), *Slavic Folklore: A Symposium*, Philadelphia, 1956.

Stewart, D. and Keesing, N. (eds), *Old Bush Songs*, Sydney, 1957.

Stewart, D. and Keesing, N. (eds), *Australian Bush Ballads*, Sydney, 1955.

Stubbes, K., *The Life of a Man*, London, 1970.

Sweeney, J., *Original Australian Verse*, Sydney, n.d. [1945?].

Tate, B., 'Thunderbolt and Morgan', *Australian Tradition*, October, 1972.

Tatum, S., *Inventing Billy the Kid: Visions of the Outlaw in America, 1881–1981*, Albuquerque, 1982.

Taylor, C. E., *The Girl Who Helped Ned Kelly*, Melbourne, 1929.

Therry, R., *Reminiscences of Thirty Years' Residence in NSW and Victoria*, London, 1863.

Thomson, B., Leader, B. and Bland, B., *Unto Brigg Fair: Joseph Taylor and other traditional Lincolnshire singers recorded in 1908 by Percy Grainger*, LP disk, Leader LEA 4050, London, 1972.

Thompson, E. P., *Customs in Common*, London, 1991.

Thompson, E. P., *Whigs and Hunters: The Origin of the Black Act*, London, 1975.

Thorp, N. *et al.* (eds), *Songs of the Cowboys*, New York, 1966.

Turnbull, C., *Kellyana*, Melbourne, 1943.

Walker, R. B., 'Bushranging in Fact and Legend', *Historical Studies* 11: 42, April 1964.

Walker, R. B., 'Captain Thunderbolt, Bushranger', *Journal of the Royal Australian Historical Society*, 43, 1957.

Wannan, W., *A Dictionary of Australian Folklore*, Sydney, 1981.

Wannan, W., *The Wearing of the Green: The Lore, Literature, Legends and Balladry of the Irish in Australia*, London, 1968.

Wannan, W., *Tell 'em I Died Game: The Stark Story of Australian Bushranging*, Melbourne, 1963.

Ward, R., *The Australian Legend*, Melbourne, 1958.

Ward, R., 'Felons and Folksongs', two lectures given at the University of Melbourne, October 1954.

Ward, R. (ed.), *The Penguin Book of Australian Ballads*, Ringwood, Vic., 1964.

Wathan, G., *The Golden Colony of Victoria in 1854*, London, 1855.

Watson, E., *Country Music in Australia*, vol 1, Sydney, 1976.

Welsh, C. and Tillinghurst, W., *Catalogue of English and American Chapbooks and Broadside Ballads in Harvard College Library* (1905), Detroit, 1968.

White, C., *History of Australian Bushranging* (2 vols), Melbourne, 1893.

White, R., 'Outlaw Gangs of the Middle Border: American Social Bandits', *Western Historical Quarterly*, 12: 4, 1981.

Wilgus, D. K., *Anglo-American Folksong Scholarship Since 1898*, New Brunswick, NY, 1959.

Williams, A., *Folk Songs of the Upper Thames*, London, 1923.

Williams, M., *Australia on the Popular Stage, 1829–1929*, Melbourne, 1983.

Williams, R. Vaughan and Lloyd, A. (eds), *The Penguin Book of English Folk Songs*, Harmondsworth, 1959.

Williams, Ralph Vaughan, The Ralph Vaughan Williams Broadside Scrapbook, Williams Library, Cecil Sharp House, English Folk Dance and Song Society, London.

Williams, S., *A Ghost Called Thunderbolt*, Woden, ACT, 1987.

Winslow, C., 'Sussex Smugglers', in Hay, D. *et al.* (eds), *Albion's Fatal Tree: Crime and Society in Eighteenth Century England*, London, 1975.

Zimmermann, G., *Songs of Irish Rebellion: Political Street Ballads and Rebel Songs, 1780–1900*, Dublin, 1967.

Index